POLICY AND MANAGEMENT
IN SPECIAL EDUCATION

POLICY AND MANAGEMENT IN SPECIAL EDUCATION

Daniel D. Sage
Syracuse University

Leonard C. Burrello
Indiana University

PRENTICE-HALL, INC., Englewood Cliffs, New Jersey   07632

Library of Congress Cataloging-in-Publication Data

SAGE, DANIEL D.
  Policy and management in special education.

  Includes bibliographical references and index.
  1. Handicapped children—Education—United States—
  Management.   I. Burrello, Leonard C. (date).
  II. Title.
LC4031.S24 1986   371.9   85-12038
ISBN   0-13-684804-4

Editorial/production supervision: F. Hubert

Cover design: Lundgren Graphics, Ltd.

Manufacturing buyer: Barbara Kelly Kittle

Printed in the United States of America

10   9   8   7   6   5   4   3   2   1

ISBN   0-13-684804-4   01

PRENTICE-HALL INTERNATIONAL, INC., *London*
PRENTICE-HALL OF AUSTRALIA PTY. LIMITED, *Sydney*
PRENTICE-HALL CANADA INC., *Toronto*
PRENTICE-HALL HISPANOAMERICANA, S.A., *Mexico*
PRENTICE-HALL OF INDIA PRIVATE LIMITED, *New Delhi*
PRENTICE-HALL OF JAPAN, INC., *Tokyo*
PRENTICE-HALL OF SOUTHEAST ASIA PTE. LTD., *Singapore*
EDITORA PRENTICE-HALL DO BRASIL, LTDA., *Rio de Janeiro*
WHITEHALL BOOKS LIMITED, *Wellington, New Zealand*

To the hundred and more graduate students
of special education administration
who have made our professional lives exciting
and from whom we continue to learn.

CONTENTS

PREFACE

Special education has remained highly visible on the public agenda since the early 1970s. As a part of the social service system in the United States, a process of evolution and maturation has occurred which presents new challenges to leadership in special education. The decade of the 1970s brought to the field dramatic change, as reflected in public attitudes, enabling legal actions and everyday practices in the service system. To personnel in administrative positions, the challenge of the era was to cope with change, at a minimum, and if possible to facilitate and guide those changes. In our previous publication, *Leadership and Change in Special Education* (Prentice-Hall, 1979), we emphasized *change* as the central theme in special education leadership. The "event" of the 1970s, the passage of landmark legislation, signaled the highpoint of the need to meet this challenge. In the intervening years, the course of the changes has become clearer, and the products of the changes have begun to stabilize.

Experience with the impact of new federal and state initiatives has permitted leadership personnel, other professionals, consumers, and the general public to gain some confidence about, if not comfort with, the evolving status of special education. Some fears that the laws could not be implemented, that paperwork and financial burdens would overwhelm the system, and that consumer demands would escalate uncontrollably have by now been confronted. At the same time, proposals to significantly reduce the potential force of the laws have also been rebuffed. The new challenge for leadership has shifted from the focus on massive change to the relative "fine-tuning" of the developing systems of service. This shift does not, however, suggest a significant decline in concern with special education as an issue on the public agenda.

The challenge for the years to come seems to focus on consolidating the achievements of the previous decade's "quiet revolution" by attending to the *quality* of programs of service and the assurance of continued *support*. Access through the schoolhouse door for children with special education needs has become largely assured. The quality of what happens once inside is much less certain. Furthermore, the flow of resources which are likely to affect program quality is subject to variance created by a multitude of other related factors.

For persons in administrative roles, concern with program quality will necessarily depend on the establishment of a framework for evaluation. A necessary complement to evaluation of program quality is a consideration of the procurement of resources to attain a desired level of service. Questions of cost and benefit and the appropriate evaluation of both quantitative and qualitative aspects of resources used and results achieved constitute the major unfinished business of special education leaders.

To address this challenge, a number of issues need to be undestood. In our perspective, the issues fall into two major domains. First, a broad set of policy issues can be identified. These have to do with establishing the scope of the field we call special education, understanding its formal and informal sources of control, its organizational structures, and its fiscal foundations. Second, a number of more specific management issues can be addressed. These are seen as involving factors which influence success in leadership, the process of human resource management, curriculum integration and development, constituency management, decision support systems, fiscal management, and finally, program evaluation. This organization of topics appears to represent the current and short-range future challenge for special education leadership fairly and, therefore, to provide a useful structure for this book. It is our hope that both the scholar and the practitioner of special education administration, and other educators as well, may find this presentation to be a help in thinking about the task before us.

Daniel D. Sage
Leonard C. Burrello

CHAPTER 1
THE SCOPE
OF SPECIAL EDUCATION

To discuss any major function of society we must first establish some definitions and parameters of the subject matter. In the case of special education, the primary policy question must deal with inherent ambiguities as to just what is included within the term *special education*. Mapping the territory can be a complex task. The inputs to the determination of parameters must be drawn from a variety of sources, and the outcomes must be recognized as having important consequences on all the policy and management questions that follow.

FACTORS THAT DETERMINE THE SCOPE
OF SPECIAL EDUCATION

The scope of special education at any time and place is determined by at least the following factors: (1) terminology, (2) philosophical beliefs, (3) history, (4) local tradition, (5) legal foundations, and (6) fiscal constraints. The ways in which each of these factors interacts to establish "the territory" are discussed in the paragraphs that follow.

Terminology

The term *special education* seems to communicate to most educators and informed laypersons an activity or domain within the total educational enterprise that is specifically concerned with students who have handicapping conditions. Among such observers the term *handicapped education* could be accepted as a synonym for special education. However, other observers may substitute a different term, *exceptional education,* with the conscious or unconscious connotation that the parameters include students who are at variance from the norm, or exceptional, in dimensions that would include the mentally gifted or talented as well. Recognition of the additional territory that such a definition implies has been incorporated into law in certain jurisdictions and will be discussed later in this chapter and in Chapter 2. The term *special needs* is also sometimes substituted for *exceptional* in designating a student who requires educational service beyond the ordinary. However, in certain jurisdictions (as in New York State), this does not suffice because a specific legal classification of *pupils with special educational needs (PSEN)* is established to define and authorize services distinct from those for *pupils with handicapping conditions (PHC),* and only the latter classification is included administratively as a part of special education.

Semantic considerations enter into this, and it is not entirely clear in some instances whether the terms used have an antecedent influence or are merely the result of parameters established by law. There is little question that the use of the term *exceptional children* has gained prominence not only because of its objective accuracy (if we do wish to encompass individual variance in dimensions other than the disabled) but because the term carries more positive connotations than the negative ones associated with "handicapped." On the other hand, the use of the term *handicapped* has undoubtedly been an important factor where the attainment of supportive legislation and funding has depended on gaining sympathy from lawmakers and their taxpaying constituents.

Furthermore, the parallel use of the terms *disability* and *handicapped,* which may be viewed by some people as synonymous, has been shown to result in quite different meanings. Social psychologists have for some time emphasized that disability is a matter of objective fact, whereas the term handicap carries an additional attitudinal interpretation of the effect of an actual or perceived status on the individual's life, as viewed by the self or by others. The point is made that a disability may become a handicap primarily as a function of how people think about it. In discussing the concept of "handicapism," the stereotyping, prejudice and discrimination practiced by society against disabled people, Biklen and Bogdan quote one activist as saying "Our bodies make us disabled, but society makes us handicapped."[1] They argue further that some of the negative loading of terminology that leads to the social phenomenon of "handicapism" can be reduced by using the term disabled rather than handicapped in referring to individuals with such conditions.

Another aspect of terminology comes into play when drawing a distinction between *special education* and *special services*. Although it is hard to find an objective reason for it, the former term had usually been reserved for those activities that have a distinctly instructional emphasis and the latter term for those supportive or ancillary functions necessary to the operation of educational programs for *all* students (including those needing special education), such as medical, psychological, social work, and counseling services. However, there has always been an ambiguous boundary between these functions, and as regulations have led to normative procedures calling for more supportive services, the inclusion of such services within the domain of what had been considered special education is understandably more prevalent. The question of whether special services are a part of special education, or vice versa, has implications that are more than semantic. The impact of these considerations will be discussed later, in Chapter 4.

Philosophical Beliefs

An important factor in determining the scope of special education can be traced to such basic issues as people's propensity to classify and compartmentalize. Schools, as a reflection of the larger society, have always ranked, graded, and segregated groups of students on whatever dimensions become most relevant for the pursuit of these organizations' objectives. The degree of segregation may vary from a particular reading group within a classroom to complete exclusion from school. The question of what degree of variance warrants a particular degree of compartmentalization is a matter of prevailing belief regarding the range of differences that can be tolerated in a particular setting. This *ecological* perspective on human variance and the identification and treatment of school children has been discussed as a part of a broadly encompassing and unifying theory for special education.[2] The parameters of special education are likely to vary as a complex function of the amount of pupil variance that exists in a community and that community's tolerance for heterogeneity. While the degree of intercommunity variation is greatly constrained by the increased universality of laws, regulations, and communication of normative practice, it is clear from incidence reports on pupils served under special education that each jurisdiction has its own norms for classification and placement.

At the extremes of human variance, the effect of philosophical belief is relatively stable and consistent. Children with unambiguously severe disabilities who clearly call for extraordinary instructional procedures are classified without question as belonging in special education. Services for the deaf and the blind, for example, are universally perceived as being a part of the special education continuum, regardless of where the services are delivered. Students whose needs fall at the margin, however, may be classified and served quite differently from one jurisdiction to another. Remedial services for students with subaverage reading skills, for example, may or may not be considered within the special education umbrella, depending upon prevailing attitude toward what is acceptable variance. Services for speech impaired students also fall within this gray area.

Statistical considerations must also be reviewed. Generally, it is thought that special education is somehow involved with a minority status. What is the "tipping point" at which a minority condition becomes sufficiently common in the total population that it is no longer extraordinary? The common cold, though a significant condition calling for treatment, does not arouse special consideration. Racial status, on other hand, will be seen as constituting a minority condition even in urban areas where the school population exceeds 90 percent black. In the case of handicapping conditions, there has been little question when the incidence of students so classified has ranged from 5 to 10 percent of the school population. But some proponents of services for learning disabled children, and others concerned with emotional disturbance, have suggested that pupils with such conditions may exceed 20 percent of the school population. Such claims understandably raise questions as to the boundaries of the special education domain. While fiscal and organizational issues must also be considered, a basic conceptual and philosophical factor may override these. How much of the territory of the educational system can special education encompass and still be *special?*

History

Normative practice as to the scope of special education has been a product of evolution. Most scholars who have reviewed this history cite

> massive neglect, denial, and rejection. For every Helen Keller and the other notable few who received intensive special help, tens of thousands of other exceptional children, both gifted and handicapped, were doomed to constricted lives . . . In a sense, the development of special education can be recounted as an assault on this discriminatory attitude.[3]

The clientele at the earliest time included only the obviously impaired, mentally and sensorially, and the organizational arrangement for service was the residential school, both publicly and privately supported. While this mode remains a significant part of the service system, it has been far exceeded by the many other models of service initiated throughout the twentieth century for an increasingly wide variety of types of individuals.

Reynolds and Birch[4] have charted the history of special education in the United States as falling into four major time periods, as follows:

Late 19th century	Residential model, with most states accepting public responsibility for the blind, deaf, and mentally retarded
Early 20th century	Community-based special classes and schools, begun within local school systems

| Ca. 1945-1970 | Proliferation of the special class model for a greater variety of pupils, with legislative support as a result of political action by organized parents |
| Ca. 1970— | More inclusive arrangements as a result of parent and professional pressure through courts and comprehensive legislation, based on civil rights principles. |

The scope of special education at any point in time, then, must be understood in terms of the accumulated history of the field as a whole, and the universal pressures of attitudes and events that are broadly communicated and, therefore, carry a general impact.

Local Tradition

In spite of mass communication and standardization throughout society, the education activity retains its strong roots in the doctrine of local control. While much of what constitutes the educational system reveals the force of ideas diffused throughout the culture, certain aspects of the total education enterprise, until very recently, were optional. The shape of the particular school system's developments in special education were, therefore, subject to local idiosyncrasies. The influence of a particular family whose child demonstrated a special need, an organization of parents with a common interest who became vigorously assertive, a professional educator who had a particular idea combined with the necessary leadership to put it into practice, or any other factors have acted to create a local slant to the scope of special education. Differences in the status and scope of special education in an entire state can in some instances be traced to a single charismatic individual. This may also be found in a single school system. Consider, for instance, the local system that developed a program for aphasic children, well in advance of the standard for the time, largely because of the presence of a professional educator whose own child had needs for such a program.

Legal Foundations

The formalization of the parameters of special education into law is a result of the preceding factors of definitional terminology, philosophical beliefs, history, and local traditions. Actions of the courts or legislatures are to a large degree a reflection of what society is ready to accept and stand behind. While those who make law may lead the rest of the community to a new understanding of the common good, they must lead from a position that is not too far advanced. Legal foundations are merely the official codification of the approximate will of the people.

The legal foundation for day-to-day local practice, whether generating from court rulings, state or federal legislative acts, or administrative regulations, is focused on delineation of *who* falls within the domain of special education, *what services* are authorized or mandated, and through *what procedures* they will be managed. In Chapter 2 we will discuss in detail each of the sources of legal control. Here, it is enough to indicate that understanding the legal base is a prerequisite to mapping the territory of special education.

Fiscal Constraints

Financial considerations are always interacting with the other aspects of policy and practice. While the definitions of who and what are often stated in ideal terms, from either the philosophical or the legal perspective, the gap between the ideal and the actual is usually a function of perceived fiscal limitations. While the courts tend to be able to view things in terms of justice, irrespective of costs, legislators and executive agencies invariably must consider the financial implication of any policy. Most statutes contain built-in price tags that have major influence in their original introduction and passage. After the fact, the realization of the intent of the statute or the regulations designed to implement it is to a large extent determined by the financial impact. The definition of a population to be served or the nature of the intended service will often be shaped, sometimes dramatically, by the fiscal gain or loss to be achieved by an administrative decision. Examples of such fiscal influences will be examined in Chapter 5.

The confluence of the six factors just discussed results in the final determination of just what constitutes special education at any time and place. Our interpretation of the most generalizable description of this status, for the United States as whole at the midpoint of the 1980s, is presented now.

MAPPING "THE TERRITORY"

The scope of special education will be described here on the basis of four significant dimensions as follows: (1) the clients served, (2) the services delivered, (3) the organizational units involved in that delivery, and (4) the personnel utilized within that organizational structure. This description will draw upon the six determining factors, illustrating each to the extent possible, but must acknowledge that it is sometimes very difficult to discriminate between and separate the influence of the various factors.

Who Are the Clients of Special Education?

The trend of the past decade or two is certainly away from describing the clientele of special education categorically. A shift in emphasis from a disability label toward a service need is clearly apparent. However, old categories are slow to fade away. Moreover, classification is an accepted means of facilitating communication, even when the risk of inaccurate communication and other negative side effects are acknowledged. In discussing the two-edged sword of classification, Reynolds and Birch point out that some form of educationally relevant classification is no doubt necessary in order to assure appropriate instruction, but whatever classification system is used, "it must give primary attention to the individuality of children and their needs."[5] In a major work that addressed this issue, Hobbs clearly states the problem:

> Classification, or inappropriate classification . . . can blight the life of a child, reducing opportunity, diminishing his competence and self esteem, alienating him from others, nurturing a meanness of spirit, and making him less a person than he could become. Nothing less than the futures of children is at stake.[6]

In spite of the recognition of this problem, the combination of history and legal factors appears to make it necessary to use labels, however stigmatic, to attain identity and, therefore, assure the establishment and funding of needed services. While there is an increasingly clear mistrust of categories and concern regarding the questionable reliability, validity, and usefulness of labels in educating children, it is equally obvious that fears of loss of support for specific programs accompany any movement to abandon such labels.

As indicated earlier, minor adjustments to specific labels, as well as major conceptual changes in classification schemes, have both been introduced from time to time, with the intention (at least in part) of reducing the negative side effects of the process. The use of the term *disabled* as opposed to *handicapped* is generally proposed as a designation that carries somewhat less stigma. Going beyond that level, conceptualization of the field as dealing with *exceptional* rather than only *handicapped* students changes both the image and the actual scope of the population concerned.

There is no doubt that to whatever extent the classification of student clientele establishes and defines the field of special education, those students who are at variance from the norm in a disadvantageous way figure most prominently in the attention of those who deal with the field, either from the inside or the outside. In reviewing the history of legislation for exceptional persons, La Vor [7] notes the statutory establishment of state schools and institutions for the deaf, the blind, and the mentally retarded in a number of states during the mid-nineteenth century and the first public day schools and classes within some of the larger city school systems in the decades just before and after the turn of the century. Again, these educational services were targeted for youngsters with sensory and mental handicaps and extended in some instances to children with crippling and severe health conditions. A notable departure was an Oregon statute in 1923 that provided for classes for educationally exceptional children, including both the gifted and the handicapped.

Whether in jurisdictions that include gifted students within the territory, or those that limit the field to the disabled, the weight of numbers and overall emphasis of programs are clearly focused on the disabled. The major consideration as to what classifications of students are included resides in state- level statutes. The state generally defines the territory as concerned with *handicapped* students or *exceptional* students. As of 1980, 19 states used the term *exceptional* and included the gifted among the types of children served. Another 17 states defined gifted and/or talented separately from handicapped, and 11 states did not define the gifted in any way. Among states providing programs for the gifted, 27 administered them through the department of special or exceptional education, and 13 administered them through a regular department of curriculum and instruction. The remainder used a variety of other organizational arrangements.[8]

The type of ambiguity and definitional limits described here are also evident in the federal policies that overlay all the state and local provisions. The *handicapped* terminology has always been present in federal initiatives, and any speculation on the possible merits of a less pejorative designation has been rejected on the basis of the loss of a clear, sympathy generating image deemed necessary for favorable statutory provisions and funding. Long before any federal legislation having a nationwide impact was passed, administrative units within the federal education establishment (the U.S. Office of Education) charged with oversight of special education were labeled with the handicapped designator. It should be noted, however, that one of the first publicly visible activities of that unit was a national study conducted during the period of 1952-1954 of the *Qualifications and Preparation of Teachers of Exceptional Children,*[9] which focused on personnel of many types, including teachers of the gifted. The continuing ambiguity was evident 25 years later when difficulty arose in deciding how to organize the responsibility for federal programs authorized under the Gifted and Talented Children's Education Act (P.L. 96-561, in 1978) in relation to the similar functions carried out by the Bureau of Education for the Handicapped.

The major federal legislation has adhered to the terminology and classifications of students associated with handicapping conditions that would demonstrably interfere with ordinary educational progress. La Vor's[10] history of legislative enactments illustrates that the early federal involvement was with the establishment of separate institutions for the deaf and the blind and that many federal initiatives arose from the desire to provide for conditions generating from military service. The expansion of this concept, which was impeded by the general resistance to any kind of federal involvement in education until the 1960s, will be discussed in greater detail in Chapter 2. But to illustrate the focus of federal laws that were enacted between 1966 and 1975, and that carried a similar definition of the intended clientele, the definition established as a product of the Education for All Handicapped Children Act of 1975 (P.L. 94-142) is quoted here, from Title XX United State Code 1401:

> (1) The term "handicapped children" means mentally retarded, hard of hearing, deaf, speech impaired, visually handicapped, seriously emotionally disturbed,

orthopedically impaired, or other health impaired children, or children with specific learning disabilities, who by reason thereof require special education and related services.

And

(15) The term "children with specific learning disabilities" means those children who have a disorder in one or more of the basic psychological processes involved in understanding or in using language, spoken or written, which disorder may manifest itself in imperfect ability to listen, think, speak, read, write, spell, or do mathematical calculations. Such disorders include such conditions as perceptual handicaps, brain injury, minimal brain dysfunction, dyslexia, and developmental aphasia. Such term does not include children who have learning problems which are primarily the result of visual, hearing, or motor handicaps, of mental retardation, of emotional disturbance, or of environmental, cultural, or economic disadvantage.

These definitions, while not precluding a state's establishing a more inclusive one, have a very strong influence on state policy in that they determine the minimal level of inclusion to which a state must adhere in order to participate in the programs that distribute funds from the federal level to assist in the provision of approved services. Persons unfamiliar with the evolution of the terms included with these definitions could rightly wonder at the extensive detail with which the category of specific learning disability is elaborated, while other terms such as visually handicapped are left without further explanation. While considerably more detail is provided in the administrative regulations developed later to guide the implementation of the law, the emphasis within the basic legal definition gives testimony to the assumption of general, common, historically based understanding of certain portions of the intended clientele. On the other hand, the meaning of the term and the scope of the concept of specific learning disability is assumed to be relatively ambiguous and, therefore, subject to distortion of the legislative intent.

The ambiguity inherent in all these definitions can be discerned from the reported figures on numbers of students served under federal categorical definitions. Although it is possible that some localities might have a greater incidence of particular handicapping conditions as a function of natural circumstances, with entire states as the reporting units, it is unreasonable to believe that great differences in the actual occurrence conditions requiring special education services would be found. It is also reasonable to expect that some differences among states would exist in services provided, regardless of incidence of need, as a function of historical development of programs prior to the last decade of heavy federal intervention. Regardless of need or the standardizing influence of the federal role, some states can be expected to be more progressively involved in the operation of service programs. One might expect that the latter factor would be associated with other demographic and socioeconomic conditions of the states, in both general educational measures and other social indicators.

Observation of data released by the U.S. Office of Special Education raises some interesting questions about each of the assumptions we have just discussed. Figures for the 1980-81 school year show that the children served, as a percentage of total school age population, comprised 8.66 percent for nation as a whole.[11] Excluding the territories and the District of Columbia (where the variation was even greater), the range served among the 50 states was from 6.5 percent in New Hampshire to 12.3 percent in New Jersey. The next to the extremes were 6.9 percent for Michigan and 11.4 percent for Massachusetts. Inspection of the entire set of figures reveals no logical explanations for the variance on the basis of such possibly related population characteristics as per capita income, median years of schooling, or minority enrollment or such resource input variables as current expenditures per pupil, pupil-teacher ratio, or expenditures as a percentage of per capita income. The fact that nearly twice as many students are identified and served as handicapped in some states as in others strongly suggests that a different standard of inclusion for the territory is being applied. A more recent report indicates an increase in percentage of handicapped children served (preschool through grade 12) in 1982-83 to 10.76 percent of the total school population. Individual state data, as a percentage of total state enrollment, were not indicated in this report.[12]

A further breakdown of similar data for the 1980-81 school year, by categories of disability, reveals an even greater discrepancy. For example, in the incidence of mentally retarded served, Alabama and Mississippi reported 4.02 and 3.10 percent, respectively, of their total school population as falling under this category, whereas Alaska and Utah claimed only .79 and .90 percent. It is quite unreasonable to think that there would be in fact four times as many mentally retarded students in one state as in another. Similarly in the reported incidence of students served under the category of learning disabled, Maryland and Rhode Island showed 5.59 and 5.49 percent, respectively, of their total school populations, while New York and Indiana showed only a respective 1.25 and 1.85 percent. Again the range is on the order of a 4-fold difference. An even greater variance is evident under the category of emotionally disturbed, where Utah and Delaware reported 2.76 and 2.14 percent of their total school populations and Mississippi and Arkansas only one-twentieth and one-tenth of one percent—a range on the order of a 20- to 40-fold difference.

While it is reasonable to expect some regional differences in actual incidence of handicapping conditions, and even more reasonable to expect different levels of intensity in programming as a function of state policy (not to mention simple reporting errors inherent in state and federal forms), these figures strongly suggest that if we attempt to use conventional classifications, the question of "Who are the clients of special education?" must be answered somewhat differently in each state. It should be noted that the figures presented are concerned with students coming under the provisions of the federal programs for handicapped and, therefore, do not reflect any state services that may exist for gifted and talented or for any other pupils who in a particular state may be considered a part of special education but do not come under the federal definitions.

Data for the United States as a whole for 1980-81 and 1982-83 showed a distribution across the reported categories of handicapping conditions for children served in all federally overseen programs (P.L. 94-142 and P.L. 89-313) as indicated in Table 1-1.[12,13]

It should be noted that the distribution reported here reflects a rather striking increase in the learning disability category since the implementation of P.L. 94-142 in the late 1970s, with a proportional decrease in certain other classifications, particularly the mentally retarded. In New York, for example, the number of learning disabled students increased by 68 percent between 1981-82 and 1982-83. This was, of course, due to a definitional change in that state, as well as to a large increase in child count within New York City, in response to pressures to catch up from a previous, relatively low proportion served.

Another issue in defining the population involves the question of age level. The degree to which a state or local system embraces the idea of preschool services, as well as programs between the ages of 18 and 21, shows

**TABLE 1-1   Distribution of Children Served,
by Handicapping Condition**

CLASSIFICATION	PERCENT OF TOTAL SERVED	
	1981-82	1982-83
Learning disabled	34.7%	40.6%
Speech impaired	28.1	26.4
Mentally retarded	20.3	18.1
Emotionally disturbed	8.3	8.2
Other health impaired	2.3	1.2
Multi-handicapped	1.7	1.5
Orthopedically impaired	1.4	1.3
Deaf	.9	.9
Hard of hearing	.9	.9
Visually handicapped	.8	.7
Deaf-blind	<.1	<.1

Source: The data in this table may be found in "To Assure the Free Appropriate Public Education of All Handicapped Children," *Fourth Annual Report to Congress on the Implementation of Public Law 94–142: The Education for All Handicapped Children Act* (Washington, D.C.: U.S. Department of Education, 1982); and "To Assure the Free Appropriate Public Education, of all Handicapped Children," *Sixth Annual Report to Congress on the Implementation of Public Law 94–142: The Education for All Handicapped Children Act* (Washington, D.C.: U.S. Department of Education, 1984), p. 3.

much greater variance than the ordinary 5- to 17-year-old group. While federal law includes children from 3 to 21 years of age, the mandate does not apply where, in the language of P.L. 94-142,

> with respect to handicapped children aged three to five and aged eighteen to twenty-one, inclusive, the requirements of this clause shall not be applied in any State if the application of such requirements would be inconsistent with State law or practice, or the order of any court, respecting public education within such age groups in the State.

Given this latitude, considerable variance can be found in the numbers of students included at these marginal ages. Incentives included as a part of federal law have not been sufficient to influence dramatically the extension of services into these ages where traditional practice and financial constraints dictated otherwise. The fact that preschool or early childhood education has not been universally adopted as a part of the general education system constitutes a major barrier to such services for the handicapped. Among all children served under P.L. 94-142 in 1982-83, only 5.97 percent were within the 3- to 5-year age span. The 18- to 21-year-age span included only 4.28 percent, leaving 89.74 percent in the 6- to 17-year-old age range. This indicates only about one-fourth as many children at each age cohort at the preschool level as compared with the school ages.

Even within the school age levels, the concentration at the elementary school years and the relative lack of programming at the secondary schools is evident in data reported by the federal General Accounting Office. Table 1-2 illustrates the percentage distribution of students served, by age level, in local education agency (LEA) programs.[14]

TABLE 1-2   Distribution of Students, by Age, in LEA Administered Schools, 1978

STUDENT AGE (years)	PERCENT	STUDENT AGE (years)	PERCENT
3	0.4	13	7.3
4	0.7	14	6.5
5	2.6	15	6.7
6	6.7	16	5.8
7	8.8	17	3.6
8	10.9	18	2.5
9	9.1	19	0.8
10	9.7	20	0.3
11	9.4	21	0.2
12	7.9		

Source: The data for this table are taken from Comptroller General, *Disparities Still Exist in Who Gets Special Education* (Washington, D.C.: U.S. General Accounting Office, 1981), p. 29.

Certain specific disabilities, such as speech impairment, deafness, or cerebral palsy, that present extremely clear needs for early intervention have tended to make up the preschool special education population. This is illustrated in the figures of children served, by category, that show that the preschool group constitutes from 14 to 18 percent of the total in the speech impaired, the multihandicapped, the orthopedically impaired, and the deaf and blind categories.[15] This rate is from two to three times the overall figures for preschool. However, when such services have been developed for these types of conditions, they have frequently been attached to a medical rather than an educational facility, further distancing preschool children from the universally recognized clientele of special education.

Within the 18- to 21-year-old population, the largest proportions (as a percentage of the total within a given category) are found among the visually handicapped, the orthopedically impaired, the deaf and blind, and the multihandicapped. But in no category does this age group account for over 11 percent of the total for the age 3 to 21 in that category.[16] Again, it is clear that the population deemed appropriately served by special education has been primarily limited to the conventional public school years. However, more recent data from a survey of eight states conducted by the National Association of State Directors of Special Education show a rapid increase in services at both the preschool and the postsecondary levels. Figures available from all 50 states show that for the period from 1976-77 to 1982-83, there was a 23.4 percent increase in numbers of preschool children served, a 69.9 percent increase in postsecondary, with only a 15.9 percent increase in ages 3 to 21 served overall.[17]

An extensive treatment of the question of clientel is covered by a report to the U.S. Congress by the Comptroller General, U.S. General Accounting Office. In an attempt to answer the question "Who gets special education?" the General Accounting Office analyzed data from some 15 evaluation studies conducted under contract with the federal government plus two data bases existing as a part of required state to federal reporting procedures. The data covered the period from 1976 through 1981 and were used to address four broad questions:[18]

> What are the numbers and characteristics of children receiving special education and related services?
>
> Are there eligible children who are unserved or underserved?
>
> Are certain types of children overrepresented in special education?
>
> What factors influence who gets special education?

Some of the major findings emphasized in the report provide documentation of the problems just cited, and point out additional ones as well. The overriding observation was that in spite of the implementation of laws and regulations from the federal level, disparities still exist as to who gets special education. Recipients tended to be young—about 67 percent being 12 years of age or younger. Twice as many males as females are represented. The predominant classifications are learning disabled (36 percent of the total served) and speech impaired (30 percent), with the majority of all served considered to be only mildly handicapped.

The analysis concluded that the proportion of children served under the learning disability label exceeded the upper limits of expected incidence and that insufficient information was available to determine exactly what types of children were being so identified. In 6 states, over half of all children served were labeled learning disabled, and in 12 additional states they comprised over 40 percent. These findings were of particular interest since it had been anticipated at the time of development of federal regulations in 1976-77 that an inordinate increase in the use of such classification would occur unless a "cap" were used limiting this designation to 2 percent of the school population. Subsequent removal of the cap had led to an expression of fear on the part of Congress that disproportionate allocation of funds might occur to a category of handicapping condition, the magnitude of which was not clearly known or understood. Data suggested that such fears had been realized and that better criteria were needed for inclusion in this category. The response of the Education Department to this issue suggested that, although some of the increase was consistent with a corresponding decrease in mentally retarded and could be attributed to the choice of a term carrying less stigma, the major factor was the inclusion of more "fringe" cases. Such cases were described as children in need of educational services but who are not actually handicapped, and who would be likely to include borderline cases such as slow learners, socially maladjusted, culturally disadvantaged, or economically deprived.[19]

Another key point in interpreting these figures is the reduction in funding of certain other federal programs, such as Title I aid to disadvantaged students. The program reduction that undoubtedly occurred in some of these related areas could be expected to have an effect of moving the boundary line in some marginal cases and thereby included more students under the handicapped classification.

It was also noted that a disproportionate share of minority children were included in certain special education programs. As compared to the white majority, the distribution of black children revealed a gross overrepresentation in programs for the educable mentally retarded and an underrepresentation in speech impaired and learning disabled. Taking all types of special education programs combined, blacks accounted for 21 percent of special education enrollment while constituting only 15 to 16 percent of total school enrollment. For Hispanics there was a slight overrepresentation in learning disabled and more so for native Americans. For Asian Americans, a disproportionate number were served under the speech impaired classification. The possible reasons for these discrepancies invite speculation. Teacher and administrator bias would seem to be suspected immediately, but complex etiological factors were also acknowledged. It was also pointed out that Indo-Chinese immigrants might be labeled speech impaired in order to provide needed language help.[20]

Sex bias in special education placement was most striking in programs for emotionally disturbed, where males exceeded females by a ratio of over 3.0 to 1. In learning disability programs, the ratio was over 2.5 to 1, and in speech impaired and educable mentally retarded about 1.5 to 1.[21] It was indicated that the categories in which the greatest imbalances appear are those where judgment of teachers and administrators play a large role in assignment of students. Possible explanations for the discrepancies in a number of dimensions include the effect of differing state policies and definitions, local school district resources, and the major impact of personal discretion on the part of school personnel in the referral and placement decision process.

What Services Constitute Special Education?

It was indicated at the beginning of this chapter that the scope of special education, in terms of both the clientele served and the services included, was determined by a variety of factors operating in concert. The legal base, which is a product of history, is also shaped in its influence on practice at a particular time and place by local tradition and policy. Just as we have seen considerable variation in persons served when examining aggregate data from the nation as a whole, we can expect to find variation in what constitutes special education services.

The cataloging of special education services has tended to focus on physical locations—the places where special education occurs. In citing the history of the field, we recognize that the earliest developments took place in separate, special schools, usually residential, both publicly and privately operated. This nineteenth-century phenomenon was followed by services offered within regular schools, but in separate special classes, as the primary mode of service during at least the first half of the current century. The activity conducted in these locations was concerned with instruction, but differentiated from the instruction that went on in other, regular schools in a number of possible ways.

One major differentiation has its focus on compensatory methodology for accomplishing common instructional objectives. In the case of programs for the blind and for the deaf, special education has consisted primarily of devising means to bypass the sensory obstacle to normal learning and, assuming more or less average intellectual capacity, the pursuit of scholastic objectives through the use of these alternate or compensatory channels of learning. The primary feature in such programs was the use of Braille and auditory communication in educating the blind, and alternate language development mechanisms in programs for the deaf. This description is somewhat oversimplified, since disability-related differences in adult life goals have always been recognized as have affective and psychosocial factors that would interact with the purely cognitive learning objectives. But within programs for the sensorially impaired, the major intent and approach in instruction could be conceived in this manner.

Quite another basis for differentiating the activities of special education from regular is the concept of differing educational goals and corresponding instructional objectives. Based on the assumption that certain irremedial disabilities preclude the attainment of normal adult life goals, special education curriculum has, for a major part of the clientele, been adapted to suit these different (reduced) objectives. Programs for mentally retarded children are characterized not only by instructional methods designed to accommodate the inefficient learning styles of such students, but also by the terminal goals of instruction. Especially with the more severely retarded, where self-help activities of daily living may be the ultimate goal and the cognitive development usually associated with school is clearly infeasible, special education is oriented around these totally different purposes.

Another characteristic of special education that has been consistently present is the focus on individualized instruction. While the ideal of recognition of individual differences among all children has been expressed throughout education, it has been most often realized within programs for handicapped children. This has in turn created a focus on the technology of instruction for a variety of student needs, as a spinoff from the highly specialized arrangements necessitated by particular disabling conditions.

Still another differentiating aspect is seen where the clientele exhibit conditions that currently preclude profit from regular instruction but are presumed to be remedial. In such cases, the focus of instruction is not only on accommodating for the existing barrier to regular instruction, but also on measures designed to alleviate (over time) the disabling circumstances. The program of special education, in these instances, can be conceived as both compensatory and therapeutic. Programs for children with emotional disturbances, with specific learning disabilities, and with speech impairments are designed with such dual objectives. Unlike the situation with visually impaired children, where the aim is normal educational attainment in spite of an unchangeable disabling status, and unlike the situation with mentally retarded children, where the aim is the attainment of appropriately altered objectives, the design of certain programs places heavy emphasis on instructional intervention that will remediate the basic problem.

These various factors that seem to differentiate special education from the normative systems of instruction have allowed the practitioners in the field to utilize an experimental approach rather frequently. The somewhat unique nature of both the learner and the teacher in special education can facilitate innovation and development of techniques that would not otherwise be risked in the mainstream. The concept of special education as experimental education has been elaborated by Burrello, Tracy, and Schultz.[22]

A significantly less predominant circumstance, but one that must be acknowledged, is the situation where a handicapping condition exists but has little or no bearing on the instructional program per se. In programs for orthopedically impaired pupils, and for other health impaired, a majority of the needs of those involved may be met by alterations in the physical environment or by the provision of services such as transportation and therapies of a noneducational nature. The inclusion of such programs within the domain of special education is rationalized on the basis of the disabling conditions found in the individuals, even though the interventions employed are not educationally specialized. This type of situation presents a complicating element in mapping the territory of special education where federal law is concerned, which will be discussed later.

Thus it can be seen that there are differing bases for defining types of services that constitute special education. The laws that have accrued over the years in each state have reflected these bases, and the combination of state law and conventional practice undoubtedly played a large part in the development of federal policy, as seen in the language of P.L. 94-142 and its administrative regulations. Special education is defined in the law (U.S.C. 1401) as follows:

> (16) The term "special education" means specially designed instruction, at no cost to parents or guardians, to meet the unique needs of a handicapped child, including classroom instruction, instruction in physical education, home instruction, and instruction in hospitals and institutions.

This definition is repeated in the Code of Federal Regulations (45 C.F.R. Part 121a) with elaboration as to the meaning of physical education, vocational education, and the status of speech pathology services as either special education or a related service, depending on individual state definitions. The matter of the distinction between special education and related services, under federal law, is of particular interest in mapping the territory. According to the U.S.C. 1401,

> (17) The term "related services" means transportation, and such developmental, corrective, and other supportive services (including speech pathology and audiology, psychological services, physical and occupational therapy, recreation, and medical and counseling services, except that such medical services shall be for diagnostic and evaluation purposes only) as may be required to assist a handicapped child to benefit from special education, and includes the early identification and assessment of handicapping conditions in children.

Again, the regulations elaborate this definition, describing in great detail the types of activities included within the scope of each of the services mentioned in the law. From the standpoint of program administration at the local school district level, any or all of these services might be considered as falling within the province of a special education department. However, these services tend to be provided rather broadly across the total population of the schools and are not exclusively directed toward pupils who are handicapped. Therefore, there is a rationale for viewing the administration of such services as a generic function, even though the linkage to special education, both in the terms of the activities and the clientele is rather strong.

This is further complicated by the fact that related services are limited under federal law to handicapped children, and handicapped children are defined as only those requiring special education. Therefore, a child who might have a disabling condition (e.g. an orthopedic impairment) that did not call for any special education would not be considered handicapped. Furthermore, such a child is not eligible to receive (as a part of a federally funded program) the related service such as transportation or physical therapy that might be appropriate. These situations are rare, and are usually resolved by determining that some form of special education is necessary, but by strict interpretation the distinction drawn between the two aspects of the total service system illustrates the ambiguity of the territorial maps and the interaction between the legal base and traditional perspectives on service.

Within the instructional realm, the emphasis on the physical location has drawn attention to the evolution of service models. Reynolds and Birch have pointed out that even after special education moved from segregated schools and institutions and became incorporated within the regular public school systems, a "two-box" perspective prevailed. Schools were seen as providing two separate educational systems (regular and special), "each with its own pupils, teachers, supervisory staff, and funding system."[23] Under such a system a child was determined to belong either to one or the other "box" with little interchange between the two. Even though some children spent more time in regular educational settings and received their special education (or services) from itinerant specialists, as was common with resource teacher services for the visually impaired and speech therapy for students needing such service, the children were seen as part-time members of the "special box." The separateness was reinforced by the training and certification of special teachers, which usually took place in academic departments away from those of the mainstream educators, with emphasis on the categorical nature of the competencies required.

The significant shift toward a "continuum of services" model that began in the 1960s and accelerated in the 1970s was primarily due to the recognition that the needs of children did not fall neatly into "two boxes" and that a much greater variety of options was called for. The idea of multiple options has been expressed in a variety of ways, with the original concept of a "cascade" of services proposed by Deno[24] and adapted by Reynolds and Birch.[25] The concept initially emphasized the various types of locations that would constitute a complete continuum of services, with the expectation that greater intensity of specialized service, associated with facilities more removed from the mainstream of education, would be required for relatively fewer children. The "floor" of the cascade was seen as the regular classroom, where most children would be served. The levels of increasing intensity of service, with correspondingly fewer children involved, were described as follows:

Regular classroom with consultative assistance	Indirect services by psychologists, resource teachers, supervisor/consultants; no direct service to child
Regular classroom with assistance by itinerant specialists	Limited direct service to child, by specialists (e.g., speech therapists, mobility instructors)
Regular classroom plus resource room help	Part-time small-group direct service in special station; categorical (e.g., blind) or generic
Regular classroom plus part-time special class	Part-time attendance in full-time special class to meet prescribed needs
Full-time special class	Direct service as part of self-contained group with similar needs
Full-time special day school	Direct service as part of large group with similar needs
Full-time residential school	Direct service encompassing more than school day instruction
Homebound, hospital instructors	Instruction provided in settings having other primary purposes
Special treatment and detention centers	Total environmental control, for primary purposes in addition to instruction

The essential purpose behind having a complete continuum of services is that the most appropriate level, or intensity, of program can be provided and placements in programs can be guided by the general principle that no greater intensity of service than is absolutely necessary will be utilized. On the assumption that specialized services are also limiting, in terms of access and participation in normal society, the principle of *least restrictive environment* is employed. The value of maximum participation and minimum segregation from the mainstream gained sufficient prominence within the culture and the professional education community to assure its codification as a key element in the federal policy encompassed by P.L. 94-142 and its regulations.

Reynolds and Birch[26] discuss a more current conceptualization of the original "cascade," based on the belief that regular schools can be made more powerful and diverse, thereby reducing the need for as many highly specialized settings. With adaptations to physical facilities, training and technical assistance to regular teachers, and a differentiated role for specialists to include more resource/consultant activity in addition to traditional direct instruction, the entire education system will be capable of responding to a greater proportion of what has been the special education population. Figure 1-1 illustrates the major principles of the instructional cascade model.

A manifestation of the acceptance of the *least restrictive environment* principle can be seen in the figures reported by the U.S. Department of Education in the *Sixth Annual Report to Congress*.[27] Data on the environments in which handicapped children were served (school year 1981-82) illustrate that

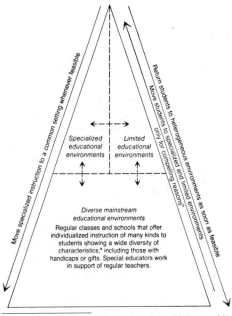

*It is assumed that no educational "place" is impervious to change and development and that through good efforts many of the varieties of specialized and intensive forms of education can be moved into a developing mainstream.

*Here, as in the case of the original cascade, it is assumed that students should be removed from the mainstream only for limited periods and compelling reasons; that their progress should be monitored carefully and regularly; and that they should be returned to the mainstream as soon as feasible. All students start their schooling in the mainstream and have a *place* there at all times, even though they may be located in a special setting for some period of time.

FIGURE 1-1
The Instructional Cascade. *Source:* Maynard C. Reynolds and Jack W. Birch, *Teaching Exceptional Children in All America's Schools* (Reston, Va.: The Council for Exceptional Children, 1982), p. 47. Copyright 1982 by The Council for Exceptional Children. Reprinted with permission.

for the most numerous types of special education students, the regular class (with supplemental part time services) constitutes the major placement mode. Considering all handicapped students combined, ages 3 to 21, 67.92 percent were served with their major assignment in the regular class. Separate classes accounted for 25.22 percent, separate schools for 5.65 percent, and other environments, another 1.22 percent.

Among the individual states and across the categories of handicapping condition, gross variations from these average figures are apparent. State figures on the use of regular classes ranged from over 83 percent in Alaska, Maine, Oregon, Tennessee, and Wyoming to only 40 to 45 percent in New York and Delaware, and under 16 percent in Hawaii. Corresponding variation in the use of separate classes and schools was evident. Separate class placements accounted for over 40 percent of enrollments in New York, Hawaii, and Wisconsin and for less than 10 percent in Nevada, Maine and Oregon. Separate school assignment figures exceeded 10 percent (twice the U.S. average) in the states of Delaware, Illinois, Maryland, and New York but were under 1 percent in Kansas and Oklahoma.[28]

These figures on educational environments are markedly slanted in the direction of regular class placement by the fact that speech impaired children (who are served from a regular class base well over 90 percent of the time) constitute such a large proportion (26.4 percent) of the total population classified as handicapped. Similarly, those reported as learning disabled (constituting 40.6 percent of the total) are based in regular classes about 80 percent of the time. On the other hand, emotionally disturbed were reported in separate classes just as frequently as in regular classes (about 40 percent of placements) and mentally retarded showed the greatest proportionate use of the separate class (about 58 percent). Again, extreme interstate variation in the use of each placement environment, within certain disability categories is evident. For example, while the states of Alabama, Arkansas, Maine, North Dakota, Oklahoma, Oregon, and Vermont show virtually all their learning disabled placements (over 95 percent) in regular classes, Hawaii reported under 3 percent in that model. The use of separate schools also shows high interstate variance in certain categories of disability. Maryland and Ohio reported over 40 percent of their emotionally disturbed as placed in separate schools, whereas Idaho, Nevada, North Dakota, and Oklahoma showed less than 2 percent of that category in separate schools.

It should be noted that the total U.S. averages of placement environments, by disability category, as presented in Table 1-3, obscure the dramatic variations that exist and only very roughly provide a sense of the nature of services utilized. The four types of placement environments likewise obscure the variety of program activities that may occur, especially in the single indicator of *regular class*. Within that setting, the services may range from occasional indirect consultation with the regular teacher to a considerable portion of time in intensive instruction with an itinerant or resource teacher. The dividing line between part-time service from a regular class base and major assignment to a special class is very unclear.

Also the figures reported above are extremely fluid where individual states are concerned. That is, data on 1982-83, as compared with two years earlier, are quite different in certain states, reflecting rapid changes in classification and reporting, and to at least some extent changes in programming practices. In the aggregate across all states, these fluctuations are much less.

What Organizational Structures Provide Special Education?

The governance and operation of education in the United States is universally recognized as a state responsibility, with the preponderance of authority delegated to local school district governing boards. The participation of state government in this shared enterprise, while varying in accordance with individual state philosophy as expressed in constitutions, statutes, and administrative regulations, tends to be concerned with the setting of standards to ensure minimum adequacy and the reduction of gross inequity in the educational programs operated at the local level. In most respects, schools belong to the local citizenry. Furthermore, education is a predominantly public en-

TABLE 1-3   Percentage of Children 3 to 21 Years Old Served in Different Educational Environments School Year 1981-1982

DISABILITY CATEGORY	REGULAR CLASSES	SEPARATE CLASSES	SEPARATE SCHOOLS	OTHER ENVIRON-MENT
Speech impaired	94.25%	4.29%	.87%	.60%
Emotionally disturbed	41.60	39.95	16.04	2.41
Learning disabled	79.80	18.59	1.40	.20
Mentally retarded	29.68	57.73	11.90	.68
Other health impaired	32.95	45.10	4.71	17.24
Orthopedically impaired	32.55	33.47	19.56	14.42
Multi-handicapped	22.36	45.53	26.62	5.49
Hard of hearing/deaf	38.88	37.06	22.99	1.07
Visually handicapped	57.78	17.76	21.18	2.28
Deaf/blind	10.47	42.53	43.91	3.09
All combined	67.92	25.22	5.65	1.22

Source: "To Assure the Free Appropriate Public Education of All Handicapped Children," *Sixth Annual Report to Congress on the Implementation of Public Law 94-142: The Education of All Handicapped Children Act* (Washington, D.C.: U.S. Department of Education, 1984), pp. 144–55.

terprise, with the role of private agencies occupying a relatively small place when comparing the United States to many other societies.

The role of federal government has traditionally been even less prominent and could be said to have been almost inconsequential before the 1960s. Until that time, the federal role had been primarily record keeping, except for the legislation of grants and other fiscal supports to stimulate educational programs focusing on specific populations and specific needs. In such instances the intervention of the federal government was usually in response to a societal need other than education, but with which an educational program could be anticipated as being a feasible part of a solution. Unemployment, economic crises, national defense, and returning war veterans have often been cited as the impetus for federal education initiatives. The dramatic change since 1960 will be discussed in detail at a later point, but it should be understood that in general, education has been and remains primarily a local function, with help and supervision from the state.

However, special education can properly be considered an exception. Some of the earliest examples of educational services for the handicapped were generated by legislative initiative from federal and state levels of government to support the establishment of institutions to meet a need assumed to be beyond the scope of local public education. Services operated directly by these higher levels of government long preceded local school system involvement. Even after the initiation of local school programs for exceptional students, special education (along with vocational education) remained one of the particular, narrow-purpose areas in which both direct and indirect intervention from higher levels of government was deemed legitimate.

In addition to the issue of governmental level, special education entails another dimension of extraordinary involvement. Within education in general, other societal agencies participate to some degree with the schools in the overall operation of the enterprise. Health, welfare, and justice agencies are typically involved with education agencies at each level of government and, depending on particular state and local policies, may play a significant role in what goes on from day to day. The interaction between these other human service agencies and the schools may be extensive where the local population is heavily weighted with students from economically deprived homes. The public health concerns of a community are often reflected in and dealt with through the clientele and personnel of the local public schools.

In the case of handicapped children, the total complex of human service needs tends to draw more heavily on the other agencies than is typical with the school population as a whole. The interaction between the families of handicapped students and health service agencies, particularly, may be closely tied to the special educational issues with which the school is concerned. The boundary lines between educational, health, and social service functions, both at the point of diagnostic assessment and treatment intervention, may need to be clarified, articulated, and monitored to achieve maximum benefit and efficiency. The vulnerability to gaps and overlaps in function is created by two factors.

First, the expectations and practices of schools tend to be increasingly concerned with more than just instructional activities. Screening for vision, hearing, and health problems, as well as more extensive assessment activities in the case of suspected handicaps, are generally seen as school functions. A wide variety of related services, including physical therapy, occupational therapy, and parent counseling, though traditionally allied to medical services, as a result of special education have also become school-based functions.

Second, educational programs must necessarily be offered in facilities operated by nonschool agencies. Hospitals and institutions operated under the jurisdiction of state health, mental health, mental retardation, or welfare agencies are mandated to provide appropriate educational programs for residents of school age. Persons detained in correctional facilities under justice departments are also recognized as including a large number of school age handicapped whose special education needs must be met. In addition, private agencies serving school age persons with medical and psychological needs in residence, must also be concerned with the provision of appropriate educational programs. Therefore, a significant crossover of responsibility and functions between education and other human service agencies must be dealt with.

Therefore, a clearly distinguishing characteristic of special education, as compared with the rest of the education enterprise, is the degree of direct involvement in the process by other than local levels of the educational system, other branches of government than education, and other than public agencies. The rationale for these differences may best be understood by considering the total service system, which is a product of the nature of the population in question and the nature of the interventions called for. Brewer and Kakalik[29] have presented a useful means of viewing the total service system, in terms of role models, functions, and rationales that drive the policy processes affecting special education. While their emphasis in this conceptualization is on the federal level, it can be shown that similar state level applications hold equally true.

Four basic aspects of government roles are identified: (1) direct operation, (2) policy and program control, (3) revenue sharing, and (4) stimulation and innovation. These roles apply across all types of government functions, but except for the purpose of illustrative comparison, discussion here will focus on human services, particularly education. The order in which the four roles are presented indicates a descending degree of overall involvement with all aspects of the activity under consideration.

Direct Operation.   As indicated earlier, local school districts are the primary government agencies involved with direct operation of educational systems. Direct operation of educational programs by the federal government are very rare, although the overseas dependent schools provided by the Department of Defense is one notable example. However, in the realm of services for the handicapped, a number of direct federal operations exist, such as the Social Security Disability Insurance program. In addition, certain special education activities are operated directly, such as Gallaudet College and its related elementary and secondary schools for the deaf, the National Technical Institute for the Deaf, and St. Elizabeth's Hospital.

The rationale for such direct operation is based primarily on the very low incidence of certain disability-connected needs and the high degree of specialization called for in responding to the needs. Economy of scale is a major consideration, as is the assumption that the benefits of knowledge and technology accrued by both the service providers and the recipients (termed "externalities" by economists) will be diffused far beyond the point at which the service is rendered. The opportunity for stimulation and innovation where specialized talent and equipment can be brought together is also a factor. Operation by the broadest (federal) level of government is thereby justified.[30]

Much more common are direct operations by state education agencies (SEAs). Examples are the numerous residential schools for the blind, the deaf, mentally retarded, and emotionally disturbed that may operate under either the education department of the state or branches of the health or welfare departments. Aside from their historical precedent, such facilities are maintained on the rationale that low incidence of certain disabling conditions and sparsity of general population mandates a catchment area as large as an entire state or major region thereof. Such economy of scale arguments are now seriously challenged as experience has been gained with less restrictive alternatives for placement, but it is clear that for some limited situations, direct state-operated programs will remain.

Long before pressures for less restrictive environments became a watchword, however, there was recognition that a centralized state operated program was too great a leap from local school district services. The parents of deaf children residing outside densely populated areas, for example, might acknowledge that, although a local program for only one or two children would not be feasible, to send a young child away to a state residential school seemed drastic. The need for something in between, based on a larger than local school catchment area, to operate highly specialized programs for the low-incidence populations, was clear. The rationale for an intermediate unit of organization is basically an extension downward of that which justifies the federal and state operations but, by being closer to the grass roots that drive education in this country, would seem to create less dissonance with the rest of the system.

Intermediate education units (IEUs) of one sort or another have been prominently used in the majority of the states for a number of purposes. For direct operation of programs, special education, along with vocational education, has provided the driving need for such organizational structures. Except for those states having county-wide school districts (such as Maryland, Virginia, and Florida) where there are no really small local organizational units, some method has been employed to bring together the local education agencies (LEAs) of a region to make special education programming feasible. A variety of legal, political, and fiscal factors have influenced the exact nature of the IEU in different states. Some of these issues will be discussed in later chapters, but the implications for direct operation of programs are virtually the same, whether the IEU is the result of informal cooperative efforts banding together a group of LEAs to share a commonly felt need or is the product of a more formal partial decentralization of the state agency (SEA).

The significance of the IEU as an organizational structure within the special education service system is not limited to direct operation of programs, but the magnitude of that aspect, nationwide, is sufficient to warrant close consideration of their presence as an influence on general policy or a reactor thereto. Estimates of the prominence of IEUs are not precise, but a survey of the membership of the national Council of Administrators of Special Education in 1982 showed that out of 1,191 persons responding, 22.7 percent were employed by IEUs. LEAs employed 55.9 percent, and the remainder were in a variety of other settings, including SEAs, federal offices, and private agencies.[31] This compares with data reported by Wyatt[32] in 1968 that indicated that about 13 percent of all special education administrators were employed by IEUs and about 46 percent in LEAs. At that time, there were relatively more employed in SEAs, state-operated programs, and private agencies, but it would appear that the magnitude of IEUs in comparison to LEAs has remained consistent.

Policy and Program Control.   The "controllership" role, as described by Brewer and Kakalik, is applicable where the governmental agency leaves the direct operation of the program to lower-level agencies or to nonpublic agencies but retains the remaining three roles. At the federal level, such a role exists when "determinations of what to spend money on, how to spend it, and how to account for it are concentrated in one definable federal unit, as are the powers to allocate enabling resources and to create and generate new approaches to manage the underlying problems."[33] Examples of this kind of role are numerous throughout a variety of human service operations, particularly where federal grants or contracts are awarded to state or local agencies to conduct a specific program, according to rather highly specified procedures. In special education, the prominent examples are (1) the basic program of Assistance to States for Education of Handicapped Children, under P.L. 94-142, or Part B of the Education of the Handicapped Act, and (2) the program of Federal Assistance to State Operated and Supported Schools for the Handicapped, under P.L. 89-313. In both instances, SEAs and LEAs receive considerable money from a formula distribution based on numbers served to assist in the operation of programs, but also must adhere to procedures designed to control that operation and promote particular policies. The broad-scale application of these two programs mark them as having significant day-to-day policy implications for virtually every school administrator.

Of lesser scope, but still important to the total perspective of the service system are other federal programs, such as Regional Vocational, Adult and Postsecondary Programs, Deaf-Blind Programs, Handicapped Children's Early Education Programs, and Projects for the Severely Handicapped all authorized by various parts of the Education for the Handicapped Act and providing funding in the form of grant awards in response to competitively submitted proposals. SEAs and/or LEAs (as well as other public and nonprofit organizations) are eligible to receive such funding to facilitate the operation of services, in accordance with federally determined and monitored guidelines.

The newness of this relationship between operators and the federal government has generated much debate regarding the reasonable balance between funding and control, intensified by shifts in general political climate in respect to the amount of government that should be "on our backs." The most pointed manifestation of this controversy was the proposed modification of federal regulations in 1982, in which support for deregulation was rationalized on the imbalance between the funds provided and the controls imposed. This is a major issue that will be discussed at greater length in Chapter 2.

The controllership role is more prominent, of course, in the relationship between state government and the local school systems, where funding and regulation have long coexisted and the administrators and policymakers at each level have become accustomed to a relatively stable balance in the relationship. And aside from the funding issue, SEA regulation of the LEA, while varying in degree as a matter of individual state political philosophy, is generally accepted as proper.

The rationale for such a relationship is most strongly based on the principles of *redistribution of resources* and *internalization of externalities.*[34] The elevation of responsibility for funding and control to a higher level of government is appropriate where pressing demand for high cost services, as well as the resources to provide them, are assumed to be unequally distributed among local jurisdictions. Concern for equality of opportunity is a driving force for government programs that provide for purchase of services. "Redress of governmental-institutional service inequities, given variations in wealth among the states and localities, is a common rationalization for formulas in grant programs characteristic of many purchase of service mechanisms."[35] In addition, the idea of responding to unmet needs translates to the responsibility for "sensing those who are in need and then accommodating those individuals, even if they cannot effectively demand service, both by broadening the scope and improving the quality of services provided them."[36] Furthermore, it is assumed that the benefits of governmental programs are spread far beyond the immediate jurisdiction and that these "externalities" to the local system, if assumed by a broader political level, become "internal" to that larger base and therefore justified, both in terms of funding and control. The principle is equally applicable among the LEA, SEA, or federal levels of government.

In discussing the controllership role, both dollars and program control have been emphasized. It is clear that the acceptable balance between these factors is a matter of individual political philosophy, and certain programs may be viewed by one person or another as being highly regulated or very open. The distinction between this role and the next identified is, therefore, rather arbitrary.

Revenue Sharing.   The major attribute of this role is the provision of funding, with relatively little control, beyond the identification of the broad target group intended to be beneficiaries of the service. No specific guidelines governing the execution of the program are imposed, and little is required in the way of accounting for how resources are actually expended. Again, the magnitude of whatever accountability is required is a matter of individual interpretation. Specific examples can be cited of programs that had relatively heavy regulation at one time but became much more open as a matter of shifts in political climate and the gradual acceptance of the program as routine. In general, most programs emanating from a higher level of government have more controls at the time of initiation, when it is assumed that leadership is required, with relaxation as implementation becomes generalized. However, some exceptions have occurred, where the initial rush to implement a program caused a distribution of funds before there was time to organize an adequate monitoring procedure. The history of the Title I program within the Elementary and Secondary Education Act of 1965 illustrates how initial lack of controls led to (apparently well-founded) fears that federal funds were being squandered in poorly conceived and operated local programs. This led to the development of more controls, which held sway for a period of years. Eventually, with the shift in political climate to less federal intervention and the establishment of "block grant" concepts, the Title I program came to approximate the ideal of simple revenue sharing, with little regulation. By contrast, proposals by the federal administration to move federal special education programs into the block grant model were rejected (after much controversy and objection from consumers and the Congress) leaving those programs with relatively greater regulation accompanying the distribution of revenue.

The general concept of revenue sharing is always based on the idea that the lower level of government will contribute a major part of the total funding for the program and that the sharing from the higher level is reasonable and appropriate because of the effectiveness with which revenues can be collected and redistributed. It is assumed that higher levels of government have more resource options from which to collect revenue and through distribution can facilitate the equalization of opportunity. This, of course, is the basic rationale on which all state aid to local education in general is based. Any added extension of the concept, or distinction in the case of special education, would be based on the belief that the demands of handicapped students constitute an extraordinary burden on the local community that should be shared by a broader base of support.

Stimulation and Innovation.   A fourth role of government, which Brewer and Kakalik describe as the "catalytic" model, is best illustrated by investments in research and development projects, in which the "primary medium of currency is information rather than money."[37] Programs that supported research on educational problems, including the education of handicapped children, were one of the first mechanisms by which a federal impact on the field could be registered. The Cooperative Research Act of 1954, passed at a time when very little support for federal involvement in education could be found, set the tone for cooperation between government and institutions of higher education in conducting research on education. Moreover, the meager appropriations that were finally obtained to implement the Act in 1957 carried a heavy emphasis on research on mental retardation. The model that has prevailed since that time, through the establishment of the National Institute of Education and the specific research branches within the Bureau of Education for the Handicapped, continues to promote the idea that a proper role of the federal government is to stimulate developments and innovations that would not occur if left to local interests. Government sponsored research impacting on the handicapped has not been limited to educational concerns. Programs focused on child and maternal health, neurological diseases, and mental health have also played a large part in what has happened at the service system level.

In addition to research and demonstration, investment in personnel development, through the provision of fellowships and traineeships, is another example of the catalytic process. Such cooperative efforts between the government and higher education result in an indirect enhancement of the service system by increasing the stock of human capital. The anticipated outcome of such investment, the dissemination of products of research and development, occurs through both the information and knowledge created and the professional personnel produced.

The rationale for investment in stimulation and innovation is "that states and locales may desire to improve the service system but (1) because of lack of start-up funds or political inertia, they have difficulty in doing so, or (2) because of lack of available knowledge about improved ways of providing services, they cannot do so."[38] For much of the research that is needed in the field, economy-of-scale or critical mass principles are applicable. Direct operators of service facilities cannot be expected to mount the kind of research efforts with their own funds that are required to impact the field as a whole. In terms of both research and personnel development, the benefits produced are subject to broad diffusion and, therefore, become "externalities" to the local jurisdiction, which can be "internalized" only by elevating the resource responsibility to the higher level of government.

What Personnel Provide the Services?

An additional dimension for defining the scope of special education, or "mapping the territory," is to consider the various professional roles or personnel classifications that make up the service providers. To a large extent, the process of administration entails the handling of human resources. In a heavily labor intensive operation such as education, and the related functions that support it, the personnel involved in large measure describe the boundaries of the system. Policy issues, therefore, may frequently include matters of role and responsibilities.

Teachers, presumably, will always constitute the major part of the work force in any educational enterprise. However, we have seen a significant general broadening of types of personnel included within the functions of all educational systems. Persons who have responsibilities for support of the teaching function are now recognized as crucial to adequate operations. Among the roles usually described as *professional* support staff to education in general are (1) administrators, at a number of levels, (2) supervisors, (3) consultants, (4) counselors, (5) psychologists, (6) health service personnel, (7) social work personnel, and (8) therapists concerned with particular technical specialties. In addition, *nonprofessional* support staff concerned with clerical, maintenance, transportation, food service, and such other operations are necessary to the system.

In the case of the professional roles at the beginning of the list, there is little question as to their being an integral part of the general system. Administrators and supervisors, regardless of level and proximity to the instructional program, are in most circumstances seen as essential to the operation, nearly as much as classroom teachers. As we move down the list of support personnel, however, there is less clarity and, therefore, some doubt about the centrality of the role to the regular operations. These personnel may be associated with technical assistance either to the pupils directly or to the general staff and, because of their technical specialty, may be seen as outside the direct business of instruction. While curricular and instructional consultants and psychologists may be perceived as being closely related to instructional concerns, nurses, social workers, and various therapists appear to be dealing with another aspect of the child.

The presence of a special education program within the system, staffed with teachers having varying technical specialties and functions that in some ways resemble the work of the support personnel, invites the question as to whether any or all of the specialists might better be considered as belonging to the special education domain. Certain personnel, such as physical and occupational therapists, are generally seen as related service staff to special education, while speech therapists are much more ambiguously viewed as either a support to general education, as special education teachers, or as related service staff to special education. How such staff are seen and organized has a bearing on the policies that govern the operation of the service system.

In addition, special education has increased the numbers and types of nonprofessional and paraprofessional personnel who may be employed in school settings. While instructional aides are to be found in small numbers throughout general school settings, the extraordinary needs of handicapped students have fostered the development of proportionately much greater use of paraprofessionals to assist the teachers.

Within particular areas of handicapping conditions, other supportive or related services personnel have become essential to the program, but they are difficult to classify in terms of their relationship to the typical instructional personnel. Interpreters and interprettutors for the deaf, mobility specialists, Braillists, and readers for the blind play an important role in a comprehensive special education program. The fact that there is no comparative role within general education for many of these types of personnel sometimes can create policy puzzles when dealing with questions of personnel management. Some of the issues in selection, certification, supervision, and evaluation of personnel in all of these ambiguous categories will be discussed in a later chapter.

When considering the personnel dimension as a factor in mapping the territory of special education, it is important to recognize that the variety of influences that determine the boundaries in other respects also play a part here. History, local tradition, philosophical, legal, and fiscal influences may interact. The personal preferences for major identification of certain professionals may coincide or may conflict with legal or fiscal consideras as to their organizational home. This is most likely to be an issue with psychologists and speech therapists, where the connections to general versus special education are particularly ambiguous. Among personnel whose major function is the provision of technical assistance, distinctions are also difficult. For example, a resource teacher/consultant whose area of specialization is with learning disabilities and is identified with the special education program may be working in a manner indistinguishable from that of an instructional specialist who consults with regular classroom teachers on the needs of disadvantaged pupils under the rubric of federal Chapter I programs and is, therefore, a part of the general system.

It might be argued that, as determiners of the scope of special education, services delivered and personnel employed amount to virtually the same thing. And this would be true to a large extent. However, since different types of personnel may be involved with the same service, and different services may be provided by the same types of personnel, it is probably useful to be aware of both dimensions and their interaction.

SUMMARY

Our intent in this chapter has been to present for consideration the multiple factors that go into the determination of the scope of special education. It should be clear that some of these factors are more rational than others. Some are more distinct than others. The scope of the field is in some cases a matter of perspective on the part of the individuals or groups who have a hand in defining it. No single determiner can explain the boundaries, but interactions between the factors may be traced as being responsible for what special education is considered to be at any time and place.

Mapping the territory is a necessary policy matter, on which many other policy considerations may be based. It may well be the number one policy issue, stimulated by the rapid growth in services delivered and dollars spent in the past decade, bringing to the surface the question, "Just how big should special education be?" Knowledgeable persons, both inside the field and out, must address the question and pursue some reasonably acceptable answers.

ILLUSTRATIVE CASE

Chris Hooker had been Principal of East High for six years and previously had served as a middle school principal, after teaching social studies for eight years at both the middle and high school levels in another school system. Dr. Hooker understood the local system but was well aware that each community and each school organization has its own culture. Chris had done a sociological study of schools and communities for the doctoral dissertation in educational administration at State University.

East High, with its 1,400 students in grades 9 to 12, is in the older section of the city and, in comparison with the district's other high school, has a sizable population of students coming from homes below the poverty level. It also has a 30 percent minority, somewhat higher than the city as a whole. The dropout rate at East High has been a concern to the Superintendent and the central office staff, and vocationally oriented programs have long been emphasized as a means of holding the line as the student population has gradually become less able or less inclined toward traditional scholarship. Chris has seen this as a major leadership challenge, particularly since the teaching staff is inclined to accept the situation as inevitable.

Because of its student mix, East High has demanded (and usually received) a good share of the support services generally authorized as a matter of district policy and for which funding assistance is possible under state law and regulation. Federally funded special projects have also been introduced and have become rather standard in the building. For example, the Reading Skills Laboratory, originally established under a Title III grant many years ago, is still staffed by some of East High's share of federal Chapter I funds. A Career Exploration Center for ninth graders, set up with a special grant from the state Vocational Education Department, was for a time a model to be envied by other schools. These have become so routine a part of the program that no one views them as "outside interventions" or remembers that they are made possible on a year-to-year basis by "soft money."

On the other hand, certain services and the personnel providing them are clearly identified as "special," and are viewed as appendages "tacked on" from the outside. The most notable are the three self-contained special classes for educable mentally retarded students, which have operated in much the same fashion since first being established in 1962. The curriculum and the schedule in these classes seem to discourage much interaction with the rest of the school, except for lunch periods and physical education. About one-third of the kids come from across town and would attend the other high school if they weren't identified as handicapped. The three special class teachers depend on the Director of Special Education from the District Office for most of their needs or the Resource Center operated by the Intermediate Education Unit; they do not turn to Dr. Hooker for much except routine supplies, health and attendance services, and emergency management situations. They generally handle their own discipline.

In addition to these programs, East High has the following personnel who might be classified as "support" to the regular classroom teachers:

2 vice principals	full time	1-curriculum & instruction
		1-administration & discipline
4 guidance counselors	full time	1 per grade level
2 school nurses	full time	covering all pupils
2 social workers	part time	shared between East and West High
2 psychologists	part time	shared between East and West High
1 speech therapist	part time	shared between East and West High

In addition, starting this September, two new staff members came aboard in the role of Learning Disability Resource Teacher. Such a program had been operating at the middle school level for a few years, but it was a new concept for the staff at East High. Chris had noted that for the past year or two some of the kids coming up from the middle schools had been receiving resource services and that on arrival at East High a few had been transferred into the special education classes. More had to "sink or swim" in what the regular curriculum offered, with poor results. Therefore, Chris had proposed to the Central Office, with the support of the Director of Special Education, that this new service be extended into East High.

The added personnel slots had been approved with relative ease since, as the Budget Manager pointed out to the board, such positions were reimbursed 70 percent from the state, and all kids served would generate more federal funds as well. The regular teaching staff at East High had acquiesced to the idea (since anything might help) but were a little vague about how the function of these teachers would be different from the long-standing special class teachers in the building.

Chris overheard a conversation in the teachers' lunchroom during the first week of school that illustrates the confusion: "Exactly what are these new special ed teachers going to be doing?" asked Bill Jones, the biology teacher.

"They're not special ed," replied Marie, who had taught math at East High for 23 years and made it a point to be precise. "They are *resource teachers,* and that means they are supposed to be available for us to send kids to for remedial help with the work in our regular classes."

"I don't think so, Marie," broke in Jane. "Someone downtown was saying that resource teachers are mostly to come in and give us advice, like consultants, and not particularly work with the kids."

"You gotta be kidding," Bill yelled. "That's no more help than the psychologists."

"Wait a minute, Bill," Marie cautioned. "Haven't the social workers been helpful sometimes, where we have been trying to get better cooperation with parents to straighten out something?"

"But are they part of our school staff, or just more Central Office Special Service, like the speech therapist?" said Jane.

"Well, the job title did say *Learning Disability* resource teacher," reminded

Marie."And that sounds like they should be *teaching,* whether you call it special ed or not. All the lousy readers we have around here sure do have a learning disability."

"But that's what our Reading Skills Laboratory is for, as long as you're Chapter I eligible," reminded Jane.

"Looks like I better get this sorted out," Chris thought, slipping back to the office."They are funded with special ed dollars, but I don't want them stigmatized like the special class teachers. And besides, I would like to have more ownership of this program. The special class teachers don't really belong. I was going to emphasize the *special service* idea, but how will that be accepted by my staff?"

"What's in a name?" Chris mused, as the door closed.

NOTES

[1]Douglas Biklen and Robert Bogdan, "Media Portrayals of Disabled People: A Study in Stereotypes," *Interracial Books for Children Bulletin,* 8, nos. 6, 7 (1977), p. 4.

[2]Steven J. Apter and Jane Close Conoley, *Childhood Behavior Disorders and Emotional Disturbance* (Englewood Cliffs, NJ: Prentice-Hall, 1984), pp. 20-23.

[3]Maynard C. Reynolds and Jack W. Birch, *Teaching Exceptional Children in All America's Schools* (Reston,VA: The Council for Exceptional Children, 1982), p. 18.

[4]Ibid., p. 20.

[5]Ibid., p. 68.

[6]Nicholas Hobbs, *The Futures of Children* (San Francisco: Jossey-Bass, 1975), p. 1.

[7]Martin L. La Vor, "Federal Legislation for Exceptional Persons: A History," in *Public Policy and the Education of Exceptional Children,* eds. Frederick J. Weintraub, Alan Abeson, Joseph Ballard, and Martin L. La Vor (Reston, VA: The Council for Exceptional Children, 1976), p. 96.

[8]Jeffrey J. Zettel,"The Education of Gifted and Talented Children from a Federal Perspective," in *Special Education in America: Its Legal and Governmental Foundations,* eds., Joseph Ballard, Bruce A. Ramirez, and Frederick J. Weintraub (Reston, VA: The Council for Exceptional Children, 1982), p. 63.

[9]Romaine P. Mackie and Lloyd N. Dunn, *College and University Programs for the Preparation of Teachers of Exceptional Children,* Office of Education Bulletin No. 13 (Washington, DC: U.S. Government Printing Office, 1954).

[10]La Vor, "Federal Legislation," pp. 96-111.

[11]Jeffrey J. Zettel, "Implementing the Right to a Free Appropriate Public Education," in *Special Education in America: Its Legal and Governmental Foundations,* eds. Joseph Ballard, Bruce A. Ramirez, and Frederick J. Weintraub (Reston, VA: The Council for Exceptional Children, 1982), pp. 28-29.

[12]"To Assure the Free Appropriate Public Education of All Handicapped Children," *Sixth Annual Report to Congress on the Implementation of Public Law 94-142: The Education for All Handicapped Children Act* (Washington, D.C.: U.S. Department of Education, 1984), p. 3.

[13]"To Assure the Free Appropriate Public Education of All Handicapped Children," *Fourth Annual Report to Congress on the Implementation of Public Law 94-142: The Education for All Handicapped Children Act* (Washington, D.C.: U.S. Department of Education, 1982).

[14]Comptroller General, *Disparities Still Exist in Who Gets Special Education* (Washington, D.C.: U.S. General Accounting Office, 1981), p. 29.

[15]"To Assure," *Sixth Annual Report,* pp. 117-118.

[16]Ibid., p. 120.

[17]Ibid., pp. 18-26.

[18]Comptroller General, *Disparities Still Exist,* pp. 12-13.

[19]Ibid., pp. 57-61.

[20]Ibid., pp. 61-63.

[21]Ibid., p. 64

[22]Leonard C. Burrello, Michael Tracy, and Edward Schultz, "Special Education as Experimental Education: A New Conceptualization," *Exceptional Children,* 40 (1973), pp. 29-34.

[23]Reynolds and Birch, *Teaching Exceptional Children,* p. 37.

[24]Evelyn N. Deno, "Special Education as Developmental Capital," *Exceptional Children,* 37 (1970), pp. 299-340.

[25]Reynolds and Birch, *Teaching Exceptional Children,* p. 39.

[26]Ibid., pp. 46-50.

[27]"To Assure," *Sixth Annual Report,* pp. 35-39.

[28]Ibid., p. 144.

[29]Garry D. Brewer and James S. Kakalik, *Handicapped Children: Strategies for Improving Services* (New York: McGraw-Hill, 1979), pp. 49-73.

[30]Ibid., pp. 62-69.

[31]David E. Greenburg, *A Planning Study Report for the Council of Administrators of Special Education* (Indianapolis: Council of Administrators of Special Education, 1983), p. 8.

[32]Kenneth E. Wyatt, *Current Employment and Possible Future Needs for Leadership Personnel in Special Education,* Doctoral Dissertation, University of Illinois (Ann Arbor, Mich.: University Microfilms, 1968, No. 68-12), pp. 48-49.

[33]Brewer and Kakalik, *Handicapped Children,* p. 51.

[34]Ibid., pp. 62-65.

[35]Ibid., p. 63.

[36]Ibid., p. 63.

[37]Ibid., p. 54.

[38]Ibid., p. 67.

CHAPTER 2
FORMAL SOURCES
OF CONTROL

In Chapter 1 we have identified major policy issues regarding the scope of the enterprise called special education. We shall now turn to the issue of how that enterprise is controlled and consider the various forces that determine what goes on within the field.

Initially, two major sources of control should be recognized and differentiated: (1) formal governance and (2) informal power and influence. While these two interact in day-to-day practice and have impact on each other, they also may operate independently. Together, they constitute the major forces for policy determination. This chapter will address the various aspects of formal governance, leaving to Chapter 3 the consideration of the nature of informal power and influence.

The official authority for what occurs within special education programs is drawn from a combination of forces and a number of levels of government. Although the concept of local autonomy carries a heavy influence in education in the United States, and boards of education in local school districts have the authority to set policy on much of the educational program, that authority is clearly delimited by the broader matrix of governing units within which the districts (and their constituents) reside. After an initial approach to the governance of education that was almost exclusively locally based in this country, the gradually increasing exercise of state-level authority through legislative bodies, courts, and units of the executive branch of government began noticeably to shape the practice of education. The avoidance of major involvement by the federal government in education was attributable to the clearly stipulated provision of the Tenth Amendment to the U.S. Constitution, which reserved to the states those powers not specifically mentioned in the Constitution.

Because of the degree to which the federal level of government has become centrally prominent in special education, and because constitutional issues have come into play, it is important to the appreciation of the controlling forces over special education that the total governance system be understood. The system is based on legal structures in which certain orderly relationships exist. These legal structures and their relationships will be outlined, with discussion illustrating the application to education, and to special education particularly.

THE LEGAL STRUCTURE

We have indicated that three levels of government operate in the exercise of most of the public activities affecting our society. Federal, state, and local agencies, with appropriate legal powers and forms to determine their activities, exist across a wide variety of public functions. While certain functions are concentrated at the federal level (e.g., national defense), others are relatively concentrated at the local level (e.g., education). While a number of functions may be executed within a single unit of government at the local level (e.g., health, social services, police, and fire within a municipal administration), the function of education is almost universally governed by a separate local agency, the school district. While the degree of independence in this respect varies among the states, and among certain large cities, this differentiating factor becomes significant in comparing the intergovernmental relations across functions within the legal structures.

In a discussion of intergovernmental policy influences on education in America, Mosher has pointed out that "the question of locus of effective power—who dominates in the partnerships or cooperative arrangements—is a matter of considerable dispute."[1] She elaborates on a view of American education by Thompson[2] that places the local school system at the vortex of interacting influence systems. As a "special" unit of government, local education is acted upon not only by the upper levels of the education system, but also by agencies of other governmental units as well as nonpublic agencies, each having a locus of identity and sources of influence at local, state, regional, and national levels.

Over each of the levels of government, the legal structure is based on four sources of authority: (1) constitutions (usually called charters at the local level); (2) court decisions; (3) statutes (usually called ordinances at the local level); and (4) administrative regulations. In accordance with the U.S. Constitution, federal statutes (or regulations or court decisions) take precedence over state and local provisions when they conflict. Similarly, state provisions take precedence when they conflict with local ones.

Constitutional Law

At each level of government the constitution establishes the primary legal basis to which all other sources of control must adhere. Constitutions are adopted at the time of establishment of the governmental unit and are amended, only rarely, by a complicated process. Constitutional provisions are therefore written in broad, general principles that will remain appropriate through changing times and conditions. Statutes and regulations must stand the test of compliance with constitutional law. The breadth of constitutional provisions necessarily contributes to their ambiguity, frequently making the test of constitutionality of statutes dependent upon judicial interpretation in the courts.

Since the U.S. Constitution does not address education as a federal concern, appeals to constitutional concepts as a source of control over educational practices have been based on fundamental civil rights that are clearly articulated, particularly those in the Fifth and Fourteenth Amendments. The U.S. Constitution has been invoked in education settings over such issues as freedom in regard to religion, speech, and assembly. With increasing frequency in recent years, the accent on civil rights and liberties has focused upon protection against governmental deprivation of such rights without "due process of law"and prohibition against a state's "deny[ing] to any person within its jurisdiction the equal protection of the laws." It is within this context that much of the force of law has been brought to bear on educational and human services practice affecting handicapped individuals.

Constitutional precedent in special education is not, however, isolated from that which has been applicable in more general settings as well. The determination of whether special education services will be provided to meet the needs of all children (including the particular needs of certain disabled, disadvantaged, or otherwise exceptional students) depends in part upon an extension of the basic legal principles upon which all public education is authorized. These basic principles include such concepts as (1) equal protection of the laws, (2) access to publicly provided services, (3) impartial due process, and (4) nondiscrimination on the basis of classification. Judicial interpretation of the Constitution and related statutes on these concepts in broadly based educational questions have been used as precedents in special education cases. While these instances will be elaborated on later, in discussing the role of the courts in this chapter, it is important to recognize that education has been ruled by the U.S. Supreme Court to *not* be a fundamental right guaranteed by the Constitution. Education is, therefore, unprotected in the manner that holds for voting, for example, but must be secured, if possible, under the equal protection or due process clauses.

State constitutions, on the other hand, speak directly to educational provisions and provide the more consistent basis for the development of state statutes and for the rulings of state-level courts. Constitutional pronouncements pertaining to the inclusion of all children, without exemption, become key to the statutory establishment of special education programs.

Court Decisions

The application of constitutional principles to daily practice in the public domain usually takes place through the medium of the court system, where judicial opinion regarding the practice and its "fit" with constitutional intent are carefully scrutinized. The most directly applicable precedent for the many judicial rulings affecting special education in the 1970s and 1980s was the landmark Supreme Court decision in *Brown* v. *Board of Education of Topeka,* in 1954.[3] Touching on a number of civil rights issues concerned with race (nondiscrimination, access to non-segregated educational programs, equal protection, etc.), the principles established have been found to be equally applicable in addressing other discriminatory classifications, most notably handicapping conditions. The notion set forth in *Brown*—that education is the means by which all other constitutional rights are secured and that education is necessary for individuals to function in a democratic society—has provided a foundation for arguing that no one may be excluded from educational programs, regardless of special or disadvantageous status. Furthermore, the notion that segregation inherently constitutes nonequality, as established in *Brown*, provides a rationale for inclusion of a variety of classifications of student, including the handicapped, within the mainstream of education.

The *Brown* case stands as a landmark, according to Turnbull and Turnbull,[4] for a number of reasons:

1. It illustrates the primacy of the U.S. Constitution as binding on other levels of government.
2. It illustrates that educational issues are essentially political policy and social issues.
3. It demonstrates the relationships between educational issues and other civil right issues that may be resolved in the courts on similar constitutional grounds.
4. It stimulated civil right activism in the development of antidiscrimination legislation at both federal and state levels.
5. It shifted the balance of influence on education toward the federal government, suggesting that few issues are "purely local" concerns.
6. It showed that although education is not mentioned in the U.S. Constitution, the principles of equal protection and due process may strongly impact public education.
7. It illustrates the manner in which a "civil action" may be brought against a

governmental unit or official by a citizen (or class of citizens) who is alleged to have been denied rights or benefits to which he or she is entitled under law.

8. It brought focus on the importance of education, the stigmatizing effects of racial segregation, and the detrimental consequences of segregation to the education of those on whom it is practiced.

9. It established that segregation, by state requirement or state sanction violates equal protection and is therefore unconstitutional.

10. The parallels between the issues of racial classification and those of other "unalterable traits" (e.g., sex, handicapping condition) are highly relevant in interpreting constitutional intent.

To appreciate the translation of the court opinion on race to that of handicapping condition, one should be aware that earlier court rulings had stood in sharp contrast. Noteworthy is the case of *Watson* v. *City of Cambridge* (1893) in which a state court supported the school committee in expelling children who persisted in disorderly conduct "either voluntarily or by reason of imbecility."[5] Also frequently cited is the case of *Beattie* v. *Board of Education* (1919) in which a Wisconsin superior court ruled that although a physically handicapped child constituted no threat, and was academically capable, his presence produced a "depressing and nauseating effect on the teachers and school children" and took up an undue portion of the teacher's time. Therefore, "the rights of a child of school age to attend the public schools of the state cannot be insisted upon, when its presence therein is harmful to the best interests of the school."[6]

A dramatic shift is evident from the attitude expressed in these cases to that in the 1970s, when the principle enunciated in *Brown* was applied to a number of decisions on rights to education for the handicapped. Basing decisions on the equal protection and due process guarantees of the Fifth and Fourteenth Amendments, courts have invoked the language of *Brown,* which said

> In these days it is doubtful that any child may reasonably be expected to succeed in life if he is denied the opportunity of an education. Such an opportunity, where the state has undertaken to provide it, is a right which must be made available to all on equal terms.[7]

In discussing the litigation that accelerated in the 1970s, Gilhool[8] defines three different lines of cases bearing on the general topic.

Right to Treatment. The first deals with the issue of right to treatment, and was initiated by the case of *Wyatt* v. *Stickney* (1972).[9] These cases are concerned with rights of institutionalized retarded persons to habilitation, care, and education within the least restrictive environment, with due regard for privacy and other basic attributes of human living. While these issues go well beyond the concerns of school policymakers or administrators, the cases illustrate many of the principles involved and the means by which the judicial system may intervene into executive branches of government. Similar examples include the Willowbrook case *(NYSARC* v. *Carey,* 1975)[10] which was resolved through a consent agreement specifying a number of remedies based on equal protection principles, including the deinstitutionalization of the majority of the residents. The case of *Halderman* v. *Pennhurst State School and Hospital* (1977)[11] also involved the ruling that institutionalization was inconsistent with individuals' rights to habilitation in the least restrictive environment.

Right to Education.   A second line of cases that are more directly involved with access to public school education was initiated by the suit brought by the Pennsylvania Association for Retarded Children against the Commonwealth of Pennsylvania *(PARC* v. *Pennsylvania).* [12] Resolved by consent agreement in 1972, this case established that every retarded child is capable of benefiting from education and set forth specific stipulations regarding the manner in which delivery of services and the procedural safeguards would be handled. The principles employed in these stipulations were to be used repeatedly in succeeding cases and in the drafting of legislation in the years that followed.

While the *PARC* case dealt only with the mentally retarded, it was closely followed by comprehensive litigation in *Mills* v. *Board of Education of District of Columbia.* [13] The court ordered in 1972 that the system had failed to provide appropriate services for all types of handicapped children and must establish hearing procedures to guard against indiscriminate suspension, exclusion, or placement of pupils in special education programs. It established that "before any handicapped child eligible for publicly supported education may be excluded from a regular school assignment, he must be furnished adequate alternative educational services suited to his needs."[14] It provided procedures for correction of official records in the case of previous expulsions that might have occurred in violation of such due process requirements. The school district was ordered to provide suitable educational programs within specified time limits, to advertise the availability of free public education, and to identify previously excluded children and inform them of their rights. Furthermore, this case directly addressed the economic issue that is often raised as a barrier to implementing programs:

> If sufficient funds are not available to finance all of the services and programs that are needed in the system then the available funds must be expended equitably in such a manner that no child is entirely excluded from a publicly supported education consistent with his needs and ability to benefit therefrom.[15]

The *Mills* case appears to have opened the door to a number of succeeding rulings, establishing that "handicapped children have a right to an education and it is unconstitutional to deny that right, that public funds must provide for educational opportunities, and that handicapped individuals or their parents or guardians have legal redress in the courts if these rights are denied.''[16] Furthermore, the success of litigation on these matters seems to have influenced the resort to the courts on additional related issues.

Discriminatory Classification.   Another line of litigation focused on the crucial issues of standards and practices used in classifying children. It should be recalled that the primary issue in the *Brown* case was one of discriminatory classification on the basis of race. Classification of children as handicapped does not occur as directly or automatically, but involves a deliberate process. The case of *Diana* v. *State Board of Education*[17] in California was the initiator of this line, followed by *Ruiz* v. *State Board of Education,*[18] and *Larry P.* v. *Riles.*[19] While the cases cited earlier had been concerned with securing a desired and presumably appropriate special educational service, this other line of litigation attacked practices of placing children into special education programs who did not belong there. In each of these cases, the state school system in California was charged with using procedures that resulted in a disproportionate number of minority group children being classified as handicapped and placed in programs that were of questionable value and carried a negative stigma.

In the *Diana* case, it was pointed out that classes for educable mentally retarded contained approximately double the number of Chicano pupils that should be expected by the proportion of such children in the general school population. It was clear that school personnel had been faced with children whose language and cultural background were significantly different from that of the typical Anglo child; the school personnel had used the special education program as the most readily available alternative to the regular classroom. It was charged that the plaintiff children had been certified as eligible for such placement on the basis of English intelligence tests, which, as the court found obvious, were totally inappropriate for making a decision regarding a status of mental retardation. The universality of such practice, wherever populations of non-English-speaking persons were found, led California to the mandate for developing test instruments and testing procedures that would be appropriate for children of other than English language and culture.

In the *Ruiz* case, group testing was a major issue since it was charged that the results from such tests tended to create a self-fulfilling prophecy when given to teachers. The demonstrated bias in such tests when used to classify pupils for special programs for the gifted led to constraints on the use of group intelligence testing. Additional strength to the arguments regarding bias in assessment and classification came from the widely disseminated findings of Jane Mercer in an eight-year study of public school and agency classification of minority children in California. Her data demonstrated that, of all agencies, the public school system was the primary labeler of individuals as mentally retarded. In elaborating on the conclusions regarding the classification of black and Chicano children, Mercer stated

We believe that psychological assessment procedures have become a civil rights issue because present assessment and educational practices violate at least five rights of children: a) their right to be evaluated within a culturally appropriate normative framework; b) their right to be assessed as multi-dimensional, many faceted human beings; c) their right to be fully educated; d) their right to be free of stigmatizing labels; and e) their right to cultural identity and respect.[20]

An extensive analysis of the courts' dealings with student classification has been discussed by Kirp. He points out that while many courts have been assertive in dealing with broad issues of school policy, they have been reluctant to intervene in matters concerning minute details within the individual school or classroom unit, which are therefore legally less manageable. However, in the domain of student classification, the courts have found it feasible to intervene, since such cases can be argued on clear constitutional standards in any of three approaches:

1. The educational harm attributable to either exclusion or assignment to slow-ability groups, or special education programs that are not only inferior, but carry psychic injury in addition to deprivation
2. The disproportionate assignment of minority group children, which creates racially or ethnically based isolation
3. The schools' procedure for determining how a particular student or class of students should be treated, irrespective of the legitimacy of the classifications themselves.[21]

The *Larry P.* case was focused specifically on black students who were placed in classes for the educable mentally retarded (EMR) in the San Francisco Unified School District at a rate three times their incidence in the general school population. It was argued in this class action suit that the students were not mentally retarded but, rather, the victims of a testing procedure that failed to account for their different cultural background. The relief sought was a moratorium on the use of individual intelligence tests for the placement of black children and a ceiling on placement of black children based on the percentage of Anglos in the total school population who are placed in such special classes. A temporary injunction in 1972 stopped the use of I.Q. tests as the main criterion for placing black students and ordered yearly reevaluation of children currently in such classes.

After much deliberation, Judge Robert F. Peckham ruled in 1979, prohibiting California school districts from using I.Q. tests in this fashion, on the grounds that the tests are culturally biased. The case had been, by this time, expanded to include all black children in the state. This decision was affirmed in 1983 by a three judge panel of the U.S. Court of Appeals for the Ninth Circuit, which held that the state did not take reasonable steps to ensure that nondiscriminatory methods were used to identify and place black students and did not make a reasonable attempt to alleviate existing disproportionate enrollment. Defendants had argued that the low I.Q. scores of black students were the result of lower socioeconomic status and that their placement was not based solely on the use of standardized test results. The court found, however, that students' school records contained insufficient evidence that school personnel had considered other factors beyond the test results in making placement decisions. Judge Peckham had noted that there is "less than a one-in-a-million chance that the over-enrollment of black children and the under-enrollment of nonblack children in the EMR classes in 1976–77 would have resulted under a color-blind system."[22]

It should be noted that during the time between the initial filing of *Larry P.* and the decision in 1979, legislation in California had brought about a different "Master Plan" for special education and a moratorium on the use of I.Q. tests for EMR placement of all children, regardless of race. These major changes were certainly influenced by the impending judicial action. However, the court concluded that these changes had been insufficient to rectify the imbalances in enrollment and that the state had failed to gather data to support the validity of the tests used and had "revealed a complacent acceptance" of discriminatory practices. Further remedies that were stipulated (1) constrained the use of I.Q. tests unless data could be supplied pertaining to the validity of proposed tests for both blacks and whites, (2) ordered monitoring and adoption of procedures to correct existing racial imbalances, and (3) mandated reevaluation (without I.Q. tests) of all black children currently enrolled in EMR classes.[23]

During the time that the case was on appeal, between 1979 and 1983, continued implementation of the Master Plan in California had resulted in the elimination of EMR as a placement classification, but state officials expressed continued concern that the prohibition of certain tests creates a "practical dilemma" in that professionals may be denied the use of a valuable tool. It should be noted that the appellate court's decision in this case is binding only on the school districts in the Ninth Circuit, covering the Western states, but such rulings tend to have considerable influence beyond the official jurisdiction.[24]

Conflicting Rulings. The impact of the courts, however, must also be viewed in light of the rulings that sometimes appear conflicting. An example in the area of alleged discrimination in testing is the case of *Parents in Action on Special Education (PASE) v. Hannon et al.* (1980),[25] which involved the Chicago public schools. In this case, Judge Grady focused on the individual test items within the instruments in question and ruled that they were not discriminatory for black children. It was his contention that although a few items in certain tests were culturally biased, this did not invalidate the tests as a whole. Therefore, such tests could be used by qualified examiners in conjunction with other criteria. The ruling of the court placed great emphasis on the school system's contention that the low scores of black students on these tests could be explained by the conditions of poverty, which tended to be associated with health problems and stimulation deprivation. It is of particular interest to note that in reaching these conclusions, the judge was responding to conflicting testimony provided by equally qualified expert witnesses and found the evidence supporting the defendant school system's arguments most convincing. The lack of consensus by experts on issues such as these brings the courts into a decision-making role on matters that involve professional standards rather than legal questions.[26]

Procedural Versus Substantive Issues.   The courts have, in many instances, taken pains to avoid ruling on issues where professional judgment was at the center of the dispute, preferring to focus on questions that more clearly involved a legal right. For example, the question of access to *some* education (or exclusion therefrom) is more readily dealt with as a legal issue than the more difficult question of establishing what is *appropriate* education.

In dealing with the definition of "appropriate," the concept of "functional exclusion" must be considered. In *Brown,* the issue was that blacks be given equal access to the same resources as whites. In *Mills,* it was that all handicapped students should have equal access to the same resources as all other students. In more recent cases, the issue has changed to the claim for the handicapped to *differing resources* for *differing objectives.* This concept was established as especially relevant in a case not concerned with the handicapped but with bilingual education. In *Lau* v. *Nichols,*[27] the plaintiffs argued that Chinese students had been "functionally excluded" since they had to attend public schools in which all instruction was in English. This case, followed by others concerned with education of the handicapped, raised the issue of exclusion from *meaningful* equal educational opportunity.

While the rulings in some of these cases have tended toward establishing means for ensuring appropriate education through timely and sufficient evaluations, individually planned programs, and periodic reviews, it is clear that the courts have been reticent to go beyond such procedural mechanisms and to make a substantive judgment about what constitutes "appropriate." This was particularly evident in the first case appealed to the U.S. Supreme Court to test the limits of the concept of appropriate education for the handicapped.

U.S. Supreme Court.   It should be noted that the cases (concerning the handicapped) discussed to this point were in state or federal district courts. The first case of this type to reach the U.S. Supreme Court was an appeal by a school district regarding the educational program for Amy Rowley. In this case the lower courts had established that a sign language interpreter must be provided by the school district for the deaf child to participate fully and profit from the educational program. There was no question of access or that various special supportive services were provided. The contention was over *how much* service was required for Amy to progress *how well* in her school program. The lower courts had ruled that the child must be provided all the services that the parents had requested in developing the individualized educational program (IEP), and the school system had appealed the ruling.

The decision of the Supreme Court in *Hendrick Hudson School District v. Rowley* (1982)[28] stated that the system was already providing "sufficient support services to permit the handicapped child to benefit educationally from that instruction." Since the services provided were apparently allowing the child to achieve passing marks and to advance with her peers, no additional services were required by law. The parents contended that Amy's intelligence was above average and that with a signlanguage interpreter her greater potential could be more fully achieved. The court noted that the legal requirement had been satisfied by the fact that *normal* progress was occurring and it is the prerogative of the state and local agencies (not the courts) to determine the best methods for providing the required services. This is consistent with a number of other cases in which the courts have refrained from dictating educational methods or judging the merits of particular instructional approaches.

Issues involving educational settings have been more readily tackled by the courts. In the case of *Springdale School District v. Grace* (1982),[29] the Supreme Court denied an appeal from a school district that had argued that the best placement for a deaf child was at a state school some distance from the child's home. The impartial hearing officer had ruled that although the child could obtain an appropriate education in either place, the local school district setting was preferable since it constituted a less restrictive environment. On a similar issue, but involving a more difficult case, the question of placement of a trainable retarded child in a local school (as opposed to a special county school) was advanced to a U.S. Court of Appeals. While a hearing officer had determined that the local school placement, in a special class, was appropriate, the Ohio State Board of Education and a district court had ruled in favor of the special county school, as long as some contact with nonhandicapped children could be assured. On appeal, the court in *Roncker* v. *Walter* (1983)[30] reversed the decision on the basis that "to the maximum extent appropriate," handicapped children must be educated with nonhandicapped. The issues of the importance of such contact and quality of services for more severely handicapped students has not (by 1985) been confronted by the highest court, but this case and a number of similar ones at the same level illustrate the general support for (but varying judgments that may be rendered regarding) the value of mainstreaming.

Other Issues.   The length of the school year has become another issue over which courts have intervened. It is clear that if a school district provides extended-year programs for its nonhandicapped students, it must not deny such services for its handicapped. In addition, it has been ruled that any school law or policy that limits the school year to 180 days (or any similar cap) is in violation of the provisions of P.L. 94-142 since it requires that schools retain sufficient flexibility to provide extra services for those who need them. *Yaris v. Special School District of St. Louis County* (1983)[31] followed a number of similar previous cases that have emphasized the fact that if a severely handicapped child will regress over the summer months, an appropriate program would necessitate provision of an extended year, and the school system must be free to elect such a program for those individuals.[32] The point is not that the courts have mandated summer programs but that states and local school districts *must not preclude* such programs as an option.

The courts have also been asked to rule on what constitutes an educational "placement." In a case involving the New York City Board of Education, the Second U.S. Circuit Court of Appeals held that "the term educational placement refers only to the general type of educational program in which the child is placed." The issue in this case had been whether the movement of a group of children from one school to another was in fact a change in placement if essentially the same program of activity was being provided in either location. It was pointed out that to consider any alteration in a child's educational program as a placement change would impair the ability of teachers to make appropriate modifications or improvements.[33]

On the other hand, the Fifth U.S. Circuit Court of Appeals ruled in *S-1* v. *Turlington* (1981)[34] that expulsion from school for disciplinary reasons did constitute a change of placement and, therefore, must follow all procedural safeguards. In this and similar cases, the courts have ruled that handicapped students could be expelled for behavioral reasons where the behavior is not a result of the handicapping condition, and if due process is observed. The problem of establishing with accuracy the connection between a child's handicap and his or her misbehavior has been duly recognized, and the courts have specified that such determination be made by persons qualified to evaluate the child's needs. This assures that such judgments will not be made arbitrarily and unilaterally by school administrators.

The issue of diplomas and completion requirements has also come to the attention of the courts, particularly as minimum competency testing has been introduced into the general school system. *Brookhart* v. *Illinois State Board of Education* (1982)[35] is one of a number of cases in which it has been ruled that diplomas could not be withheld, even though handicapped students failed to pass the otherwise required minimum competency tests. The major rationale in these decisions has been that handicapped students had not received sufficient notice of the requirement. The validity of this argument cannot be expected to endure, however, and other statutory and regulatory provisions are being made to deal with this issue. It can be seen that the judicial system has paved the way in establishing connections between constitutional rights and day-to-day practice in the delivery of public services for the handicapped. To decide every service issue in the courts, however, would be extremely awkward. Statutory provisions have always been the major control mechanism for practice, and those legislative initiatives flowing from court decisions have become the major force for change at both the state and federal levels.

Statutory Code

In contrast to the policies generating from court cases and the rulings of a single judge or judicial panel, laws passed by a legislative body presumably reflect the policy intent of a large group of individuals, elected to officially represent the will of the people. The legislative process involves the writing of proposed laws, or statutes, in the form of bills that receive study, debate, and testimony from interested parties and revision before finally being voted upon by the elected representatives. In addition, the required endorsement of the proposed legislation by the chief executive further broadens the presumed base of acceptance of the policy before it becomes law. This process of statutory development operates in basically the same manner in all states and in the U.S. Congress. The assumption of broad, representative input to legislative acts provides the rationale for expecting the statutes generated from this process to be implemented in accordance with the intent of those initiating and approving them. Being more focused and specific to a particular purpose than constitutional provisions, statutes provide authorization for certain things to occur; however, they are usually not sufficiently detailed to be totally explanatory or self-enforcing. Statutes generally set forth broad principles permitting, authorizing, or mandating activities in the jurisdiction concerned, but leave to the executive branch of the government the responsibility for determining exactly how to carry out the understood intent. The degree of detailed specificity included within a statute is often an issue of controversy, and the achievement of an optimal level of detail enters significantly into the chances of bills becoming laws and, after the fact, laws being implemented. These factors are particularly apparent in some of the statutes passed in the area of special education in recent times.

State Initiatives.   At the state level, a rapid upsurge in legislative changes marked the decade of the 1970s. While almost every state legislature had periodically added and modified existing statutes with some degree of regularity during the 1940s, 1950s, and 1960s, the focus of that period's legislation tended to be on incremental expansion and addition of services, the securing of somewhat more favorable fiscal provisions, and the development of standards for the delivery of quality instruction to the handicapped. There was encouragement and, in many cases, incentive for local school systems to improve their service offerings. However, strongly worded mandates for comprehensive service for all conditions and degrees of handicaps were rare. By contrast, legislative activity in the early 1970s was so pronounced that by the close of the 1975 legislative session, 46 states had some form of mandatory legislation.[36] However, it was recognized that exemption provisions and loopholes allowed for considerable slippage in the realization of full services.

The newer legislation of the 1970s tended to focus on the policy of guaranteeing service for *all,* with no child excluded from services or education for any reason whatsoever. Due process protections, growing out of the upsurge in court actions at the time, also were frequently found in most of the legislative changes. Attention to the principle of least restrictive environment and maximum feasible normalization, which had not been evident before the 1970s, was increasingly found. Fiscal modifications, with increases in funding, occurred in virtually every state.

Legislation concerned with statewide planning was passed and advisory councils were authorized, bringing such provisions to a total of 23 states in 1972. Provision for preschool services, very rare before 1970, were also introduced in nearly half the states. In summarizing the effects of this upsurge in state legislation, a major point is that by the time federal legislation was passed in 1975, the states had taken affirmative action of a similar nature to a very large extent.

In accordance with the Tenth Amendment, education is basically a concern of the states, and federal intervention has been limited to issues where equal protection principles have been prominent. Exceptions have been noted where, to meet certain other social concerns, federal initiatives to promote and facilitate particular educational objectives have been advanced.

Federal Initiatives. Discussing the federal role in a historical context, Kaestle and Smith[37] mention the popular notion that federal aid to education has tended to occur in connection with incidents of national crises, many of which have been war related. They cite the Morrill Act, providing aid to higher education, passed during the Civil War, and the Smith-Hughes Act for vocational education (directly affecting elementary and secondary schools) passed during World War I. The Lanham Act, which introduced the concept of aid to federally impacted areas (largely due to military bases and private defense contractors), was passed at the beginning of World War II and expanded during the Korean emergency. The cold war is credited with influencing the National Defense Education Act in 1958. These federal programs have tended to be limited in scope, enabling rather than mandatory, and always supplemental to the major state and local role in providing education. Combination federal-state programs in vocational education had long been a source of support to local schools, but these had been highly categorical and were not accompanied by significant federal intervention. Departure from this stance dates only from 1965.

It should be noted that certain items of federal legislation concerned with education of handicapped children predated this point. However, these initiatives offered *indirect* support in that they dealt with the funding of research on the problem, the training of personnel to work in education of the handicapped, and the development of instructional materials, specifically for the deaf and the blind. This earlier legislation, dating from 1954 to 1964, contained no provision for funding or otherwise intervening in local school system special education programming. While aspects of these earlier federal programs have been retained as parts of more expansive provisions in recent years, their magnitude has been overshadowed since the early 1970s by both the dollars involved and the impact of the federal presence on the education community and the general public.

The Breakthrough.   The Elementary and Secondary Education Act of 1965 (ESEA, P. L. 89-10) was again a response to a social concern, with its major focus on problems of poverty and its mechanisms designed to supplement local practice. Consistent with the observation that federal interventions to education have been associated with war and other national crises, this initiative, occurring concurrently with the Vietnam involvement, was a major part of what Lyndon Johnson proclaimed as our "war on poverty." However, the scope of ESEA, the magnitude of federal funds distributed, and the extent to which its mechanisms intervened with state and local educational practices clearly constituted a breakthrough in legislative history. ESEA broke the logjam on federal involvement in local education. Certain principles set forth in the implementation of the law have become a part of standard interaction between levels of government in the delivery of education services. Many of those principles have later become reflected in policies and procedures in special education as well. Some of the parallels between ESEA and the later federal legislation concerned with the handicapped are particularly relevant.[38]

1.   Focus on a *disadvantaged* population. The acceptance of a role for the federal government in facilitating the achievement of equal opportunity for a class of students whose characteristics mark them as having a distinct disadvantage in utilizing the existing system of public education.

2.   Focus on *individual* child needs. The recognition that compensation for disadvantaged status requires a focus on the student and his or her needs rather than on a standard curriculum and delivery system.

3.   Focus on *planning*. The importance of systematic planning in the development of programs of intervention for the individual student, the local school system, and the state program.

4.   Focus on *consumer participation*. The recognition that parents and other citizens of the community affected by a program should have an active voice in the planning, execution, and evaluation of what occurs.

5.   Focus on *personnel development*. The recognition that to accomplish the task required the recruitment and/or training of new personnel to perform different functions than had been typical in the educational system.

6.   Focus on *public/nonpublic cooperation*. The adoption of the"pupil benefit theory," which permits public schools to act as a "public trustee" in the provision of services to children in nonpublic schools.

7.   Focus on *supplementation* of regular school services. The development of the concept of comparability, which assures that federal funds will purchase only those services that are above and beyond those normally provided for *all* students by regular state and local resources.

8. Focus on *evaluation and accountability.* Acceptance of the importance of including an evaluation mechanism, with monitoring that includes participation by parents and/or direct consumers of the service.

These aspects of ESEA have been carried forward into much of the legislation concerning federal involvement in education. Title VI, which was added to the original ESEA by amendment in 1967, extended certain provisions of the Act to cover services for handicapped students and thereby became the forerunner of two major federal civil rights initiatives—the Rehabilitation Act of 1973 (P.L. 93-112) and the Education for All Handicapped Children Act of 1975 (P.L. 94-142).

Concern for the Handicapped. The prohibition of discrimination against the handicapped is the major focus of P. L. 93-112, through its Section 504, which though constituting a very broad umbrella, is unusually brief in its statement that

> No otherwise qualified handicapped individual in the United States, as defined in section 7(6), shall, solely by reason of his/her handicap, be excluded from the participation in, be denied the benefits of, or be subject to discrimination under any program or activity receiving federal financial assistance.

The programs referred to include education, and since virtually all education agencies receive some form of federal assistance, this policy has direct application to education of the handicapped as well as to the full range of other public services (such as health, welfare, and employment) and to all ages of participants. Much more of the implications of this statute will be discussed later under the topic of administrative regulations.

A more narrow target is addressed by P.L. 94-142, which deals only with *education* and with handicapped persons from *3 to 21* years of age. The Act reflects the intent of Congress to ensure that a free and appropriate education and related services be provided to *all* handicapped children. The major provisions of the Act include

1. Grants to states to assist in providing mandated programs
2. The requirement of state plans and local applications to receive the allocated funds
3. State and local procedural safeguards for students and their parents
4. To the maximum extent appropriate, education within the least restrictive environment
5. Procedures for nondiscriminatory evaluation and assessment of students
6. The development, implementation, and periodic review of an individualized educational program for every handicapped student
7. A comprehensive system of personnel development for each state
8. Cooperation between state and local education agencies and those other public and private agencies concerned with handicapped children

9. Involvement of parents in the approval of assessment procedures and in determining how and where children will be served.

Within these broad parameters of statutory control, the articulation of federal, state, and local policies and procedures are carried out. The details that determine day-to-day practice must be provided by administrative rules and regulations. It has been noted, however, that as compared with many federal statutes, and certainly as compared with the degree of intervention from the federal level with which state and local school administrators were accustomed, P.L. 94-142 is rather highly prescriptive. Although the Bill passed the Congress by a comfortable margin, in retrospect it should be recognized that such specificity, entailing such intrusion on previously held autonomy, was a significant change in intergovernmental relations in the educational domain. The reactions from the education community in the decade since the Act's passage demonstrate the effect of that change. Proposals to modify the statute have come from a number of quarters, but the political process for any proposed changes to be successfully undertaken has forestalled attacks on the statute very effectively.

The Nature of Federal Intervention.   The criticisms of P.L. 94-142 as an externally intrusive policy were not unique to the issue of special education, but were consistent with long-standing attitudes of the education community regarding its status as a "special" government. Mosher points out the tendency of educators to adhere to isolationist politics, with a "hostility to general governmental controls and competition for resources with other public services."[39] Furthermore, she cites the observations of political scientists regarding the effects of cooperative federalism that were evident in the general government programs of earlier decades. Distinctive features that appear relevant to the more recent involvement in special education include the following:[40]

1. *A bypassing tendency.* Grants in aid from the national government to local agencies, bypassing traditional political jurisdictions, such as the states.
2. *A skewing effect.* The slanting of local and state program support to command federal matching funds and pursue "what is hot," regardless of actual local needs.
3. *Fractional responsibility.* The tendency in grant-supported programs do develop specialized roles and personnel without accountability to mainline organizational units.
4. *Demonstration and activist programs.* Development of programs outside existing functional networks, that compete with established programs for grass roots support.
5. *Planning and administrative support.* The encouragement of planning efforts at state and local levels to elevate levels of service to nationally recognized standards.

These tendencies and others of a similar nature have been cited by analysts of the impact of ESEA on local education, from which many parallels may be drawn to special education. Some of the most pronounced cited by Mosher are as follows:[41]

1. The insensitivity of federal policymakers to the diverse capabilities of recipient agencies, their need for planning time, and the difficulties of articulating inter-level fiscal and personnel practices

2. The disappointment over shortfalls in funding from the expectations envisioned from original authorizations

3. Invasions of local turf on such matters as designated target beneficiaries and mandated collaboration with nonpublic schools, parent advisory groups, and other agencies

4. The clearly evident lack of trust among legislators, the executive branch, and the scholarly community that the educational establishment would carry out programs as intended

5. The resort to narrow, special-purpose grants rather than broad discretionary ones, as a means of maintaining control where trust was lacking

6. The rise of numerous vested interests at local and state levels around earmarked funds, with a need for communication with Washington to keep funds flowing.[42]

Still another perspective on the intergovernmental relationships that may facilitate or block the intent of legislation designed to modify local practice in the schools has been expressed by Wayson, reflecting on the impact of ESEA. In discussing the sources of power and control, he made the point that changes in education do not occur through adoption by a central office of a local school district but by the personnel who make decisions in school buildings and individual classrooms:

> The three levels are interdependent but operate in such a way that each controls its own realm and has only nominal or, at best, only partial power over the realms controlled by the others. Each exerts its own controls, and imposes its own sanctions. Each has its own territory, its own prerogatives, its own traditions. Each is much more autonomous than either folklorists, researchers, or the participants themselves recognize. The fact remains that teachers and principals—not higher-ranking officials—make the decisions that determine whether a reform will be successfully implemented.[43]

This view, in contrast to that of ambitious promoters of reform legislation, suggests much more modest changes as an anticipated outcome of federal policy initiatives. Sarason and Doris have also discussed the expectations that may be held for legislated reform, pointing out, "When we endeavor to make a change in our schools, we fail to recognize that the *structure* of the schools was developed in relation to earlier societal problems, and that these structural characteristics will be effective obstacles to our efforts at change."[44] Given these recognized limitations, it may be useful to reiterate the major goals of the statutory measures that have been legislated and to examine the apparent results.

The Goals.   Lynn makes the point that "Judging by the legislative history, the goals of the individual congressmen and senators who voted for the new law were pragmatic and concrete. They wanted to provide financial assistance to states that were under pressure to expand special education opportunities."[45] They saw the need to serve those children not being served and to increase the adequacy of existing services, but they were also very conscious of the need to keep some constraint on potential demands on the federal treasury and to avoid undue interference in state and local decision making. While the major controversy focused on financial authorization levels, there was also recognition that it would be very difficult to specify procedures that would achieve the assurances of service without committing the federal government to objectionable intrusiveness.

There was relatively less debate over the delivery system, which was the chief concern of parents and their advocates, who saw the law "as the capstone of a revolution that had been in the making for nearly a decade in the schools, courts, state legislatures, and Congress."[46] They had expectations that the new law would create a different philosophy, more accepting of deviation, and mandating an end to the artificial segregation that had characterized special education in the past. We are reminded by Sarason and Doris, however, that

> Change in societal attitudes and social policy was spearheaded by a dedicated minority relying on political pressure and the courts; but at every step of the way, this minority encountered opposition, especially from personnel in schools, institutions, and state agencies who saw how drastic the proposed changes would be for them.[47]

In describing the nature of these changes, Lynn points out that rather than sending difficult children off to psychologists, classroom teachers "had to become knowledgeable about the difficulties and to shed the stereotypes that contributed to discriminatory or invalid labeling and placement."[48] Furthermore, regular classroom teachers had to learn a new relationship with special educators, as partners rather than as competitors, and to become responsive to parents while being aware of the rights of both parents and children. The features of the law promote its basic goals, in that

1. It reinforces changes already underway in the legal framework of special education that recognize and enforce the rights of children and their parents.
2. The financial aid formula is an incentive for states to serve larger numbers of handicapped children with special programs and support. Funds are available under the Act only for children who are enrolled (although not necessarily served) in public school and only for costs that exceed the per pupil average expenditure in the local school district.

3. The Act fundamentally alters decision-making processes and power relations between and among parents, regular teachers, and special education personnel. Quite simply, parents now have the opportunity to exercise greater influence over decisions affecting their children. Teachers no longer can be so arbitrary in expelling students from class or labeling them as retarded.[49]

Some Problems. In spite of these significant benefits from the law, a number of problems are obviously inherent in its provisions. Some of the most prominent are

1. Raised expectations which cannot be fulfilled for a variety of reasons, not the least of which is the predictable shortfall between authorization and appropriation levels of funding
2. Increased incentive to label children as handicapped, particularly the least expensive to serve, to take advantage of available funds based on "head counts"
3. An emphasis on resource inputs, rather than outcomes achieved, in the approach to financial incentives
4. An expression of the philosophical value of least restrictive environment, without a clearly demonstrable effective method of accomplishing the ideal
5. A vulnerability to focus on "the easy ones" when carrying out the general intent of mainstreaming, leaving more seriously involved students in environments as restrictive as ever
6. A vulnerability to "backlash" from both taxpayers and professionals whose roles and/or autonomy are threatened
7. A focus on procedural safeguards and processes which obscures attention to substantive program quality
8. Insufficient attention to the need for changes in the preparation of teachers, both regular and special educators, which is the source of attitudinal and organizational resistance to change.[50]

Outcomes. A great number of studies have been conducted in the years since 1975, when P.L. 94-142 was passed. The federal government alone sponsored from four to nine different studies in each of the years from 1976 through 1984 as a part of the mandate within the law to evaluate its effects. These studies provide the data for the annual Reports to the Congress. Closely related are numerous studies initiated within individual states, reflecting on the combined impact of the federal law and statutory developments at the state level. Interpretations of these data have led to conclusions about the outcomes from statutory reform that, though containing some ambiguities, exhibit a good number of fairly consistent findings.

1. Increasing numbers of children are being identified as possibly handicapped, assessed, and programmed for service.
2. Numbers found to be in need of service have not reached previously anticipated levels.
3. Greatest increases have been in mildly handicapped students, who might not have been regarded as handicapped previously.

4. Increasing varieties of service options are found, with greatest growth in students placed in regular settings, while receiving supplemental instruction and related services.

5. Increasing numbers of more severely handicapped are served in private placements with public support.

6. Procedural safeguards in student assessment and program decision processes have become technically sophisticated, complex, and time consuming but are accepted as valuable and necessary by most participants.

7. Participation in the processes is passive by most regular teachers and parents, when it occurs at all.

8. School personnel are increasingly conscious of the parent role (though largely symbolic) and make an effort to observe appropriate procedures.

9. Effective use of due process by parents is predominantly an upper-middle-class phenomenon.

10. Alternatives to expensive due process hearings are being explored and increasingly used.

11. The majority of due process hearings have dealt with parent requests for more restrictive (usually private) placements than those proposed by school personnel; parents (particularly the well informed, relatively affluent) tend to win such cases.

12. Greatest hesitancy from school systems has concerned the provision of related services, where high cost and ambiguity of eligibility is most pronounced.

13. Interagency relationships between schools and other health and human service programs, particularly where funding responsibility is an issue, remain confused.

14. Availability of personnel with required technical competency is a problem in many less attractive localities.

15. Support for inservice upgrading of personnel, both regular and special education, is insufficient; this has become an issue in negotiations and political platforms of teacher organizations.

16. The demand for thorough, individualized processing of pupil need is constrained by the realistic organizational demand for efficient management of labor intensive procedures; this is particularly problematic in large systems having great numbers of eligible students.

17. The Individualized Educational Program (IEP) process, originally viewed quite negatively, has become recognized and accepted as valuable, even though it is often no more than a "paper exercise" with modest instructional utility.

18. Communication among all parties of the service system has increased along with record keeping to document it and all other procedural matters.

It is generally concluded by most observers that given the sweeping scope of the federal law, its implementation has occurred surprisingly well, with many of the most fearfully anticipated problems being met, solved, or otherwise accommodated. Almost exactly eight years after the passage of P.L. 94-142, the Congress reaffirmed the general intent of the federal role in special education. On December 2, 1983, President Reagan signed P.L. 98-199, the Education of the Handicapped Act amendments of 1983, which included major features as follows:

1. Restoration of the National Advisory Committee on the Education of Handicapped Children and Youth
2. Permission to use federal funds under the preschool incentive grant program to serve handicapped children below age 3
3. Establishment of grants to states for developing and implementing comprehensive plans to provide early childhood education to all handicapped children from birth
4. Expansion of model demonstration postsecondary education programs, including vocational, technical, continuing, and adult education
5. Establishment of a new program to stimulate and improve secondary special education and transition to postsecondary education, vocational rehabilitation, continuing education, employment, independent living, and other adult services
6. Refocusing of personnel preparation resources on the preparation of special education personnel and requiring colleges and universities receiving grants to meet state and professionally recognized standards
7. Establishment of grants for parent training and information
8. Establishment of a new clearinghouse for dissemination of information on federal laws, career and job opportunities in special education and available services and programs in postsecondary education for the handicapped
9. Emphasis of federal research on the improvement of teaching methodology and curriculum and the application of new technologies toward improved instruction.

It should be noted that the thrust of these amendments is on some of the services that have been most difficult to move forward, at the preschool and at the secondary and postsecondary age levels. A major issue that will probably remain controversial is the degree of administrative regulation that is necessary and appropriate to carry out the intent of this or any other law.

Administrative Regulations

As we indicated earlier, statutes are usually designed for broad authorization of desired policies, with the expectation (and authorization included within the statute) that additional necessary details may be taken care of by regulations developed by the executive branch of the (state or federal) government. In the case of education, the task of regulation development and implementation rests with the office of the chief executive for education, at this time the Secretary of the U.S. Department of Education. In each state a similar responsibility rests with the chief state school officer (by whatever title) as representative of a state board of education or other policymaking body (the exact designation of this group again varying from state to state).

The process of regulation development typically starts with an expression by the professional staff of the executive agency as to what rules, regulations, or guidelines are needed to permit reasonable execution of the intent of the law. Advice may be sought from informed sources outside the government in the drafting of proposed regulations, and technical guidance by legal experts within the agency must always attend the process. Public exposure of proposed regulations, to gain additional advice and to gauge potential reaction and acceptability of the proposal, is a standard procedure in most jurisdictions. This may be done by public notice (as in the *Federal Register*) inviting written comment or testimony at public hearings scheduled at times and places presumably to allow adequate input. Such procedure then leads to revision and adjustment before final adoption by the official policy body or chief executive.

The interval between passage of a new statute and the adoption of administrative regulations, in cases where policies and practices of operating systems are likely to undergo extensive change, may extend over a considerable period of time that may be filled with controversy. The lesser scope of the impact of regulations at the state level, as compared with the federal, permits the necessary negotiations and compromises to be accomplished with reasonable dispatch, but in some instances it becomes politically mandatory to introduce a timed phase-in of new regulations in order to secure initial agreement and set the stage for future implementation. Some of the policy changes covered by state level regulatory developments of recent years have been, as with the federal developments, of major interest to a variety of constituents, thereby sparking time consuming controversy.

Two Examples.   At the federal level, two cases illustrate the nature of the process. The Education for All Handicapped Children Act, Public Law 94-142, became law by presidential endorsement on November 29, 1975, after passage in both houses of Congress by a large majority. The development of regulations, as authorized in the Act, proceeded over ensuing months, with a draft of proposed regulation published in the *Federal Register* on December 30, 1976. Comments and testimony were received dealing with virtually every aspect of the proposed regulations, until the final draft was ready for adoption and publication in the *Federal Register* on August 23, 1977. Given the extent of detail and potential impact on state and local educational practices, the 21 months required to get from law to regulation in this case appears reasonable. Both the law and the regulations are long and prescriptive. The law extends over 40 pages of the United States Code, and the regulations (including comments regarding the proposed draft and responses of the executive branch in justifying the final draft) occupy nearly 100 pages of the Code of Federal Regulations.

The parallel case of Section 504 of the Rehabilitation Act of 1973 presents a somewhat different example. This Act was passed on September 23, 1973 and covered a number of provisions pertaining to vocational rehabilitation. The part of the Act dealing with nondiscrimination, Section 504, was only a brief paragraph, but it emphasized a civil rights issue, going beyond the social welfare provisions of the rest of the Act. The development of regulations in this case included the participation of staff of the Office of Civil Rights. The scope of the forthcoming regulations would cover a wide variety of life needs, including access to education and all other public services as well as employment and architectural barrier issues.

Since the section of the law itself was rather "open ended," development of regulations required consideration of a vast number of issues. Defining the population covered by the law was a problem, only partially addressed by language included in the Rehabilitation Act Amendments of 1974 that indicated the inclusion of "any person who (A) has a physical or mental impairment which substantially limits one or more of such person's major life activities, (B) has a record of such an impairment, or (C) is regarded as having such an impairment."

This definition led to consideration in the regulation writing of whether certain individuals, such as alcoholics, drug addicts, or homosexuals were to be included as "handicapped" under the law. Decisions on these questions rested on differing opinions as to logic, precedent, and public image. The determination to include alcoholism and drug addiction, but not homosexuality represents a "best compromise" from the arguments advanced by various advocacy groups. There was no question that many conditions create a barrier to access and, therefore, become a handicap primarily because one is "regarded as having such an impairment" rather than because the condition constitutes an objective physical or mental limitation. It was recognized that homosexuals experience this status from the perspective of much, but certainly not all, of society. On the other hand, there is much more agreement within the medical field and among those having the conditions, as to the diseased status of alcoholics and drug addicts.

Other major questions addressed in the Section 504 Regulations concerned the relationship of its provisions to other federal initiatives that were also in the process of being interpreted. Right to treatment, for individuals in institutions was covered by the Developmentally Disabled Assistance and Bill of Rights Act (P.L. 94-103), and while Section 504 spoke to guarantees of "equal" rights of the handicapped to whatever is provided to other persons, it did not intend to establish "substantive" rights to treatment. Similarly, the parallel intent of P.L. 94-142 to guarantee educational access created areas of overlap, particularly on definitions and procedures, necessitating coordination between the Bureau of Education for the Handicapped (responsible for administering P.L. 94-142) and the Office of Civil Rights (responsible for Section 504).

These considerations, the complications of attaining consistency in definitions and procedures among the relevant laws and their regulations, not to mention the uncertainty of the potential costs of implementation, inhibited progress on the writing of regulations for Section 504. Proposed rules were published in the *Federal Register* on July 16, 1976, leading to over 700 written comments from the field and testimony at 22 public hearings conducted around the country. The controversial nature of the provisions and their potential impact again delayed final action until political pressure and demonstrations by consumers and advocates (including wheelchair sit-ins at government buildings) forced adoption by the administration. Final regulations were published in the *Federal Register* on May 4, 1977, nearly four years after the passage of the original law. In this case, regulations to administer a section of a law only one paragraph in length covers over 40 pages (including appendices of comments and explanatory content) of the Code of Federal Regulations.

Format.   In view of the impressive volume of content comprising at least these two examples of regulations, it may be useful to examine the format of such publications. Federal and state regulations tend to follow a similar structure, the nature of which may be illustrated by the table of contents of the final regulations under P.L. 94-142, Title 45, Code of Federal Regulations, Part 121a. With the organization of the new U.S. Department of Education in 1980, a recodification of all educational regulations has resulted in these now appearing at 34 C.F.R. Part 300. However, the regulations are most frequently referenced in accordance with their original designations.

In accordance with typical format, an initial statement (Subpart A— General) sets forth the purpose, applicability, and general provisions of the regulations and includes definition of terms as used throughout the rest of the document. Such definitions frequently constitute a major portion of regulations in which it is anticipated that obscure and specialized language must be used to establish the scope of the provisions in question. In this instance, 12 terms are defined, including such possibly obscure or ambiguous ones as "free appropriate public education" and "related services" as well as presumably well-established concepts such as "parent" and "state."

The remaining parts of the regulations spell out the substantive requirements:

SUBPART B—STATE ANNUAL PROGRAM
PLANS AND LOCAL APPLICATIONS

These sections deal with the required content of plans that states must submit annually in order to be a participant and thereby receive available federal funds, as well as the content of local educational agency applications (again for funds) and the procedural requirements controlling such local participation, including public participation in the adoption of such plans.

SUBPART C—SERVICES

These sections detail the ingredients of a free, appropriate, public education; set forth priorities in the use of funds; establish the process and content of individualized educational programs; outline procedures for direct service by state agencies where local agency services are precluded; and establish the state's responsibility for a comprehensive system of personnel development.

SUBPART D—PRIVATE SCHOOLS

These sections cover procedures for children in private schools, distinguishing between the situation in which such children are placed or referred by public agencies and those who are enrolled without public agency involvement but to whom the agency must provide needed service.

SUBPART E—PROCEDURAL SAFEGUARDS

These sections outline the due process procedures for parents and children, including protection in evaluation, confidentiality of information, and hearings; the use of least restrictive environment in placement considerations; and the responsibility for such procedures at local, state, and federal levels.

SUBPART F—STATE ADMINISTRATION

These sections cover the state agency's responsibility for program monitoring, adoption of a complaint procedure, use of federal funds for state administration, and the operation of an advisory panel.

SUBPART G—ALLOCATION OF FUNDS; REPORTS

These sections detail the formulas and procedures for allocation and distribution of federal funds to agencies within the state and outline the contents of various required reports to the federal government.

The volume of detail as well as the extensive scope of these regulations for P.L. 94-142 have been cited from many quarters as the extreme example of overly intrusive federal activity. Although directly concerned consumers and their advocates, as well as most professional special educators, have seen the regulatory process as necessary, the general educational administrative establishment quickly recognized that the degree of prescription, when weighed against the level of support, was somewhat unusual. Individuals and groups such as the Council of Chief State School Officers, perennially conscious of the balance of power and funding among federal, state, and local levels in many aspects of the education system, were able to point to special education as the prime example of creeping (or perhaps galloping) federalism.[51] Congressional support for the principles involved has remained consistently strong, however, and unlike some other policies in which regulation had introduced much more prescriptive detail than that found in the original statute, supporters of P.L. 94-142 have been able to attest accurately that the law itself contained most of the detail and, representing the intent of Congress, had broad grass-roots support.

The Regulatory Burden.   Aside from the particular case of this federal initiative, however, scholars of social reform and intergovernmental relations have frequently cited the problem of "regulatory unreasonableness" where either federal or state government gets involved in program operation at "the street level." Kagan points out that standards promulgated by the government to control schools often require investments of local resources as well and "thus shift responsibility for deciding the precise trade-off among conflicting claims on scarce resources away from local administrators to government officials in Washington or state capitals."[52] Since school systems are highly diverse, regulations that may be appropriate to ensure service adequacy in one place may be unnecessary in another. In contrasting educational regulation to that imposed on business (e.g., by the Environmental Protection Act or the Occupational Safety and Health Act), Kagan argues that more discretion is granted to "the regulated" in education. To an extent, schools are able to plan their own programs and execute them in accordance with broad procedural structures. In addition, sanctions for violations are more limited and less automatic. That is, school officials may face a threat of cut-off of federal funds, but are not subject to personal criminal prosecution for violations, and withholding of funds is seldom used, since to do so would usually only worsen a bad situation for the students involved. Furthermore, regulatory failures are less dramatic in education than in business and, therefore, regulators are more likely to recognize that given the uncertain technology of education, there is room for reasonable differences of opinion as to means to an end.

On the other hand, this "open-endedness" of standards also permits clients and advocates to take the public agencies to court for failure to pursue statutory goals and provides "more discretion for ideologically minded enforcement officials and judges to read their own substantive views into the law, even to the point of unreasonableness."[53] The lack of a fixed standard for "appropriate" education has certainly allowed educators to make decisions that have led to appeals, litigation, and legalization of the special education process. Furthermore, there is the general assumption that since the emphasis in regulation is on procedural rather than substantive standards, accountability is problematic. Since tangible outcomes are illusive, we must compensate by overloading on process, with documentation and reports to assure that the process has occurred. The development of the IEP and other due process steps illustrates this.

A major problem is the balancing of regulatory intensity to monitor those systems that might neglect minority needs if left alone, without stifling the conscientious activity of the others by overbearing surveillance. To the extent that such regulation is overdone, an undue focus on literal compliance is found, with less attention to substance and quality considerations. If it were believed that school systems were uniformly bad in their execution of programs coming under the intent of the law, then intense accounting for regulatory detail would be appropriate. However, this is probably not the case. School systems vary extensively on this dimension, and there is good reason to fear that regulatory zeal may yield diminishing returns when the focus on details of compliance intrudes upon time that could be spent on substantive matters.

In reporting on the implementation of laws and regulations in suburban districts of the state of Massachusetts, which paralleled but preceded the federal initiatives, Weatherley and Lipsky indicate that in spite of only moderate monitoring efforts by the state, school personnel focused in an all-consuming fashion on the bureaucratic details required to "process" routine cases in order to have some time to deal with those cases that were sufficiently problematic to warrant their professional attention.[54] Examining implementation factors in the City of Boston in 1977 and 1978, Bourexis found a similar situation, with personnel struggling to keep up with (though overwhelmed by) the details that mere compliance with procedures demanded, with no time left to attend to program quality considerations.[55]

While it is generally observed that school system personnel, particularly the special educators, have responded to the heavy burden of regulation with valiant effort and only mild resentment, the presence of even this level of reaction runs the risk of stimulating a backlash when added to a general political thrust toward decentralization and a reduced federal role in education. When such a situation exists, "the bitterest fruit of legalistic regulation has been an undiscriminating "deregulation" movement that threatens to undermine the positive contributions of the programs."[56] Given such risks, the argument for flexible regulation (or flexible enforcement of regulation) becomes very persuasive. In the relatively uncertain technology of education, where differences of opinion regarding "most appropriate" are the rule and cost-benefit analysis is virtually impossible, Kagan suggests that such flexibility, though fraught with many other risks, is a goal worthy of serious pursuit:

> Constructing criteria for such nonuniform treatment and developing a legally defensible rationale for a flexible mode of implementing regulations and broadly-stated student rights are important goals for the regulation of schools and businesses alike. The alternative, as suggested earlier, may be continuing political backlash and wholesale "deregulation" that throws out the baby of progress with the bathwater of regulatory unreasonableness.[57]

Deregulation. It would appear that the conditions just described have been prevalent with respect to federal regulatory activity in general, and to P.L. 94-142 in particular, at the time of Reagan's inauguration in January 1981. Upon the appointment of Terrel Bell as Secretary of the Department of Education for this administration, one of the first actions (true to the President's campaign promise to "get government off our backs" was the withdrawal of the rather prescriptive (*Lau*) regulations dealing with bilingual education. Although protested by some advocates who charged that bilingual students would be harmed, the education community and consumers in the main accepted this change toward local autonomy in the choosing of methods for educating such students as reasonable, even though it symbolized a position on political philosophy more than pedagogical judgment.

Similarly, the movement to collapse a large number of federal education programs into much fewer "block grants" under the provisions of the Education Consolidation and Improvement Act of 1981 was a strong signal to allow greater discretion at the local level regarding the use of federal funds for the administration of programs authorized to pursue a variety of national priorities. Discussing the place of categorical grants when rethinking the federal role in education, Levin cites the nature of complaints and contradictions that accompanied the dramatic expansion of the federal financial involvement from 1965 to 1980.[58] He points out the doubts regarding the efficacy of certain categorical programs, the concerns that in spite of rules to the contrary, federal grants were being used to supplant local and state funding, and perhaps of greatest influence, the fact that administrative regulations connected to each categorical grant program created a duplication of paperwork. The potential for wasted resources under existing procedures and the promise of savings in administrative costs (however exaggerated) provided a potent argument for consolidation, as did the presumed opportunity for decisions about the use of funds to be made closer to those who are affected by them.

Opposing arguments focused on the fact that federal categorical grants were established in the first place because state and local education agencies were not providing for special educational needs. To turn decisions over to locals would run the risk of federal block grants being used to replace state and local funding, at the expense of the needs of the poor, minorities, and the handicapped. The strength of these opposing arguments, and the lobbying power of special education interests were apparently responsible for modifying the original intent of the Reagan administration to include all categorical education programs within the block grant package.

As a result, the final shape of the Education Consolidation and Improvement Act included two chapters, with the major intent of financial assistance to meet special educational needs of disadvantaged children (the old Title I program) constituting Chapter I and over 30 other existing programs collapsed into a single block under Chapter II. These latter programs included virtually all of the remaining titles of the Elementary and Secondary Education Act, plus certain programs under the National Science Foundation Act, the Alcohol and Drug Abuse Education Act, the Higher Education Act, the Career Education Incentive Act, and the Follow Through Act. All programs encompassed by Education of the Handicapped, including the major Part B (P.L. 94-142) Assistance to States for Education of Handicapped Children, were excluded from the consolidation and permitted to remain in their independent categorical status, with all existing regulatory provisions intact.

Coincident with the block grant movement, and pursuant to a January 1981 Executive Order from the President, the Department of Education set forth a "general objective to reduce the burdens and costs of existing and future regulations."[59] The Order called for a review of regulations promulgated by the Department to pursue the President's goals to

Avoid unnecessary regulation
Reduce compliance requirements
Increase agency accountability for regulatory actions
Ensure that societal benefits of the regulations outweigh the cost to society
Eliminate burdensome, unnecessary and unproductive paperwork
Minimize the cost of rule making to the federal government
Ensure that the Department is only collecting information it needs to collect
Specifically, reduce burdens to small entities.

This review process, as exercised by the Office of Special Education and Rehabilitative Services (OSERS) immediately focused on the Part B (P.L. 94-142) regulations. The process involved analyzing and comparing statutory and regulatory provisions to identify places where the regulations may have gone beyond the statutory mandate, researching the legislative history and judicial precedent to determine whether such extensions in the regulations might be justified, and summarizing and analyzing comments received from various relevant sources outside the government, with the end purpose of identifying regulatory provisions that might be overly prescriptive, ineffective, or unnecessary for fiscal accountability and program evaluation. The product of this effort was to develop and propose amendments to the existing regulations that would be consistent with statutory purposes and requirements while relieving educational agencies of burdensome requirements of fiscal and compliance paperwork, liberating them from unnecessary federal direction and control, yet continuing to protect the rights of handicapped children to equal educational opportunity.

As an outcome of the review process, OSERS identified 16 "targets of opportunity for deregulation" falling within the four general areas of definitions, grants administration, services, and procedural safeguards. These targets were selected on the basis of attention that had been brought to them through public comment, litigation, problems in plan approval, complaints from the field, difficulties in enforcement, paperwork demands, and so on. Problems with definitions focused on "special education," "handicapped children," "related services," and "specific learning disabilities." Concerns in the area of grants administration included state plans, local education agency applications, state advisory panels, allocation of funds, and reports. Problems in the area of services focused on the scope of free, appropriate, public education, extended school year programs, suspension and expulsion, out-of-state placements, individualized educational programs, services to children placed in private schools by their parents, and the comprehensive system of personnel development. The procedural safeguards area included concerns about due process, nondiscrimination in evaluation procedures, least restrictive environment, and confidentiality of information.

In sum, the areas identified for modification (in the direction of less regulation) constituted a major portion of the power and thrust of the program. Approximately a year passed after the release of the initial review of the regulations, which permitted considerable in-house assessment of the degree of feasible deregulation. A retrospective view of this period suggests, however, that the political press for less government from the Whitehouse overwhelmed the usual good judgment of the bureaucrats within the federal educational establishment as to the public acceptability of any proposed change, and insufficient input was obtained (or paid attention to) from the field.

Reaction.   At any rate, when the notice of proposed rulemaking was published in the *Federal Register* on August 4, 1982, with public hearings scheduled for the following month, the response from the field was of a magnitude unparalleled in federal education history. Consumers, advocacy organizations, and, to a lesser extent, special education professionals directly and through congressional representatives made known their displeasure with the proposed deregulation. Within a week, the Senate Subcommittee on the Handicapped held a hearing to determine the likely impact of the proposed deregulation, and shortly thereafter the Senate, by a vote of 93 to 4 attached a rider to the Supplemental Appropriations Bill calling for a halt in the implementation of the changes until the Congress had the opportunity to review and possibly exercise a legislative veto over them. This reaction, the ensuing testimony in the hearings, and the written response from the field led to the Secretary of Education withdrawing six major areas of the proposal on September 29 and postponing rewriting of the regulations until comments from the field could be studied. In the ensuing months, over 23,000 communications were received, far surpassing the response to any other piece of federal education policy. For almost another year, the Department voiced the intent to rewrite and submit modified deregulation proposals but finally acknowledged in late 1983 that no further efforts would be made to diminish the basic P.L. 94-142 regulations.

This scenario rather clearly demonstrates the balance of forces that act upon the control of public policy. The trade-offs in the case of an obviously intensive and extensive degree of official governmental regulation of local education practice, in which two branches of government were on opposite sides of a political and philosophic issue, were in the final analysis determined by the action of informal influence sources. The following chapter will consider more of the nature and impact of such sources of informal control on public policy in special education.

ILLUSTRATIVE CASE

As Director of Special Education in Metropolis, Dale Walker is recognized as one of the leaders among administrators in the state of LaFayette. During the past ten years in this position, Dale has frequently been active in affairs of governance of special education in the state, serving as legislative committee chairperson for the LaFayette Council of Administrators of Special Education before being elected to the presidency of that organization. Therefore, it was not unexpected when Dr. Walker was invited to membership on the Advisory Committee to the State Education Department, convened by the Assistant Commissioner for Special Education.

This is a critical time to be on such a committee, as new legislation was passed last year in LaFayette, largely designed to close a few remaining gaps between the state's statutes pertaining to special education programming and those emanating from the federal offices. This legislation had modified some definitions regarding handicapping conditions, clarified some of the authorized services, and cleaned up some due process procedures, none of which raised much controversy. Dr. Walker had spoken in support of the bill covering these changes, but there was little opposition, and the legislature had passed the bill easily. Since there appeared to be only routine budgetary implications, the Governor had signed the bill into law with no concerns.

One section of the law, however, now appears to be destined for greater controversy that had been anticipated. This section, generally overlooked at the time of the bill's discussion, authorized the State Education Department to study means of organizing instruction in special education programs that might emphasize the *functional needs* of pupils rather than their *category of disability*. Furthermore, the Department was authorized to develop and promulgate regulations that would assure the implementation of all aspects of the legislative changes, including this "functional needs" policy.

Therefore, the State Education Department has charged its Assistant Commissioner for Special Education to develop such regulations, with appropriate participation and advice from the field, which especially includes the Advisory Committee. Initial meetings of the Committee found considerable interest in the concept of functional needs, with some members focusing on the corresponding deemphasis on disability classifications. As Professor Jones, a Committee member from State University put it, "We now have a mandate to move to noncategorical programming and get rid of some dysfunctional, stigmatizing labels!" Other more conservative members, though acknowledging the authorization to use regulation to implement the intent of the Legislature, were steadfast in their cautionary perspective of "Not throwing out any babies with the bathwater of clinical categories." After all, special education has enjoyed rather favorable support in LaFayette which has escaped the trauma of "wrenching reorganization."

As usual, Dr. Dale Walker was found in the middle, arbitrating between these two positions, not because of any special skills as a mediator, but as a matter of honest uncertainty regarding the trade-offs. Dale could hear a variety of arguments with equal clarity. The special education system had been based on the assumption of specialized needs of children being met by highly specialized professionals who knew the technology of instruction for particular disabilities. The state standards for program organization (grouping, teacher certification, supervision, instructional materials, etc.) reflected this assumption and had served quite well. On the other hand, there is no disputing the charge that the system sometimes appears to have "hardening of the categories." With the growth of the *resource model,* as opposed to self-contained special classes, and with the increased emphasis on learning disabilities and corresponding lower incidence of students identified as mentally retarded, it certainly made sense for instructional grouping (and all other aspects of state standards) to focus on the functional needs rather than the categories.

With this backdrop of competing considerations, the development of proposed regulations has proceeded and a first draft circulated among all school district superintendents, special education administrators, teacher organizations, and consumer advocate organizations. In essence, the draft allows (but does not require) school districts to group special education pupils for instruction without regard for diagnostic category of disability as long as "due consideration is given to the similarity of needs in terms of (1) scholastic performance, (2) social development, and (3) physical development." It also proposes that where groups consist of more than one type of disability (under the old categorical labels), the teacher's certification may be in any of the categories represented. In short, Dale observed, the proposal does not force any change in practice but emphasizes flexibility and local prerogative to try new organizational arrangements.

Reaction has been mixed, but swift. The local superintendents (especially those from smaller districts) favor the increased flexibility, noting that the new regulation would permit much more logical and efficient organization for instruction. Some special education administrators and consumers are in agreement that this flexibility would facilitate serving children in a less restrictive environment and permit the assignment of teachers in accordance with subtle interests and capabilities not always reflected in certification classifications. Perhaps the strongest reaction has come from the few large school systems in the state, most notably Dale Walker's own city of Metropolis. As the state's major urban center, the LaFayette United Teachers are well represented, and a subcommittee for special education includes teachers on Dale's staff. The LUT position, as articulated in the press by the spokesperson for the special education subcommittee is as follows:

1. Noncategorical grouping will require teachers to cope with intolerably varying types of problems.
2. Teachers will be forced to teach "out of field," subverting the basic intent of special education training.
3. School districts will be permitted to "pack" classes as an administrative means of cost cutting, at the expense of quality instruction for those who need it most.
4. Supervision and technical assistance to teachers will be ineffective due to dispersal of pupils with common disabling conditions.
5. Federal reporting procedures require child identification by category. Classes and teachers should be organized accordingly.

After this initial reaction, the first draft of the proposed regulations is to be studied, redrawn if deemed appropriate, and resubmitted for public comment at hearings around the state. While the staff of the State Education Department has the major responsibility for the process, the members of the Advisory Committee (including Dale Walker) will be expected to play a key role in recommending revisions, explaining the finished product, and presumably defending it. Dale believes that the thrust of the new regulations are heading in the right direction. But resistance will be strong—especially right at home.

Is LaFayette ready for this much progress? How much regulation is desirable? How much is possible?

NOTES

[1]Edith K. Mosher, "Education and American Federalism: Intergovernmental and National Policy Influences," *The Politics of Education,* Seventy-sixth Yearbook of the National Society for the Study of Education, Part II (1977), p. 119.

[2]John Thomas Thompson, *Policy Making in American Public Education* (Englewood Cliffs, N.J.: Prentice-Hall, 1976), pp. 17-35.

[3]*Brown* v. *Board of Education,* 347 U.S.483, 493 (1954).

[4]H. Rutherford Turnbull and Ann Turnbull, *Free Appropriate Public Education: Law and Implementation* (Denver: Love, 1978), pp. 12-16.

[5]*Watson* v. *City of Cambridge,* 157 Mass. 561, 32 N.E. 864, 865 (1893).

[6]*Beattie* v. *Board of Education,* 169 Wisc. 231, 232, 172 N.W. 153, 154 (1919).

[7]*Brown* v. *Board of Education* (1954).

[8]Thomas K. Gilhool, *The Right of Access to Free Public Schooling for All Children: Special Education in Court,* Vol. 2, in the Leadership Series in Special Education, eds. R. A. Johnson, J. C. Gross, and R. F. Weatherman (Minneapolis: University of Minnesota Press, 1973).

[9]*Wyatt* v. *Stickney,* 344 F. Supp. 387, 392 (M.D. Ala. 1972).

[10]*New York State Association for Retarded Children* v. *Carey,* 393 F. Supp. 715 (E.D. N.Y. 1975).

[11]*Halderman* v. *Pennhurst State School and Hospital,* 446 F. Supp. 1295 (E.D. Pa. 1977).

[12]*PARC* v. *Pennsylvania,* 343 F. Supp. 279, 302 (E.D. Pa. 1972).

[13]*Mills* v. *Board of Education of District of Columbia,* 348 F. Supp. 866 (D. D.C. 1972).

[14]Turnbull and Turnbull, *Free Appropriate Public Education,* p. 37.

[15]*Mills* v. *Board of Education* (1972).

[16]C. Lamar Mayer, *Educational Administration and Special Education: A Handbook for School Administrators* (Boston: Allyn & Bacon, 1982), p. 108.

[17]*Diana* v. *State Board of Education,* C-70, 37 RFP (N.D. Calif. 1970).

[18]*Ruiz* v. *State Board of Education,* C.A. No. 218294 (Super. Ct. Sacramento, Calif. 1972).

[19]*Larry P.* v. *Riles,* 343 F. Supp. 1306 (N.D. Calif. 1972).

[20]Jane R. Mercer, "A Policy Statement on Assessment Procedures and the Rights of Children," *Harvard Educational Review,* 44 (1974), p. 132.

[21]David L. Kirp, "Student Classification, Public Policy and the Courts," *Harvard Educational Review,* 44 (1974), pp. 7-52.

[22]*Larry P.* v. *Riles,* 343 F. Supp. 1306, 502 F. 2d. 963 (N.D. Calif. 1979).

[23]Barbara J. Smith and Josephine G. Barresi, "Interpreting the Rights of Exceptional Citizens Through Judicial Action," in *Special Education in America: Its Legal and Governmental Foundations,* eds. Joseph Ballard, Bruce A. Ramirez, and Frederick J. Weintraub (Reston, VA: The Council for Exceptional Children, 1982), pp. 74-75.

[24]Susan G. Foster, "Court Finds I.Q. Tests Racially Biased for Black Pupils' Placement," *Education Week,* February 8, 1984, p. 5.

[25]*Parents in Action on Special Education (PASE)* v. *Hannon, et al.,* C.A. No. 74 C 3586 (1980).

[26]Smith and Barresi, "Interpreting the Rights," p. 77.

[27]*Lau* v. *Nichols,* 414 U.S. 563, 94 S.Ct. 786 (1974).

[28]*Board of Education of Hendrick Hudson Central School District* v. *Rowley,* 50 U.S.L.W. 4925, 4932 (U.S. June 28,1982).

[29]*Springdale School District* v. *Grace,* No. 80-1777 (8th Cir. Nov. 8, 1982).

[30]*Roncker* v. *Walter,* 700 F. 2d 1058 (6th Cir. 1983).

[31]*Yaris* v. *Special School District of St. Louis County,* 558 F. Supp. 545 (E.D. Mo. 1983).

[32]*Battle, Bernard and Armstrong* v. *Kline et al.,* C.A. nos. 78-133, 78-132, 78-172 (E.D. Pa. 1980).

[33]*Concerned Parents and Citizens for the Continuing Education at Malcolm X (P.S. 79)* v. *New York City Board of Education,* 629 F. 2d 751 (2d. Cir. 1980).

[34]*S-1* v. *Turlington,* 635 F. 2d (CA 5,1981).

[35]*Brookhart* v. *Illinois State Board of Education,* 534 F. Supp. 725 (C.D. Ill. 1982).

[36]HACHE, *Questions and Answers: The Education of Exceptional Children* Report No. 73, (Denver: Education Commission of the States, 1975).

[37]Carl F. Kaestle and Marshall S. Smith, "The Federal Role in Elementary and Secondary Education, 1940-1980," *Harvard Educational Review,* 52 (November 1982) pp. 390-392.

[38]Samuel Halperin, "ESEA: Decennial Views of the Revolution, I. The Positive Side," *Phi Delta Kappan,* 57 (November 1975), pp. 147-150.

[39]Mosher, "Education and American Federalism," p. 101.

[40]Ibid., pp. 109-110.

[41]Ibid., pp. 114-115.

[42]Rufus E. Miles, Jr., *The Department of Health, Education and Welfare* (New York: Praeger, 1974), p. 164.

[43]William Wayson,"ESEA: Decennial Views of the Revolution, II. The Negative Side," *Phi Delta Kappan,* 57 (November 1975), p. 153.

[44]Seymour B. Sarason and John Doris, *Educational Handicap, Public Policy, and Social History: A Broadened Perspective on Mental Retardation* (New York: Free Press, 1979), p. 156.

[45]Laurence E. Lynn, Jr., "The Emerging System for Educating Handicapped Children," *Policy Studies Review,* 2, Special no. 1 (January 1983), p. 35.

[46]Ibid., p. 36.

[47]Seymour B. Sarason and John Doris, "Mainstreaming: Dilemmas, Opposition, Opportunities," in *Futures of Education for Exceptional Students: Emerging Structures,* ed. Maynard C. Reynolds (Reston, Va.: The Council for Exceptional Children, 1978), p. 7.

[48]Lynn, "The Emerging System," p. 37.

[49]Ibid., p. 39.

[50]Ibid., pp. 42-43.

[51]Joseph M. Cronin, "The Federal Takeover: Should the Junior Partner Run the Firm?" *Phi Delta Kappan,* 57 (1976), p. 500.

[52]Robert A. Kagan, *Regulating Business, Regulating Schools: The Problem of Regulatory Unreasonableness,* Project Report No. 81-A14 (Stanford, Calif: Institute for Research on Educational Finance and Governance, 1981), p. 29.

[53]Ibid., p. 34.

[54]Richard Weatherley and Michael Lipsky,"Street Level Bureaucrats and Institutional Innovation: Implementing Special Education Reform," *Harvard Education Review,* 47 (1977), p. 171.

[55]Patricia S. Bourexis, "Implementation Factors Related to Schools' Compliance with Special Education Policy" (Unpublished doctoral dissertation, Syracuse University, 1979).

[56]Kagan, *Regulating Business, Regulating Schools,* p. 56.

[57]Ibid., p. 66.

[58]Henry M. Levin,"Categorical Grants in Education: Rethinking the Federal Role," in *IFG Policy Perspectives* (Stanford, Calif.: Institute for Research on Educational Finance and Governance, Spring, 1981).

[59]Office of Special Education, *Briefing Paper: Initial Review of Regulations Under Part B of the Education of the Handicapped Act, as Amended* (Washington, D.C.: Department of Education, Office of Special Education and Rehabilitative Services, September 1, 1981).

CHAPTER 3
INFORMAL POWER
AND INFLUENCE

Control over special education is not limited to the legal entities that constitute formal governance. As in any organizational system, the influence of informal forces is significant. Special interests typically play an important part in the determination of what educational administrators experience in their day-to-day work. Within *special education,* the nature of these forces may be somewhat unusual, and of surprising potency. Such interests, sometimes bolstered by a coalition of groups or by an established advocacy posture, have become quite common. And these influences (both internal and external to the educational system) often compete with and sometimes overwhelm the legal determinants of practice.

Attention to and utilization of special interest groups may be a key consideration in personal and organizational goal attainment. A sensitivity to some of the particular interests of individuals and groups who identify with certain exceptional populations is a relevant concern to both special and general administrators. The groups are of three general types: those made up of *consumers*, those representing *professionals*, and those focused solely on *social advocacy*. While there may be some overlapping membership, each type has attributes and perspectives that should be understood.

CONSUMER GROUPS

Parents are generally seen as being the consumer, standing in proxy for the child's interests in special education. Parent organizations have tended to be centered on specific classifications of disability and have promoted their interests on the basis of rather narrowly defined needs and populations. Born of a self perception as an oppressed minority, parents of handicapped children who successfully organized to gain strength in numbers have often perceived their organizational power to depend on maintaining a specific and concrete identity rather than risking becoming diluted through affiliation with more broadly defined groups. This may be seen as a "circle the wagons" perspective and was probably more characteristic of the early history of such organizations, when few battles had been won, than is presently the case. Any trust in coalition could not be developed until some success in organizational accomplishment had been demonstrated. While a large number of groups having a specific disability orientation may be identified, three examples will be presented here to illustrate the typical attributes of consumer organizations. Each of these organizations has a national headquarters office and affiliated state and local chapters in many locations. The strength of affiliation varies among the different national organizations, and within each group the degree of identification with the central office varies from one locality to another.

The National Association for Retarded Citizens

Established in the early 1950s as the National Association for Retarded *Children* (NARC) and made up largely of parents of mentally retarded persons, with minimum participation by professionals, NARC has maintained a significant influence on legal progress at both state and federal levels, but has also been a consistent force in the development and operation of local direct service programs. Advocacy at the local level has sometimes resulted in the establishment of their own private service programs, but has frequently supplied the necessary pressure within the local political structure to cause public services to be initiated, regardless of legal mandates.

The NARC is not a monolithic group, and its posture varies significantly from state to state and among localities. In the main, however, its membership has tended to adhere to the assumption that their cause will not be well represented by any other more broadly based group. It is not uncommon, where local chapters of NARC have established and are operating their own private service programs, for there to be competition among the varied private and public services, with a clearly felt threat to the "association" sponsored service when other options become available. This is probably due in part to a general concern for loss of control, but it is also clearly a concern about protection and safety for the children, who are seen as very vulnerable.

The Association for Children
with Learning Disabilities

The ACLD was established in 1963 and followed much the same course of political activity as the earlier NARC, influencing state and federal legislation and subsequent regulation regarding publicly mandated and supported service programs. The ACLD was much less inclined to establish its own direct service facilities (although in some locations this was done) than to focus on the influence of public policy. This difference is in part attributable to its distinctly less severely handicapped population, as compared with the constituency of the NARC, but it is also probably due to its later establishment, at a time when the promise of public provision was more clearly visible and the need for privately sponsored service less critical.

The interest of the ACLD in maintaining an earmarked status for its population in laws and regulations is quite clear. As a group with a more newly established and somewhat ambiguous identity, there was a need to distinguish sharply the nature of the problem and the prescribed interventions from that of the other, more familiar classifications of handicap. It is evident that the element of perceived stigma also plays a part here, as a function of the social desirability of certain labels. The enrollment of students from higher socioeconomic levels tends to be heavily weighted toward the learning disability label, while the mental retardation label is found in greater frequency among the less affluent. It is clear that these differences are not due exclusively to clinically observable status of the students, but to social-psychological factors in the adult community as well. Concern regarding the overuse of the learning disability label was particularly noted by the superintendent of the Philadelphia city schools, who called for an investigation of the classification system in 1984. It was noted that there had been a 496 percent increase in that district's learning disabled population between the 1977-78 school year and 1983-84, accompanied by a 70 percent decrease in educable mentally retarded over the same period.[1] Less dramatic, but similar, trends have been noted nationally.

The National Society
for Autistic Children and Adults

This organization was established in 1965 and is smaller than the others in its membership and the population it represents. As with the learning disabled, autism is a condition not well understood by laypersons or many professionals. Its definition and classification required much complicated (and recent) argument just to deal with it in state and federal law and regulation. An amendment to existing federal regulations was published in January 1981, officially deleting autism from the "emotionally disturbed" category and adding it to the category of "other health impaired" under the definition of handi-capped children. In explaining the change, the *Federal Register* acknowledged the "expanded knowledge of autism gained through our contracts with and knowledge provided by the National Society for Autistic Children."[2] The in-dividuals concerned differ from those represented by the other organizations in that the condition is exclusively a severe one, with which most schools would deal only in a most restrictive fashion until very recent times.

For these reasons, the Society had a major challenge both in establishing an identity and in assuring appropriate inclusion within existing special edu-cation program provisions. Furthermore, the ambiguities about etiology cre-ated social-psychological complications. Prominent beliefs regarding causation initially suggested that autism was caused by parents who rejected their chil-dren and that parents and children required treatment as mentally ill persons. Recent research has placed great doubt on that hypothesis as more constitu-tional and chemical factors have been identified. Much of the Society's current effort has become focused on overcoming the burden of inaccurate belief re-garding the nature of its parent membership and its children, as viewed both from within and without. A statement of definition of autism, appearing prominently at the front of the organization's annual report states, "Autism is a lifelong brain disorder that inhibits or distorts understanding of what a person sees, hears, or otherwise senses. It causes severe problems in learning, communication and behavior. *Nothing psychological* has been shown to cause autism."

Other Consumer Organizations

Other organizations of a similar nature, representing the interests of par-ticular disabled individuals, and to a major extent with a focus on children, include:

Epilepsy Foundation of America
International Association of Parents of the Deaf
National Association for Visually Handicapped
National Easter Seal Society
United Cerebral Palsy Associations, Inc.

Each of these maintains a national office as well as local and state-af-filiated chapters. They vary widely in the degree to which they concentrate on operation of services at the local level versus a focus on political and social advocacy. Information on these and other organizations concerned with hand-icapped persons, including addresses and telephone numbers of their offices, is published in a government directory.[3]

An issue with each of the consumer organizations discussed here, and probably with most of those concerned with disabled persons, is the dilemma regarding the merits of minority status. The groups exist because their members have previously had a problem—an unmet need. As the group succeeds, some of the needs may be satisfied as a result of unified effort, hard work, and sacrifice. Although the factors that created the unmet need have been reduced, and the minority status has been ameliorated by acceptance and inclusion, there is still a concern about equal status and the adequacy of attainments achieved. Therefore, while it might be appropriate to abandon the minority identity, it is not quite safe to do so. This ambivalence is sometimes seen by representatives of the majority establishment as an inconsistency or erratic behavior on the part of consumer groups.

There is no question regarding the power that such groups have been able to bring to bear on both individual cases in which advocacy was needed to bring about a resolution and on more large-scale political action to modify the formal governance structure. The role of consumer organizations in causing the individual citizen (usually a parent) to grow from a focus on a single child with a (however critical) need to becoming a leader of a social movement has been repeatedly documented. Turnbull and Turnbull[4] have collected the personal accounts of the experiences of persons who are both parents and professionals and who vividly relate their own process of change in the way they perceived their situation. In many instances, consumer organizations play a part in the parent's interaction with the social system confronting the family of the handicapped child.

THE CONSUMER-PROFESSIONAL CONFLICT

One theme running through the accounts of consumers (parents) who are also professionals is the internal conflict, particularly felt by those whose professional roles are in a field directly or closely related to services for handicapped children. This would be most pronounced in the case of the special education teacher who becomes a parent of a handicapped child, the pediatrician, psychologist, social worker, or child development researcher. To a lesser degree, general educators, attorneys interested in civil rights issues, the clergy, and other human service professionals find themselves behaving in accordance with their role as a professional at one point and as a parent-consumer of social services at another. The issue of professional legitimacy comes into play here, as well.

In discussing the problem of leadership in community organization, Biklen[5] points out that consumers groups depend on voluntary participation by individuals of all sorts, including professionals whose field of expertise may or may not be related to the issues about which the consumers are interested.

There are two sides to the problem. Where the professional is not "in his field," the public (and especially the establishment against which the consumer organization is contesting) tends to discount that person's legitimacy as compared with experts in the field. The case of Benjamin Spock's activism in organizing against the war in Vietnam and the reaction it created, is cited as an example of this phenomenon. In our society, with its emphasis on credentials, people are expected to stay in their own domain of expertise. On the other hand, when the professional is "within his field," there is the problem of the individual having to place the substance of the issue ahead of the inclination to be cooperative and loyal to the "guild" or system in which one's professional colleagues conduct their affairs. The obstacles to a professional educator functioning as a member of an advocacy-oriented consumer organization are extremely pronounced when that organization is challenging existing educational services.

Another aspect of the consumer organization as an influence on the service system is the differentiation between the various groups who are in the business of "doing good." Biklen describes the place of charitable organizations as the initial source of leadership in social reforms, followed by professionalism, and finally community organizing as social roles.[6] In pointing out how the charity model went wrong, he indicates that while the general concept and practice of being charitable and helping one's neighbor remain valid, the institutionalization of charity results in quite a different thing. Charitable organizations have always tended to see their role as differentiating between the worthy and unworthy."Charity, with its characteristic moral imperialism, assumed that people suffered as a result of their own failings or by fate (old age, disability, abandonment, and neglect) and not of social injustice (economic exploitation, class origin)."[7] The dramatic dollar growth of the "charity business" in this country over recent decades has not seen any major change in the attitudinal factors that drive its success, and its tendency to treat symptoms rather than possible causes of the social problems. They depend for their fundraising success on appealing to the public's feelings of guilt and pity.

> On balance, charity, both in its historic and present-day form, has failed to achieve the ends espoused in its noblest ideals—relief with dignity, greater independence, and equality. While no one would deny that charity has relieved immediate human suffering, few would contend that it has altered the structural social conditions which cause human suffering.[8]

Professionalism, as a means of influencing social reform, has gone beyond charity in improving the quality of life. However, it also has sometimes resulted in the attainment of displaced goals. In reviewing the classic attributions of professionalism (pursuits that are essentially intellectual in character, autonomy and responsibility, specialized knowledge, practical application of that knowledge, transmission of the knowledge and skills through an organized brotherhood, and altruism regarding serving the public interest) Biklen points out the increasing skepticism regarding their universal validity. The conflict between public interest and self-interest that may be manifested in the tendency to inflate the image of intellectual pursuit, exaggerate the specialized knowledge, restrict its communication, and demand autonomy without risk can be seen in the tendency for professional societies to seize and maintain control over institutions that purport to serve the public. The basic conflict between the professionals' pecuniary interest and their altruism shapes their behavior toward attending to "paying clients" more than to the reform of social systems.[9]

The conflict in the consumer-professional role is further demonstrated when one attempts to identify organizations that are devoted to special interests of certain populations. It was noted that those organizations listed and described here (NARC, ACLD, NSACA, and others) were made up primarily of consumers. However, they do not exclude from membership those individuals who have only a professional or general interest in the welfare of the group. These organizations could be classified as charitable groups and would certainly qualify as such legally. However, to the extent that they have mounted an activist stance in the influence of public social policy, they have gone far beyond the classic charity.

There are actually many more organizations that could be listed and described as having an interest in the provision and improvement of services for various types of disabled children and/or adults but whose membership is more heavily weighted toward professionals. Such organizations may legitimately describe their purpose as advocating for better conditions for the clients they represent, through the promotion of more and better services. However, to the extent that they include a mixture of consumers and professionals, their basic goals and activities must be interpreted differently. While we do not mean to suggest that professional altruism for the public (or client) interest is a totally lost commodity, the presence of a professional interest influences the nature of an otherwise consumer-oriented organization.

PROFESSIONAL GROUPS

The professional groups that can be expected to have an impact on special education policy are of two general types, those representing the teacher and administrator organizations as a whole and those concerned with the specialty of education of the handicapped. There are relevant subdivisions within each of these that also must be considered. It must be recognized that professional organizations almost always have a dual purpose. While a primary purpose is always the welfare of the client population with which the professionals are concerned, a secondary, and possibly conflicting purpose is the welfare of the individual professional. It is also obvious that the overall interests of the various groups may carry some inherent intergroup conflict. The nature of these intragroup and intergroup conflicts should be understood as they affect special education policy.

Teachers' Organizations

Whether officially designated as unions or not, teachers' organizations have been quick to respond to issues brought on by changes in public policy concerning education of the handicapped. A major issue has been whether the inclusion of such children in less restrictive or mainstream settings would constitute an unreasonable expectation for regular teachers. The pronouncements of the union on such matters frequently have expressed a skeptical position that mainstreaming was a thinly disguised ploy of school boards to save money at the expense of teachers. When more charitable, unions have pointed out that unless proper training could be provided for regular teachers, and appropriate supportive services to aid such teachers in handling of handicapped students, the union must consistently resist efforts of school systems to implement the inclusion of such children.

Teachers' unions in certain locations have clearly stated this position in terms of guaranteeing the welfare of all children, protecting them against the possibly pecuniary interests of taxpayers and school boards. But they have also argued strongly for the teacher's voice in decisions about pupil placements. It has been pointed out that in the procedural guarantees of the Individualized Educational Program (IEP), the parent and the school administration together have more say than the teacher in what the programming arrangements will be. To rectify this, the New York State United Teachers, for example, have proposed that a union representative be a regular member of each local district's official placement decision group. The presence of special education teachers within the membership of local unions has in some instances placed such teachers in the middle on issues where the interests of handicapped children and those of teachers in general seemed to be in conflict. On the state and national level, union organizations have exercised a strong voice in reaction to legal and regulatory proposals. A Teacher Network for Education of the Handicapped, operating out of the national office of the American Federation of Teachers, is designed to serve as a clearing house for concerns of special education teachers, and has a particular focus on larger urban school systems where the union is most strongly represented.

Special Educator Organizations

Associations comprised strictly of special education personnel have experienced some of the same dilemmas as the consumer groups, in regard to the relative benefits of broad versus narrow identity. The issue has been whether there is more in common among the concerns of teachers of students with varying exceptionalities, or more that is uniquely associated with a particular condition. The Council for Exceptional Children (CEC), as an umbrella organization attempting to represent professionals across a wide spectrum (including the gifted and talented), has been able partially to resolve this issue by the use of divisions within the organization that are focused on particular interests. These interests are both disability related (e.g., Division for Physically Handicapped, Division on Mental Retardation) and functionally oriented (Council of Administrators of Special Education, Teacher Education Division). However, there have been recurring conflicts over the degree of affiliation, with proposals to secede from the larger group and with the establishment of new divisions as particular previously unrecognized interests are identified. The status of a division to reflect the interests of personnel concerned with the learning disabled has been a most notable conflict, as that group mushroomed numerically and evolved conceptually in recent years.

Within some states and localities, completely separate professional organizations have maintained some prominence, usually where a group has concluded that their specific interests were not well represented by the existing organization or that participation was stifled by the magnitude of its membership. Special education teachers have often charged that their major organization (CEC) is irrelevant due to its domination by university professors and administrators. At the same time, special education administrators in some instances have demonstrated their parochial orientation by disaffiliation from the major organization (Council of Administrators of Special Education) and establishment of independent alternative groups that presumably better satisfy their purposes.

Much of the dissension regarding professional organization can be attributed to the differences in the degree to which individuals view their role as being an integral part of some larger scheme of educational practice or a relatively isolated and unique activity. Social status also may play a part in the choice of primary identity. Among persons who are involved with services to special populations, there are those who view their technical role as being more associated with medical, psychological, or social work fields than with education. These views tend to be reflected in the choice of organizational membership.

The importance of the various consumer and professional groups lies primarily in the power and tendency of such organizations to advocate for particular interests. Special interests may weigh heavily in policy decisions and everyday practice. An understanding of the most prominent perspective of each group may be of crucial importance to administrators in negotiating decisions and in managing practice. Central to such understanding is a sensitivity to the conflicts among interest groups as well as the ambivalence that often exists within the membership of a single group.

ADVOCACY ORGANIZATIONS

A major role of most of the organizations discussed in the preceding paragraphs is to advocate not only for the interests of the clientele who are the recipients of professional services but in some instance for their own membership as well. However, the last decade has seen increasing growth in organizations devoted exclusively to advocacy for individuals or groups who are in apparent need. On the assumption that classes of persons exist with similar needs and similar inability to speak effectively for themselves, agencies have been established, many with assistance grants from branches of the federal government as a part of the social legislation of the late 1960s and 1970s, to provide guidance and training to individuals or groups for securing their civil rights. Such agencies have generally displayed an activist posture, going beyond the attainment of specific needed service and focusing on more long-range change in the system.

Organizations that are independent of the service system may be able to intercede for parents in securing services from the system and at the same time help to educate both the consumer and the service provider as to the issues in dealing fairly with each other. While the list of organizations serving an advocacy function may be very long, examples of those specifically established for this purpose and having played an important part in influencing policy include the following:

Center for Law and Education
Guttman Library
6 Appian Way
Cambridge, MA 02138

Center on Human Policy
Syracuse University
Syracuse, NY 13210

Children's Defense Fund
1520 New Hampshire Ave., NW
Washington, DC 20036

Closer Look Information Center
　for the Handicapped
P. O. Box 1492
Washington, DC 20013

Mental Health Law Project
1220 19th St., NW
Washington, DC 20036

National Center for Law
　and the Handicapped
1235 North Eddy St.
South Bend, IN 46617

The training and information dissemination function of such "professional advocacy" organizations marks their posture as being somewhat more specialized than either the consumer or the professional groups discussed earlier. These organizations have developed the technology of advocacy and the process of transmitting it. Literature from such sources includes guidance on practices calculated to help individuals not only secure services personally due but also to change the social system in the process. One such "manual" written from the parent's perspective instructs the reader on appropriate alliances, identification of community needs, knowing those who resist change, learning to use power, and concrete steps for action. It analyzes the use of demonstrations, letter writing, public hearings, symbolic acts, negotiation, lobbying, boycotts, publicizing model programs, and legal action.[10]

Similar publications serving as guides to parents in securing the rights of their children include works that focus on understanding bureaucratic systems and the personnel who inhabit them. Cutler points out the common "snow-jobs" used by establishment personnel to resist change and to forestall legitimate requests for services and instructs parents on effective ways to deal with the system (as well as strategic errors to avoid).[11] She details specific skills in using the telephone and writing letters, collecting and maintaining appropriate records, using certified mail, and enlisting appropriate organizational and political allies.

In a similar guide, Anderson, Chitwood, and Hayden[12] outline for parents the necessary steps in working through the process of referral, evaluation, the eligibility decision, the placement decision, development of the IEP, and monitoring the service program. Suggestions are given regarding items that the parent should insist on at each step and the considerations in going to a hearing, when disagreements cannot be resolved.

Certain advocacy organizations have a specific focus on the needs of handicapped children, or other disabled persons, while many maintain a much broader program, concerned with the interests of any group that appears to have needs in obtaining fair treatment in society. An example of the latter is the Center for Law and Education, located at Harvard, which over the years has dealt with such concerns as Indian education, vocational and career education, migrant education, compensatory education for the disadvantaged (Title I), desegregation, tracking, sex discrimination, student records, and corporal punishment, as well as education for the handicapped. Most advocacy centers feature a strong legal component, though many do not maintain an attorney on full time staff. The focus of a particular organization may be suggested by its title, but this is by no means consistent. The organizations listed here maintain a nationwide scope, but may in practice tend to also engage more intensively in actions near their geographic base. Other groups are organized exclusively for a regionally constrained thrust.

An example of an activity executed by a local advocacy center, Advocates for Basic Legal Equality, Inc. (ABLE), a legal services program based in Toledo, Ohio, was a training program to prepare advocates to help parents of special needs children in 14 counties in northwest Ohio. As a part of a Handicap Education Advocacy Project, the trainees received basic information on state standards for special education, federal laws and regulations, psychological testing, and development of the IEP. The program also included assertiveness training, role-playing sessions, and discussions on the role of the lay advocate. It was noted that almost two-thirds of the trainees were themselves parents of children with special needs. One member explained her involvement as stemming from an eighth grade graduation ceremony that included both hearing and hearing-impaired students, but in which no interpretation was provided for the 15 hearing-impaired students, "who were made to feel and look foolish because they didn't hear their names called and didn't know when to go forward to receive their diplomas."[13]

Variations on this theme, both in terms of the motivating force behind individual interest in advocacy and the programs of action carried out by organized advocacy groups, could be found repeated frequently throughout the country. The success of such activity in influencing the service system at the local level and public policy in general is obvious. One possible limitation on the potential impact has been the difficulty in mounting a consistently coordinated attack.

COALITIONS

It was mentioned earlier in this chapter that consumer organizations have frequently hesitated to affiliate outside the particular interest with which their primary identity is associated. The factors that create this resistance are many, including such rational concerns as strategic maximization of impact by maintaining a target that is clearly identifiable and understood in the public mind. However, mistrust of broader affiliation is undoubtedly also due to less defensible concerns over image and turf, not to mention the ego of individual organization leaders.

Efforts to overcome this problem have been attempted, with temporary and partial success. An Organization of Organizations for the Handicapped, for example, was formed in New York State in the early 1970's, which permitted some coordinated identification of needs and planning. It remained on the scene long enough to support and participate in the drafting of state legislative initiatives that were of major interest at the time. Its viability faded, however, as immediate objectives were accomplished and the awkwardness of its breadth was too great in view of the heterogeneity of interests represented. Renewed interest in issues surrounding proposed state regulatory changes in 1981, however, led to the forming of a Coalition of Concerned Organizations for the Education of Children with Handicapping Conditions. This group, comprised of over 20 child advocacy, parent, and professional organizations, including the New York State United Teachers, was successful in persuading the state's Board of Regents to delay implementation of certain revisions in regulations and conduct a study of school systems that had chosen to use the proposed regulations during an earlier optional time period. The difficulty in sustaining concerted activity, in view of varied perspectives and individual subgroup interests, seems to be overcome only when a near crisis of mutual concern is confronted.

Advocacy organizations have experienced the same problem, to a lesser degree. The generic interest in advocacy, rather than a specific population in need, has permitted a somewhat more coordinated effort, especially when generally recognized crises have occurred. A successful instance of coalition on a national scale was demonstrated in 1980 when a group of 13 separate advocacy organizations (having both national and local orientation) combined to form the Education Advocates Coalition. The focus of concern was the perceived lack of progress in implementing the intent of the Education for All Handicapped Children Act (P.L. 94-142). The Coalition gathered data on the status of local practices throughout 11 states, and evaluated the activity of the federal Bureau of Education for the Handicapped. The report published by the Coalition listed 10 major problem areas in which the federal agency's failure to develop policies and compliance procedures had led to confusion and delay in parents' efforts to obtain mandated services. They charged that

1. Thousands of children remain on waiting lists for evaluation and placement.
2. Institutionalized children are routinely excluded from any kind of schooling or are denied appropriate services.
3. Many children are denied "related" services essential to enable them to benefit from their special education program.
4. Handicapped children are unnecessarily segregated in special schools.
5. Black children are misclassified and inappropriately placed in classes for the "educable mentally retarded" at a rate three times that for white children.
6. Handicapped children are illegally suspended or expelled from school.
7. Many students in special education classes do not have the required individual evaluations and program plans or have "canned" rather than individual plans.
8. Seriously handicapped children are denied education beyond the 180-day school year.
9. Children placed out of their homes or without parents are deprived of all advocacy in decisionmaking about their programs and placement.
10. Parents are inadequately informed of their right to participate in evaluation and placement decisions for their children.[14]

The impact of this report, along with other sources of criticism regarding the administration of P.L. 94-142, stimulated a response from the federal agency, resulting in the establishment of a task force that studied the charges of the Coalition, in addition to a report prepared for the Civil Rights Transition Task Force for the new Department of Education, and a draft report by the Council of Chief State School Officers. This task force then developed a set of policy recommendations, published October 15, 1980, which included a Memorandum of Understanding between the Office of Civil Rights and the Office of Special Education regarding the responsibilities of each agency for implementing both P.L. 94-142 and Section 504. The Memorandum specified procedures covering enforcement, data collection, policy development, and technical assistance activities. It was stated that these procedures would permit better targeting of compliance review activities on the basis of priority problems identified by parents and advocates, and through joint planning efforts and better coordination in the handling of complaints, needed data could be obtained while reducing the burden on state and local agencies, as well as providing better technical assistance to those agencies for the resolution of implementation problems.[15]

The success of the federal offices in subsequently realizing such worthy objectives is open to interpretation, but there is no doubt that the plan and the attempted efforts were in direct response to the pressure from the field, the informal sources of influence. It would appear that the consumer-advocate group, in this instance strengthened through an identified coalition, was the primary force. Closely following, however, was the force of a professional interest group, the Council of Chief State School Officers. The forces from these two groups, with generally opposing interests, together with the forces generating from the Congress through the oversight hearing process, converged to cause the forging of a federal policy that would impact on every local school system.

It should also be noted that two years later, when the federal Department of Education attempted to modify significantly the regulations governing P.L. 94-142 (discussed in the previous chapter), the storm of protest that resulted in withdrawal of the proposed changes came most convincingly from the consumer advocate groups. While professional special educators (teachers, administrators, and higher education personnel) joined in support of consumer interests, the message from other educator groups was more divided. General administrators at both the state and local levels were understandably attracted to the idea of less oppressive federal intervention. This created some interesting interplay between some organizations. The membership of the Council of Administrators of Special Education, for example, while supporting better programs and procedures from much the same perspective as consumers, and also constituting a strong professional affiliation with the rest of the special education community, could scarcely avoid being influenced in their official stance by their alignment with the membership of the American Association of School Administrators. Similarly, those comprising the membership of the National Association of State Directors of Special Education (presumably special educators at heart) are employed directly by the individuals who make up the Council of Chief State School Officers. The latter organization tended to have a strong interest in state, rather than federal, prerogatives in the regulatory process. The public position taken by some of the special education organizations was understandably the product of philosophical and political compromises. Thus, the balance of forces from professionals on the issue of federal deregulation was somewhat equivocal. It was, therefore, the voice of the organized consumer that tipped the scales and convinced the educational establishment as a whole that the principles set forth by litigation, legislation, and regulation of the past decade should remain solidly in place.

SUMMARY

In this chapter we have presented a description of three identifiable types of interest groups that from time to time play a large part in the determination of social policy through their interaction with the official, legal, governance structures of our public institutions. While the deregulation dilemma of 1982 provides a dramatic example of the interworkings of formal governance and informal influence as sources of control of the system, it should be understood that a similar blending of forces probably occurs to some degree every day, at every level of the service system. Working within such multiple forces is a fact of organizational life.

Attempts to change public policy are inescapably complex ventures. Such attempts take place in economic, political, and social environments that virtually ensure that tensions will be present at the time and place of policy implementation. Since the policy process involves interactions of individuals and groups, we can expect these interactions to reflect all the idiosyncrasies of human behavior. These processes have been discussed extensively by such policy analysts as Wildavsky.[16] In a similar analysis of the processes involved in the implementation of federal policy regarding intermediate care facilities for the mentally retarded, Wickham-Searl points out that as a result of these interactions, "the activities of implementation often contradict original policy intent: unanticipated events steer policies from intended courses in unexpected ways."[17] In that study, four principles were identified that were clearly present in the case under study (Intermediate Care Facilities for the Mentally Retarded) and that tend to inform social policy in general. The four principles were described as follows:

1. Policies reflect their historical heritage. Changes in social policy emerge incrementally.
2. Tensions exist between concepts of social reform and fiscal conservatism; economic concerns usually dominate reform efforts.
3. Many social policies continue long-established traditions of institutional bias. Alternatives to institutions tend to reflect economic interests rather than reform intentions.
4. States are politically powerful in federal-state partnership programs. In the political process of social policy, certain key individuals are highly influential. These individuals represent states' interests rather than federal or beneficiaries' interests.[18]

In this example of policy implementation, differing interests of the state level program administrators, the consumer advocates, and the conceptualizers of general policy reform were very evident. The relative power and influence of each group at each stage of the policy process could be traced, as in the case of the deregulation of P.L. 94-142, and virtually every instance of policy development, adoption, and implementation could be determined. As was indicated at the beginning of this chapter, a sensitivity to the forces behind the influence of such interest groups may be an important key to program administration.

ILLUSTRATIVE CASE

Green Meadow Central School District has maintained a vigorous program of cooperative school-community partnerships, enhanced in the recent past by the public's attention to school quality brought forth by the "reports" from numerous national task force groups and commissions. Reading closely the comments and advice in the "popular" education press, such as *Kappan,* Superintendent Lee Brown had vowed to make Green Meadow a model in working with the business community to improve the school system.

The description of the work of the California Business Roundtable sounded most exciting, and, while a long way from Green Meadow, Superintendent Brown felt that the influence of the business leaders in promoting a statewide educational agenda was the type of thing that could work locally also. Attention was paid to minimum graduation standards, beefed-up state testing, curriculum guidelines, stronger attendance and disciplinary laws, a longer school day and year, deregulation of state restrictions on teacher dismissals and layoffs, and new concepts of teacher training. And, in response to the opportunity to have such influence, business leaders had apparently been instrumental in getting significantly larger school finance appropriations passed.

While Lee Brown and Green Meadow could hardly be expected to cause their whole state to follow the lead of California, the local initiative was off to a good start. The Chamber of Commerce had convinced some of its most dynamic leadership to work with Lee in setting up a Partnership for School Improvement, and the first thrust of this PSI had been to examine graduation standards. As Partnership Chairman Bradley Strong had stated in a recent news release, "Business firms who employ Green Meadow graduates in the future will know what a high school diploma means—that the youngster has attained a reasonable standard of literacy."

Moreover, the teacher and building administrator representatives on the PSI seemed to be getting along famously with the business people. So far, everything on the agenda had been well received by the Teachers' Organization. The mutual interest in improved standards provided a sound basis for cooperative problem solving. The feedback from the general public had never been more favorable.

Lee's euphoria was therefore jarred by a letter received from the president of the local Association for Retarded Citizens, which read, in part, as follows:

Our membership has been duly appreciative of the progressive stance of the Green Meadow Central Schools, under your leadership, in seeing that regular high school diplomas have always been awarded to the members of the special education classes. We are keenly aware that such recognition of their accomplishment of the objectives set forth in each student's Individualized Educational Program, as opposed to some "second class" symbol, goes a very long way toward enhancing the self esteem of our children.

We are therefore quite concerned about a bill being proposed in the state legislature which, as presently drafted, would prohibit the award of diplomas to any students who have not passed the state minimum competency tests. We understand that one version of the bill mentions the awarding of a "Certificate of Attendance," while another version makes no mention of any symbol of completion. Our local chapter, as well as the State Federation for Retarded Citizens, finds all such proposals unacceptable. It is apparent that the decision of the U. S. Supreme Court to refuse to hear an appeal from New York on essentially the same issue, has played a part in the current initiative in our state.

We are therefore launching an attack on this most damaging proposal. We have considerable strength among our statewide affiliations, but we will also need the support of forward-looking professional groups and individuals as well. We are aware that not every school district has been as enlightened as Green Meadow on this issue, and therefore we look to school administrations such as yours to stand beside us as an example of what can and must be maintained. We are sure that we have your private, personal good will on this, but we expect to also need your public testimony.

We anticipate a legislative hearing on this bill during the next month, and we intend to send a delegation from our local chapter to join the state officers in testifying at the Capital. Could you accompany us? We know of no better spokesperson from the professional side of this issue.

Superintendent Brown recalled some nagging thoughts of inconsistency that had been troubling, from time to time, but which had been dismissed since it seemed like two completely separate issues. But was it? After all, how many special education "graduates" apply for jobs in the community? But shouldn't they be able to? Will more in the future? We have been placing special education kids in work-study situations which lead to permanent employment sometimes. Is this going to be a problem? Lee didn't really know.

NOTES

[1]Vernon Loeb,"Philadelphia to Study Classification of Learning-Disabled Pupils," *Education Week,* April 25, 1984, p. 1.

[2]"Technical Amendments to P. L. 94-142 Regulations," *Federal Register,* January 16, 1981.

[3]*Directory of National Information Sources on Handicapping Conditions and Related Services* DHEW Publication No. (OHDS) 80-22007 (Washington, D.C.: U.S. Government Printing Office, May 1980).

[4]H. R. Turnbull and A. P. Turnbull, *Parents Speak Out* (Columbus, Ohio: Charles E. Merrill, 1978).

[5]Douglas P. Biklen, *Community Organizing: Theory and Practice* (Englewood Cliffs, NJ: Prentice-Hall, 1983), pp. 88-89.

[6]Ibid., p. 64.

[7]Ibid., p. 67.

[8]Ibid., p. 74.

[9]Ibid., pp. 75-83.

[10]Douglas P. Biklen, *Let Our Children Go: An Organizing Manual for Advocates and Parents* (Syracuse, NY: Human Policy Press, 1974).

[11]Barbara C. Cutler, *Unraveling the Special Education Maze: An Action Guide for Parents* (Chicago: Research Press, 1981).

[12]Winifred Anderson, Stephen Chitwood, and Deidre Hayden, *Negotiating the Special Education Maze: A Guide for Parents and Teachers* (Englewood Cliffs, NJ: Prentice-Hall, 1982).

[13]"Lay Advocates Trained to Serve Parents in Ohio Special Ed Project," *Center for Law and Education, Inc., Newsnotes,* No. 31 (January-February 1983) (Cambridge, Mass.).

[14]*Report by the Education Advocates Coalition on Federal Compliance Activities to Implement the Education for All Handicapped Children Act (P.L. 94-142)* (Washington, D.C.: Children's Defense Fund and Mental Health Law Project, April 16, 1980).

[15]*Final Report to the Secretary of the Task Force on Equal Educational Opportunity for Handicapped Children* (Washington, D.C.: Office of Special Education and Rehabilitation Services, October 15, 1980).

[16]Aaron Wildavsky, *Speaking Truth to Power: The Art and Craft of Policy Analysis* (Boston: Little, Brown, 1979).

[17]Parnel Wickham-Searl, *The Shaping of a Federal Policy: Intermediate Care Facilities for the Mentally Retarded* (Unpublished doctoral dissertation, Syracuse University, 1984), p. 2.

[18]Ibid., pp. 165-166.

CHAPTER 4
ORGANIZATIONAL STRUCTURES

Within any enterprise, the issue of organizational structure can have a significant effect on how the system operates in carrying out its mission. The design of the structure is of considerable importance to the administrative process since it affects just how the major administrative tasks may be executed. The structure may be established as a product of careful planning in which a clear purpose or mission guides determination of its shape, or it may merely be a reflection of traditional patterns, following lines of least resistance. In either case, persons concerned with the policies that guide organizational goals and the management of the activities that pursue those goals have a stake in the administrative structure of the organization.

In discussing the general purpose of organizations, with a particular focus on the administration of schools, Morphet, Johns, and Reller emphasize that organizations must make provision for decision making concerning which goals, purposes, objectives, policies, and programs will be accepted by the organization as legitimate.[1] They point out that the primacy of decision-making processes as the central core of administration has been fully elaborated by Griffiths, who set forth the assumption that the specific function of administration is to develop and regulate the decision-making process in the most effective manner possible. He posited that the structure of an organization is determined by the nature of its decision-making process and that maximum organizational achievement is related to the congruency of the formal and informal organizations. Furthermore, the proper role of the administrator is seen as controlling the decision-making *process* rather than making the decisions.[2]

The process of decision making is inherent in pursuing the purpose of any organization, which is, in general, to provide the procedures by which its members can achieve their common goal. These include, at minimum, procedures for

1. Selecting a leader or leaders.
2. Determining the roles to be played by each member of the group
3. Determining the goals of the group
4. Achieving the goals of the group.[3]

In the field of special education, the question of how the enterprise should be organized has been subject to certain long-standing dilemmas as well as to some rapidly changing legal and philosophic trends. As we discussed in Chapter 1, the perennial ambiguities concerning the scope of special education—that is, the boundaries among special education, general education, and other human service functions, are manifest in the search for optimal organizational structures to administer the enterprise. A fundamental question is the degree to which special education should be seen as unique and therefore differentiated from other human services or as only a minor variant within the broad scope of education and related social services. A secondary question to be addressed, irrespective of the answer to the first, concerns whether the enterprise is primarily focused on instruction (and variations within that function) or on a variety of support services to the broad range of habilitation, of which instruction is only one (though very important) part. Both questions bear heavily on how special education is organized at various times and places.

Furthermore, the question of organizational structure is of interest at various levels of the total societal system. At the grass-roots level, where direct service providers are face to face with clients (we are not limiting the consideration solely to teachers and children), the issue of how these personnel relate to others in the immediate system is a matter of organizational concern. Among the various units comprising a local service system, for example, a school district or combination of local agencies, the structure has a major influence on how planning, communication, and all other administrative functions are executed. The issue remains relevant at higher levels of government—the state agencies responsible for education and certain other social services, as well as those at the federal level. Whether we are considering the supervision of a speech therapist employed in a regular elementary school or the organization of cabinet level departments of the federal government, there are similar structural issues that are important to effective operation.

While ambiguities regarding the scope and purpose of special education have always existed, thereby leaving the issue of optimal organization poorly and variously resolved, the area of special education, no matter how it was conceived, was at one time too small to be of much concern to anyone. Only since the 1970s has the field been large enough to warrant serious thinking about structural design. In addition to rapid growth in numbers of clients, service providers, and organizational units, significant trends in philosophic perspectives, buttressed by legal developments, as well as increased pressures to educate all students more effectively, have together created a need to rationalize just how it is all put together.

CONSIDERATIONS FOR ORGANIZING

The primary consideration in any organizational structure is whether the existing design facilitates, permits, or hinders "getting the job done." However, "the job" may be multifaceted and it may not always be clear what the highest-priority aspects of the organization's purposes are. Within special education, one may reasonably argue the relative merits of technical skill attainment versus social assimilation of the students involved. The argument for students is easily extended to include the question of whether these two differing goals are in fact compatible and what effect administrative structures may tend to have in enhancing either of them. To place the issue in perspective, Is the special education student's growth affected by, for example, whether the teacher is supervised by a building principal rather than by a central office special education supervisor? Or is the growth of the individual student at a particular time and place of less consequence than the impact that the supervision of the teacher might have on the way special education is perceived in the educational establishment and the community? While it may exaggerate the possible influences, this example represents one of many dimensions on which basic questions of optimal structure should be considered.

Given the primary consideration of getting the job done, a host of secondary issues becomes evident. It may be assumed that organizational structures should be calculated to facilitate at least the following:

1. Systematic program planning (comprehensive, groups, and individuals)
2. Efficient ongoing operation (day to day management)
3. Fiscal accountability (budgeting, managing, monitoring)
4. Influence on staff personnel (selection, supervision, evaluation, development, retention)
5. Effective communication among all relevant parties (professionals, clients, and public)
6. Consistent evaluation (program quality and individual student progress).

Beyond these necessary elements for general organizational effectiveness, some particular considerations for a special education service system would also probably include the following:

7. Thorough assessment of group and individual needs
8. Procedural safeguards in assessment and programming decisions
9. Least restrictive appropriate environment among program alternatives
10. Reduction of stigmatizing consequences of special classification
11. Consumer participation in all aspects of the service delivery process
12. Acceptance of human variance within school and society.

Given this variety of legitimate objectives to influence the structure of the service system, the development of an optimal design is understandably complex. It is not surprising that the structures are determined more often by default than by design.

Special educators can credit themselves with having led in the development of ideas that later became standard practice throughout education as a whole. The concepts of individualized instruction, certain technologies for delivering instruction in spite of unusual obstacles, and the whole philosophy of students' rights, which affect the entire educational establishment, have largely been the product of the advocacy thrust of the professionals and clients concerned with exceptional students.

In contrast, in meeting the challenge of developing organizational structures for administering programs, special educators have not been particularly creative. Considering the demand for innovative structures that the wide variety of service needs imposes, the administrative organization within most systems remains (with a few exceptions) surprisingly routine. In most cases, existing organizational structures have been the product of reactive circumstances rather than proactive planning. Especially in moderate-to large-sized school systems, where special education in some form has long been established, the structure for its administration has tended to reflect the accidental presence of individual personalities to fill specialist roles and the idiosyncratic perspectives of key general organization leaders.

Creative development in organizational structure has occurred, however, where there has been the necessity of setting up entire new organizations. The driving force in such instances has been to create a viable unit within the array of a total service system. For example, the problems of rural, sparsely populated regions, where the issue has been the aggregation of sufficient population base for the provision of services, have resulted in the development of cooperative systems organized under joint agreements between school districts or intermediate education units that have at least made the question of rational administrative structure clear. In other isolated instances such as a major shake-up in the administration of an established system, a reaction to a significant legal problem, or unusually progressive policy leadership, systems have undergone careful study and planning of improved structures.

Unit Magnitude

In considering what goes into appropriate organizational structures, the size of the unit, generally determined by the state government as well as by population density factors, must play an important role. For example, the governance unit for the state of Hawaii, in which the entire state is a single school district, removes from consideration certain issues of revenue collection and resource distribution but leaves to other administrative policy groups questions of how best to manage the operation. The structure of school districts in a number of states (e.g., Florida, Maryland, and Nevada) is made coterminous with the county as a legal entity, which has the general effect of making fewer, larger, administrative units. Other states in which local "town" governance is a major part of the cultural heritage (e.g., Illinois, Nebraska, California, and Texas) tend to have significantly more (in these examples, over 1,000) districts, with many being very small. The geographic expanse of each state, of course, also plays a part in determining the number of governance units. As one would expect, Rhode Island and Delaware have relatively few districts, 40 and 16 respectively, whereas Nevada's 17 districts and Alaska's 52, when compared with Texas's 1,101, must be viewed with recognition of the population density factor. The country's urban centers will have large school systems (as measured by enrollment) regardless of the state's school governance system, purely as a matter of population density.

General school consolidation has reduced the number of school districts in the United States from about 120,000 separate units in 1940 to under 16,000 in 1980. Data reported by the U.S. Office of Education in 1976 showed that the 187 "large" (over 25,000 enrollment) districts, constituting only 1.1 percent of the total number of districts in the country, enrolled 28.3 percent of all the country's children. Conversely, 4,464 districts (constituting 27.3 percent of the total) enrolled fewer than 300 children each, thereby accounting for only 1.2 percent of the country's total enrollment. It should be clear that when considering questions of organizational structure, we must recognize that a relatively few school systems are responsible for a large proportion of the nation's students. If we are to focus on the school system when thinking about viable organizational structures, we must remember that over half the legal entities for operating schools in the country are so small as to enroll less than 1,000 students. On the other hand, if we are to focus on where the children are, nearly half attend school systems of at least moderate (over 10,000) enrollment.

The perspective on organizational unit size becomes especially important as we consider the viability of systems for the delivery of special education services. What constitutes a "critical mass" for a special education organization? To provide for every imaginable contingency, even very large systems may need to "go outside" to secure appropriate services. However, it has been recognized that systems enrolling over 25,000 students should be able to provide for virtually every child's needs within the system. The degree to which smaller systems must secure services outside their own organization depends upon a number of contingencies and has varied considerably as a function of changing attitudes regarding integration and the doctrine of least restrictive environment.

It was pointed out in Chapter 1 that educators had long recognized a need for some type of mechanism to pool the needs of many smaller school districts. While this need extends to vocational education and certain other support activities (such as pupil personnel services, research, data processing, and instructional resources and materials) that may be provided more effectively and efficiently with a larger student population base, special education has tended to be the major stimulator of multidistrict organization. Historically, interdistrict contracts, wherein larger districts agreed to serve handicapped children from neighboring smaller districts, led the way to informal cooperatives in many states, in which a modest amount of systematic planning among a collection of small districts permitted the establishment of a much more complete array of services than would have occurred on any single district's initiative. Although interdistrict contracting and informal cooperatives remain as one type of service mechanism, the more formalized cooperative, legally established as an intermediate education unit (IEU) between the local districts and the state education agency (SEA) have become the major means of organizing for service delivery to small districts. The driving force for the formation of such units, whether stated openly or not, has been the implicit goal of achieving capacity programming in a manner possible only in large systems while retaining the benefits of the smaller local education agency (LEA).

The Status of Intermediate Education Units

Intermediate units vary among states on a number of dimensions, such as scope of program involvement, governance, fiscal base, and organizational structure. In a report prepared for the American Association of Educational Service Agencies, Levis[4] cites a number of studies dealing with the various types of units that it is suggested, can best be identified by the title Education Service Agency (ESA). The most recent (1981) data indicate some type of regional agency in 39 states. A 1979 study by Stephens Associates identified three basic ESA patterns:

Special district. A legally constituted unit of school government between the SEA and a collection of LEAs, usually established by the state, or by the state and client LEAs together, to provide services to both the SEA and the LEAs. Eleven states were reported to have this model.
Regionalized agencies. ESAs established as a regional branch of the SEA to deliver services to LEAs. Four states were reported to have this model.

Cooperative agencies. Two or more LEAs sponsor an ESA to provide one or more common services, exclusively for the member schools. These are found to some degree in 13 states.[5]

The same publication noted that in 1975 the official names for regional education service agencies in various states included the following:

Cooperative Educational Service Agency (CESA)—Wisconsin, Indiana, and Georgia

Area Education Agency (AEA)—Iowa

Educational Service Unit (ESU)—Nebraska

Intermediate Unit (IU)—Pennsylvania

Educational Service Center (ESC)—Texas

Intermediate School District (ISD)—Washington and Michigan

Regional Educational Service Agency (RESA)—West Virginia

Boards of Cooperative Services (BOCS)—Colorado

Boards of Cooperative Educational Services (BOCES)—New York

Intermediate Education District (IED)—Oregon

It is noted that some states have more than one type of ESA and that classification is rather difficult. Organizational and financial characteristics were compared among the systems in eight states that have legislatively mandated statewide networks of ESAs (Georgia, Iowa, Nebraska, Pennsylvania, Texas, Washington, West Virginia, and Wisconsin) and those in four states functioning under permissive legislation (Colorado, Michigan, New York, and Oregon). A high degree of variation was noted in most characteristics, with commonality found only in the method of selection of the chief administrator, the eligibility to receive federal grants, and the authority to enter into service contracts with constituent LEAs. Most states did not specify a minimum enrollment for the agency, but among the five that did, the lower limit ranged from 4,000 in Colorado to 50,000 in Texas, suggesting quite different concepts of scope and relationships between the ESA and its constituent systems.

Much of the variance may be attributable to the initial purposes for which intermediate agencies were established in each state. In New York, for example, the Board of Cooperative Educational Services (BOCES) placed major emphasis on direct instructional services in special and vocational education for LEAs too small to provide their own efficiently. The entry into increasing varieties of administrative and support services came later. By contrast, the Texas Regional Educational Service Centers have always emphasized support services, with little involvement in direct operation of instructional programs. The differences in functions obviously influence the numbers and types of staff employed. A reflection of the emphasis on direct program operation can be seen in the fact that in 1975, 67 percent of all ESA/IEU staffs in the nation were in three states: New York, Pennsylvania, and Michigan.

Regardless of the programmatic scope of the IEU, there are certain inherent organizational problems. The IEU cannot avoid being perceived as a "limited-purpose" structure when compared with the regular LEA. The IEU development tends to be in response to an unmet need, usually centered on a particular service. As a result, the IEU, in focusing on that service, cannot become an integral part of the entire educational system, which places its personnel in a role tangential to the major business of the regular school system. Personnel employed by the IEU may be identified only with the special-purpose program and may suffer the same "second-class citizenship" status as the students for whom services are provided.

The legal governance structure of the IEU varies from state to state. Where the agency is an integral part of the state-to-local chain of command, serving as an extension of the SEA into the field rather than merely a cooperative group LEAs, the capacity of the administrator to impact the direct service field is enhanced. However, this "official" status also carries the disadvantage of putting the IEU apart from, and somewhat superordinate to, the mainstream system. The governance structure will certainly influence the degree to which regular educators and consumers feel that the special education program operated by the IEU is accessible, integral, and relevant.

The ultimate in separate governance, and a unique model for dealing with the problems of population base and "critical mass," is the St. Louis County (Missouri) Special District. Established by special state legislation in 1957, the district has legal, fiscal, and governance structures similar to all other school districts in the state but geographically overlays all the regular school districts in the area. Its ability to operate programs independently of local district constraints earned the system praise for two decades as the ultimate solution to programming problems of small school districts. However, the separation from mainstream educational programs was recognized as a barrier to interaction, constraining flow among levels of the continuum of special services and exerting a negative influence on least restrictive alternatives in programming decisions. With the philosophic shift at the beginning of the 1980s, this perceived barrier became the basis for litigation against the state of Missouri that was expected to have far-reaching implications for organizational structures of this type.[6]

The "special purpose" status of the IEU is also reflected in its fiscal base, which in most states sets it apart from the mainstream of state to local revenue collection and expenditure and renders it dependent upon tuition payments for contracted services. This difference in basic funding structure may have both positive and negative implications, but the fact that the system and its funding are specialized constitutes an articulation problem with the educational system as a whole.

The one thing that appears quite clear is the steady growth of IEUs, both in numbers and the responsibilities they carry out. Forecasts regarding their role point to still broader functions in the future, in research, technology, staff development, and similar administrative services, with somewhat less emphasis on direct operation of programs of instruction. However, in states where numerous small school districts are an embedded part of the culture, the role of some type of ESA/IEU as the service provider for low-incidence handicapped students appears long enduring.

The question of optimal enrollment and organizational unit structure for special education service delivery is not limited to the small district and the use of service agencies or other intermediate units. In larger school systems as well, one must consider how to organize the administrative units for most effective and efficient management and operation.

Emphasis on Form

One approach to organization of program may be based on some form of client or service classification, delineated either on statistical incidence, clinical disability, or type of service delivered. Students with handicapping conditions that occur in very low incidence, for example, in much less than 1 percent of the general school population, should probably be assigned for administrative purposes to the broadest-based, centralized service delivery unit. *Incidence-based* organization assumes that a client population requiring similar types of services should consist of at least 100 pupils (ages 3 to 21) in order to constitute a viable planning and service unit.

Application of this incidence criteria would probably result in centralized (or cooperative) administration for programs for orthopedically handicapped, trainable and profoundly retarded, autistic, multihandicapped, home and hospital bound, visually impaired, and severely hearing impaired. Service by decentralized regions of large systems (or independent small systems) would be viable for the educable retarded, emotionally disturbed, specific learning disabled, speech handicapped, socially maladjusted, and gifted. It should be evident, however, that classification difficulties will occur as we attempt to differentiate among levels of hearing impairment, mental retardation, and so on, because depending on where the line is drawn on the severity continuum, a classification may fall into either low incidence or high.

Another approach would ignore incidence rates and organize solely around *clinical disability* classifications. Such a plan would permit the deployment of instructional and supervisory expertise to the units at which the population was served. While this would result in much the same assignment between organizational units as the statistical approach, it could realize a benefit based on the presumed common need of a disability group, regardless of degree of severity. This approach tends to break down, however, in that optimal service planning for very-low-incidence students (e.g., profoundly mentally retarded) calls for a much larger organizational unit (perhaps 50,000 enrollment base) than is required for the mildly mentally retarded (where a 5,000 student population base may be quite sufficient).

A third approach would classify the type of *instructional service,* ignoring both incidence and clinical disability. Such an approach is viable only where the total system can adopt a full continuum of services. Under this plan, all services that are delivered in an essentially self-contained mode, isolated from the mainstream, would be operated by the centralized unit. Services that are most articulated with the mainstream, such as resource teachers, itinerant teachers, and consultants, would be administered by decentralized units, where proximity to regular teachers and administrators could be optimized.

In each of these three approaches, it is assumed that persons responsible for special education will be employed at both the centralized (or cooperative) unit and at the localized (or independent district) level and that the assignment of responsibility can be attached to programs of services and/or classifications of children.

Emphasis on Function

A different approach to organization may focus on the processes that constitute the leadership role. A simple division into administrative and supervisory processes has often been used to identify two levels on an organizational hierarchy and may provide a basis for distinguishing between those functions that can best be executed from a broad, centralized unit and those that should take place closer to the point of delivery. However, given the obviously trivial nature of certain administrative tasks and the relatively crucial impact of technical supervisory processes on the quality of service delivered, the inherently implied hierarchical relationship between administration and supervision may not provide the most useful "handle" for distinguishing functions or their optimal organizational locus.

In large school systems where a two-layered (or more) organizational structure for general program administration is required, in moderate-sized systems where the central office-building level interaction is the issue, or in small systems where some services may be procured from another (intermediate) agency, a rationale for identifying and understanding different functions and locating them organizationally is probably helpful. The distinction that has been drawn in conceptualizing and presenting this book—into *policy* and *management* issues—may lend itself well to this question.

Looking at the scope of leadership functions associated with any organization, certain processes fall logically into the domain of the broadest, most centralized units, whereas others fit into the directly operational level. Policy development, for example, surely is a function of the central office. In contrast, personnel selection usually needs to be carried out by administrators closest to the field of action. As we move from general principles for all organizations to educational particulars, including the mission of special education, the determination of each level's processes becomes less clear. At the central level, we could place those functions concerned with planning, development, and evaluation, leaving decentralized units with the functions of management and direct supervision. The distinction of each level's responsibilities is blurred by the broad scope of certain concepts. For example, while planning would normally be concerned with overall long-range programmatic issues, daily operational survival also includes planning. Similarly, the evaluation process is normally concerned with programs calling for a broad-scale central perspective, but specific units to be evaluated (for example, instructional personnel) would best be examined by leadership staff (managers) nearest the action.

According to this model, therefore, we would see planning and policy development as it relates to resource allocation, curriculum, and general program evaluation occurring at the most central level. This would include budget development and staff allocation as well as inservice development of existing staff. The functions of program advocacy, public relations, and interagency liaison would also probably be best executed from the broadest central level.

At the localized level, the operational management functions would include personnel selection and assignment, personnel evaluation, case management and pupil placement, instructional supervision, resource management (including such tasks as materials and facility procurement), and consumer (parent) relations. Complete dichotomization, of course, would never be possible or desirable. Managers should not have to execute programs that they had no voice in developing. Input to policy must include the management perspective. Conversely, localized personnel should seek the counsel of central administrators as they undertake such management tasks as personnel evaluation. The crucial consideration is that the responsibility be fixed at one level for each function, leaving few functions in an ambiguous shared domain. Even if both levels must be involved in a particular activity, the division of authority should be clear.

MAJOR ORGANIZATIONAL ISSUES

Examples of systematic study of the issue of optimal administrative structures that can be drawn from both recent and past events will illustrate some important considerations. These examples concern large systems, where the issue of organizational structure has been deemed worthy of intensive deliberation. Certainly the effect of such structural choices is not negligible in smaller systems, but it is the larger systems that tend to have enough at stake to invest seriously in questions of organizational structure.

The Centralization Question

One issue that confronts service systems of all sizes but has been of particular interest to larger systems is that of optimal centralization. This is not limited to the public school sector, since any branch of a multilevel service system has a similar question about the degree to which the several units of the lower level should operate autonomously or be controlled by the central higher level agency. The issue is basic to state and local relationships within the educational establishment, but it is also applicable to health, welfare, and all other social services. Within the educational system, however, the issue becomes even more pronounced since local school districts typically consist of a number of units (individual buildings) to which considerable autonomy is extended. For the general educational program, in spite of certain centralized functions such as fiscal controls, personnel management, and broad curricular oversight, school units tend to operate with great independence. The view of schools as "loosely coupled systems" has been well documented.[7]

However, superimposed upon this general program are the special education needs of certain students, calling for a program that for a number of reasons may suggest the need for a greater degree of centralization. The logical press for (relative) centralization of special education is obvious on the grounds of the statistical minority status of the population. That is, whatever basis for optimal organizational unit size is applicable for the general school population, a different catchment base must be recognized for handicapped students, particularly where low-incidence severity levels are concerned. Furthermore, apparent needs for technical expertise, specialized materials, and other factors may also press for some level of centralization.

In this context, then, a series of related questions may be asked that bear directly on the centralization issue. For example:

1. To what extent can special education be administered from the individual building level?
2. To what extent can a general school principal provide necessary program supervision?
3. What support services can best be provided from a central district level?
4. What services can be procured only from beyond the central system?
5. What relationships may be applicable among school building enrollment, district enrollment, community resources, and the incidence and degree of exceptionality in question, and the answers to questions 1 through 4?

The centralization question can probably best be viewed as the choice of an optimal point on a continuum rather than as a choice between dichotomous alternatives.

A Classic Example.   Well before the rise to prominence of special education as a major policy issue, the Los Angeles City school system, on hiring a new administrative head of special education in 1960, commissioned a study of the merits of various designs for relating the individual school building administrators to the central office of the system. As in most very large systems, the general-special interaction was further complicated by the presence of a two-layered general administrative framework, in which some of the responsibilities of the central superintendency are delegated among geographically designated regional administrative offices.

The key questions in this study focused on (1) the placement of the central administrator of special education within the overall hierarchy, (2) how this position would relate to other central office administrators having either generic operational or specialized staff responsibility, and (3) how the several school building administrators would relate to the various central positions concerning both general and special education matters. Again, the issue was complicated by the existence of two types of schools—most with a few special education personnel providing services within a regular building, but a few cases with buildings devoted entirely to special education services. While the "special school" model is found much less frequently now than at the time of this study (the early 1960s) it is still an administrative problem that requires a solution.

The study drew on expert opinions of professors of educational administration, leading professors of special education, and state education agency officials, as well as the experience of other large systems as reported in an extensive national sampling. The study demonstrated extreme ambiguity regarding the merits of various alternative models proposed.[8] The essential questions were whether the line of responsibility upward from the building principal should be exclusively through the *general* administrators in the regional and central offices, whether the central *special* education administrator should be the line authority for special school principals, or whether some type of divided line of responsibility should be used, and how these lines should be differentiated in those buildings housing both general and special education programs. Opinions of respondents tended to fall along professional identity lines, with generalists and specialists each favoring more authority for their own groups. Reported practice placed special education administrators in advisory or staff relationships with school personnel in two-thirds of the systems, but in positions with line authority over special education schools and classes in the other one-third. Analysis of the possible alternatives and the trade-offs involved in each illustrate the anticipated gains in control over special program operations, as well as the presumed benefits of technical expertise where the central special educator has a line or shared responsibility. This is obviously counterbalanced by the tendency to "disown" programs for which responsibility is lacking or diluted and by the loss of opportunity to integrate the special education operation within the mainstream. To put the alternatives into the simplest terms, the trade-off may be between emphasis on special education as "a part of" or "apart from" the rest of the system. While many other things in addition to formal administrative organizational structure influence that dichotomy, it is clear that such a structure may reflect, reinforce, or help to create a desired philosophical position.

A More Complex Question

An additional variable influencing the issue of generalist authority is the emphasis on special education as an instructional versus a support service. In discussing this question, Howe strongly advocates the linkage with instruction, pointing out that line managers (those in charge of building principals) are the persons who can have an impact on the system as a whole.[9] This relates to the preferences expressed by incumbent special education directors (in the study of that role by Kohl and Marro) for a change from the traditional specialist-staff position to one directly connected to line administrative operations.[10] It was noted in that study that directors felt their responsibilities far exceeded their authority and that they were seeking for a way in which to increase status. This group was, however, clearly divided on whether their situation would be most improved by affiliation with curriculum and instruction or with special services departments.

It is clear that, given the trend toward increased integration, the idea of achieving authority through a separate line administration for special education is out of the question. Howe concludes that a shared authority system is most viable and argues that identification with instruction rather than special services provides the firmest anchoring of the program within the mainstream. On the other hand, models have been developed that conceptualize special education as a broad, supportive service for all students and implement that concept by encompassing the various units of the organization that deliver the entire continuum of services. It is this type of structure that we have argued holds the best promise for the future.

We have given examples of school systems that attempted to incorporate these general principles, with a number of variations, in our earlier work.[11] In each of the systems presented at that time (Madison, Wisconsin; Minneapolis, Minnesota; Houston, Texas; and Boston, Massachusetts), some important, common elements were noted. In those instances, a change was made to (1) reduce the emphasis on segregated programs and establish a more complete range of services along an entire continuum and (2) discard the medical categorization or specific defect approach to service delivery and emphasize an ecological, systems-based approach to instruction, supervision, and overall management. These examples were cited because they represented some of the most progressive, and deliberately planned, efforts at organizational change. In the first three, the movement occurred in the early 1970s, well ahead of the broad-scale policy awakening and was truly "on the cutting edge." The Boston example occurred slightly later (1976-1979), and the changes were driven by more overt reactive forces. Since it was the product of the most extensive planning effort, and encompasses a composite of issues and principles that are worthy of study, the reorganization in Boston will be described with some detail here.

The Boston Model. Prior to the initiation of the major planning effort, the Boston public schools (with approximately 78,000 students) had a typical structure of special education leadership. Departments based primarily on classifications of disability were led by specialists with expertise in such handicaps. Impetus for change of that traditional structure came from studies by both internal and external evaluators of the administrative process. The focus of such studies on the special education service delivery system was accentuated by the passage of legislation (Massachusetts Chapter 766) that was well ahead of that of most states in its deemphasis of categorical classifications of children and programs. A suit against the system in the state court supplied added pressure to move the system into compliance with the new state (and later federal) regulations. Reorganization was seen as one necessary step in solving a host of policy and management problems. Some assumptions identified early in the planning process were the following:

1. Decentralization of the Department of Special Services will lead to more effective service delivery as well as to greater accountability.
2. The central office must be capable of providing the necessary technical and expert support to the districts to maximize program implementation.
3. The central office must be capable of monitoring the implementation of policies and procedures regarding special services and make appropriate modifications when necessary.[12]

An additional assumption in the Boston case was that the central administrative unit overseeing special education services would also encompass those related functions, that is, health, attendance, psychological assessment, and counseling, that in many systems were not organized integrally with the major instructional aspects of special education. The conceptualization of a total range of services that cut across the entire student population, but had proportionately greater concern with those with special needs, was made more concrete by the regulations implementing the state law. These regulations prescribed broad multidisciplinary input to the evaluation and placement decision process, which argued forcefully for closer coordination between the instructional and the related supportive services affecting the special needs population.

As in most school systems of its size, the decentralization motivation in Boston was well established as a means of extending the image, and to some extent the reality, of local community voice in school affairs. In this highly politicized urban area, decentralization was carried to an extreme in that the resulting nine community districts were each much smaller than would be deemed appropriate by scholars of urban system organization. However, this structure made possible the appointment of a coordinator for special education in each district, responsible to the community district superintendent, for a fairly small (about 8,000) population base. The major role of this position was to coordinate and monitor the process of pupil assessment, educational planning, and placement on a districtwide basis, in accordance with central office procedures and state regulations. Further extension of the decentralization process was accomplished by the appointment of a person within each school building (under the building administrator) to accept and process referrals for assessment, coordinate the writing of educational plans, and facilitate all other aspects of service delivery within the assigned building.

Superimposed on this system was a central Department of Special Services that was reorganized to discard disability classifications and feature administration according to level of service offered. Three major areas were created, each constituted by two or more units responsible for particular functions, bearing the following organizational titles:

1. Student Support Services (Educational Investigation and Measurement, Pupil Adjustment Counseling, Guidance, Core Evaluation Teams, Health Services, and Attendance).
2. Special Schools and Programs (Boston Special Schools and Programs, Contracted Educational Services).
3. Mainstream Programs (Resource, Interlevel, and Itinerant Programs).[13]

Each of the areas was headed by a Director who reported to an Associate Superintendent for Special Services. Under the three Directors were Associate Directors for each major function. As illustrated in Figure 4-1, the personnel on levels A, B, and C constituted the management team whose functions would be from 70 to 100 percent administrative. The personnel on levels D and E, by contrast, would have less than 50 percent management function, since their role was to provide supervision and technical assistance.

This plan utilizes the idea of horizontal and vertical teams, in which each level is expected to exercise coordinative functions. Personnel on levels A, B, and C would be concerned with both horizontal and vertical coordination within and among the departments in the areas and units represented. By contrast, personnel on levels D and E would be primarily concerned with indirect horizontal coordination (between operational areas) and direct horizontal coordination (within each operational area or organizational component). The model emphasizes a *functional* design strategy in that personnel at the upper levels would be responsible for planning, supervising, and evaluating programs across all geographic regions and program categories. However, personnel at the lower (D and E) management levels can be described as operating within a *matrix* design strategy since they would be responsible to both the general administrative staff at the regional level (building and Community District) and to the central special education management at level C.

The net effect of having both functional and matrix designs utilized in the same system is twofold:

1. With a functional design, conflicts may arise between the community superintendent and management personnel at levels A and B over the distribution and direction given to centralized personnel working in the community districts, since these superintendents would have little authority over personnel distributed and directed out of central office.

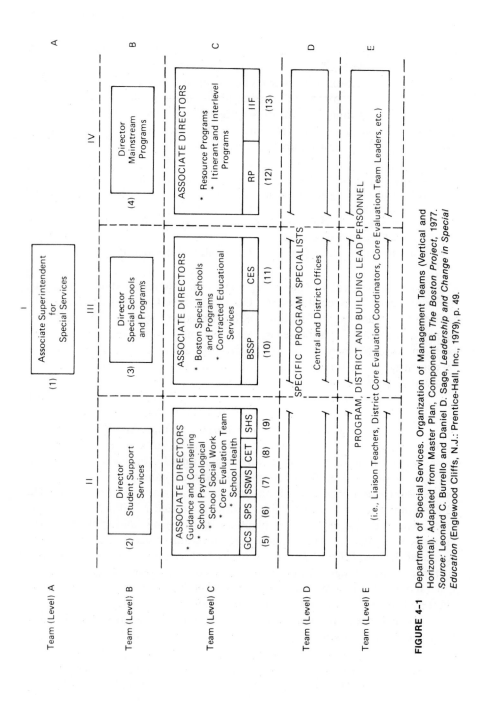

FIGURE 4-1 Department of Special Services. Organization of Management Teams (Vertical and Horizontal). Adapted from Master Plan, Component B, *The Boston Project*, 1977. *Source:* Leonard C. Burrello and Daniel D. Sage, *Leadership and Change in Special Education* (Englewood Cliffs, N.J.: Prentice-Hall, Inc., 1979), p. 49.

2. With a matrix design, personnel at management levels D and E must deal with conflicting priorities in their daily activities, created by the dual authority structure over them, that is, the community superintendent and the central special education management staff at levels B and C.

It should be noted that although this description of a model is placed in the context of one setting (Boston), where it was planned, adopted, and implemented, the concepts are generalizable to any system of sufficient magnitude to warrant more than a handful of leadership personnel in special education and services. In the Boston instance, the design employed numbers of personnel that could well be judged unrealistic, if not excessive, for the size of the system. However, this must be understood in light of the crisis situation that existed at the time—an embattled urban school system trying to catch up in response to the pressures of court orders, and an entrenched bureaucracy in both general and special education based on outdated concepts of management and service delivery. Furthermore, these personnel and the relatively high status (Associate Superintendent) of the leader were justified on the basis of broad, multiple functions of instruction *and* supportive services incorporated in the department.

However, as is typical in large urban systems, the political volatility of the school and community environment led to a series of changes in the governing board and the upper levels of general administration. This culminated in the abandonment of the Special Services Department organization before its implementation could be fully realized and the departure of many of the key management personnel. In three of the four cases cited earlier for their innovative organizational developments (Minneapolis, Houston, and Boston), the experience has been rather shortlived, with the new structures evaporating quickly under politically pressured leadership personnel mobility. The exception to this dismal history of organizational innovation (Madison) and the circumstances that in our opinion may have permitted that system to continue without major setbacks, will be discussed at this point.

Integrated Student Services

We have indicated that the process of introducing changes in organizational structure in special education systems has been subject to multiple forces of legal pressure, professional interests, bureaucratic constraints, and political vagaries. Furthermore, some of the examples pointed out in our earlier publication, as well as those discussed here, were seen as "grand ideas" that failed to reach fruition or to endure long enough to really demonstrate whether the concept was sound. On the other hand, one example that can be cited illustrates an evolution and development along fairly consistent conceptual lines for a period of over a decade. This example of special education organizational development will be described in an effort to show many of the same guiding ideological principles discussed earlier, but with some additional speculation regarding the factors that have allowed this system to move toward a goal without noticeable detours or retrogression.

The Madison Development.   In our earlier work, we included a discussion of how the Madison (Wisconsin) Metropolitan School District (MMSD) had succeeded in moving (from about 1972 to 1977) from a categorical disability model of administrative and programmatic organization to a regional plan with a special education coordinator in each geographic area to facilitate the provision of direct services to *mildly* handicapped children and to support the general school program for all children.[14] It should be noted that the attempt to rely *solely* on regional coordinators for the supervision of all special education services was not deemed successful, and was, therefore, modified after one year. The resulting model used a combination of functional organizational structures and a self-contained structure within and between regional and districtwide service domains. In the regional service areas (where self-contained units could complete all tasks through the resources organized within the region), special services were organized providing for a variety of specialized inputs (functionally organized and distributed across buildings within the region) for the general programs in the region. The regions could also share, on a functional basis, specialized resources among each other and with other supportive divisions districtwide. A districtwide unit, initially set up to handle services for the severely handicapped, became unnecessary after 1977 with the system's success in integrating all severely handicapped children into the regular school-based programs of the four regions.

In accordance with the continuous, long-range development endeavor of MMSD, a working document for in-house study and planning was disseminated in 1982.[15] This document, which addressed issues concerning the *total* mission of the system, not just the special education services, set forth six major goals:

1. Maintaining and improving the instructional program
2. Maintaining and improving the integration of the instructional program
3. Maintaining and improving the management of human resources
4. Maintaining and improving the physical facilities of the district
5. Maintaining and improving a public information and public relations program
6. Making the organizational changes necessary to implement the total plan.

It was noted that the plan was the product of interaction, both formal and informal, of the Board of Education, members of the professional staff, and the community over a period of several years. Two of the goals listed are of particular relevance to the organization of special education services and should be discussed in some detail here.

The goal of an *integrated instructional program* is based on the rationale that since a variety of options are necessary to meet the individual learning styles and needs of all students, the educational program must include a comprehensive but flexible range of programs and service options. Four variables that inhibit or enhance the maintenance and improvement of an integrated program were cited:

1. *Resources.* Provision of equal opportunities requires unequal distribution of resources. In addition, an integrated program is generally more costly.
2. *Parallelism.* The lack of equal opportunity, which has fostered special advocacy groups, that secured special legislation and funding sources, has led to development of special management structures and delivery systems that tend to be parallel to, rather than a part of, the existing instructional program.
3. *Advocacy.* While advocacy is healthy and necessary, specific interest groups that lead to parallelism foster lack of ownership of special programs by school personnel.
4. *Attitudes/Ownership.* Lack of ownership among school personnel regarding students who differ from the norm is in part an attitudinal factor, which is difficult to modify when parallel structures exist to take care of these differences.

To pursue the goal of an integrated instructional program, a number of objectives were proposed:

1. To improve the process of integrated decision making and advocacy for programs. It was noted that an integrated instructional program could not function with parallel decision-making structures and that a plan was needed to set priorities, delineate role expectations between principals and instructional coordinators, provide staff development, and coordinate instructional goals.
2. To develop an effective process for setting priorities for block grants (former categorical programs). With increased options (and decreased funding) for certain special programs, a process was needed for instructional priority setting on the allocation of grants that would assure attention to mandates, unique needs, and necessary safeguards.
3. To improve the integration and service delivery of optional programs within the total instructional program of the school district. The several alternative programs leading to high school completion, designed to address the needs of students requiring different teaching and learning styles (not handicapped students) must be coordinated and articulated with the regular instructional program.
4. To improve support to regular classroom instruction relative to the impact of an integrated educational model. The need for staff development was recognized, as was the need for technical assistance to support individual teachers who educate students with special or exceptional needs.
5. To improve the staff's knowledge and skills regarding the function of assessment in instructional decision making. Staff development efforts, specific to the process of modifying problems in learning through the interactive nature of assessment and instruction, is crucial to the overall goal.
6. To develop an effective district plan concerning student support services. Since the individual school is not a large enough unit from which to generate the full continuum of student support services, yet recognize the strengths of a decentralized model, it is important to achieve a balance between school-based and district level service provision.[16]

The achievement of these objectives, and the goal of an integrated instructional program, would require the attainment of another major goal, the *reorganization of the management components of the district.* The rationale for this goal included recognition of the need to continue the vertical K-12 coordination of program, which had been enhanced by the geographic area approach but had been reduced from four to two areas. However, the complexity of the programs precluded the Area Directors from providing sufficiently comprehensive supervision, evaluation, and coordination of staff and program. Therefore, an increasing need to provide horizontal coordination was cited to integrate various special programs into the total program. This called for additional management resources and a redefinition of the roles of existing staff.

The programs supported by advocacy efforts and special funding, which had developed parallel leadership structures, were now seen as needing to consolidate and integrate with the mainstream organizational structure. The problem of crises management, as a result of reduction in staff and growing complexity of parts of the organization, also called for added human resources, redefinition of functions, and reassignment of existing personnel. In view of these considerations, objectives for reorganization of the management structure were set forth as follows:

1. To continue to emphasize the vertical coordination of personnel and program
2. To place additional emphasis on the horizontal coordination of personnel and program
3. To improve the supervision and evaluation of administrative staff
4. To increase administrative resources in support of the planning, coordination, and priority setting functions of the district
5. To redefine roles of existing staff so that they can accomplish assigned responsibilities and better use the talents they possess
6. To become more humanistic and less mechanistic in the management of human resources in the district
7. To eliminate organizational parallelism through the continued integration of program
8. To maintain program advocacy where it is needed
9. To provide additional management resources to components of the organization that are becoming increasingly complex and important to the operation of the district
10. To define the appropriate functions of the principal as an instructional leader and to support staff development programs necessary to implement those functions.[17]

The action plan to pursue these objectives called for modifying the role of the Assistant Superintendent for Instruction (who was "spread too thin") to permit more time for coordination and planning functions and to modify some of the functions of the two regional Area Directors. This entailed establishing three directorships for districtwide horizontal coordination of programs. The resulting table of organization, finalized the following year (August 1983), is shown in Figure 4-2. The chart illustrates that two of the Directors had primarily vertical responsibilities whereas the others were given horizontal functions. Each Director supervised coordinators responsible for various programs, either regionally or districtwide. The Department of Curriculum and Staff Development and the Department of Human Relations constitute fairly minor realignment of previous functions and relationships. However, the newly established Department of Integrated Student Services is of greatest interest to the concepts with which we are concerned here.

The conceptual underpinnings and rationale for this new department and the scope of responsibilities encompassed were explained by the planning document:

> Continued advocacy is important to providing programs for exceptional children. However, it is important that those programs be integrated into the total instructional program and not be parallel to it. Present attitudes in the staff and community regarding the Specialized Educational Services Department seem to

FIGURE 4-2 Organizational Chart, Instructional Services Division, Madison Metropolitan School District. *Source:* Madison Metropolitan School District, *Exceptional Education Handbook* (Madison, Wisc.: The District, August, 1983).

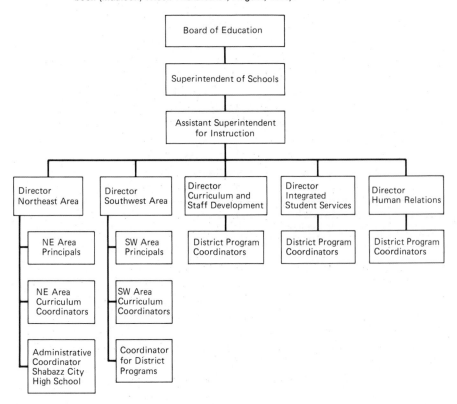

reinforce the concept of parallelism. It is almost impossible to place programs that meet the special needs of children within the SES Department because of the perception that all programs in the Department deal with children who are handicapped. Therefore, the name of the SES Department will be changed to the Department of Integrated Student Programs, and programs coordinated by the Department will be expanded. These programs will include the alcohol and drug abuse program, family change task force, student support services including health, the talented and gifted program, and others. In addition, the Director of the Integrated Student Programs Department will take on additional responsibility for supervising and evaluating principals of elementary schools wherein there is a large program dealing with the special needs of children.[18]

To illustrate the internal structure and responsibilities of personnel within this new department, the organization chart for that unit is displayed in Figure 4-3. It should be noted that the six coordinators are all concerned with districtwide activities, many of which would be included within conventional handicapped education program definitions. Other functions within the department are supportive and related services, as well as those programs con-

FIGURE 4-3   Organizational Chart, Department of Integrated Student Student Services, Madison Metropolitan School District. *Source:* Madison Metropolitan School District, *Exceptional Education Handbook* (Madison, Wisc.: The District, August 1983).

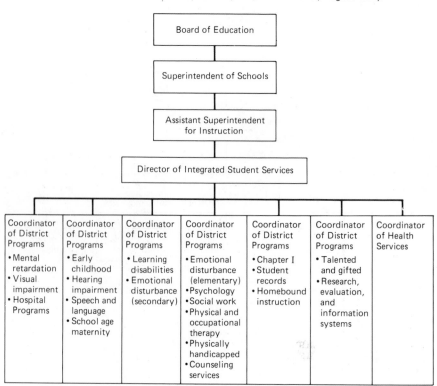

cerned with needs of special students who would not be classified as handicapped.

A complete listing of the programs, services, and functions of the department is shown in Figure 4-4.

As indicated earlier, the most striking aspect of this example of organizational change, beyond the rather significant conceptual expansion and integration of special education, is the fact that development has maintained steady growth, consistent with a basic theme, over a long period of time. This may raise the question of why Madison, as compared with the other cases cited, has provided a more favorable climate for innovations. The obvious difference in size of the system (under 25,000 enrollment), and the concomitant ease of communication and manageability of the bureaucracy, can be presumed to render it much more receptive to change than would be the case in Boston or other larger cities. But other factors undoubtedly have allowed MMSD to be recognized as a major generator of educational innovation, particularly in special education.

A case study of the MMSD by Muoio,[19] which was initiated prior to the

FIGURE 4-4   Integrated Student Services, Madison Metropolitan School District, adapted from *Exceptional Education Handbook,* Madison Metropolitan School District, September, 1983.

Integrated Student Services

DISTRICT STUDENT PROGRAMS	DISTRICT STUDENT SERVICES
Chapter I	Health
Talented & Gifted	Psychology
Exceptional Education	Social Work
Summer School (Regular & Special)	Counseling
Diploma Completion Program	Physical Therapy
	Occupational Therapy
	Speech & Language Therapy

DISTRICT INFORMATION SERVICES

Student Records and Data
District Achievement Testing
District Research and Evaluation

ADDITIONAL SERVICES AND FUNCTIONS

Alcohol and Other Drug Abuse
Family Change
Staff Development Task Force
Multidisciplinary Team Process Committee
Federal Curriculum and Research Grants (Exceptional Educ.)
Leadership and Management Teams
MMSD/UW-Madison Teacher Training

most recent phase of its organizational development, was prompted by the recognition that this system had successfully introduced the innovation of serving severely handicapped students in least restrictive environments far in advance of the legal mandates and social policy pressures to do so. In her analysis of the factors that may have contributed to innovation receptivity, she noted that certain characteristics of the community, the school district, and the change process itself had favorably influenced what has happened there. Being both the state capital and the site of a major university, the community has a relatively high average income and proportion of white-collar residents, a growing population, and a populist sociopolitical history, which provides "fertile soil" for innovation. The size, organizational structure, lines of communication, participatory decision making, and posture regarding staff development enhance the school district's capability for implementation of change. The strategies for change involved support from high-level administrators and the development of linkages and interrelationships, bringing together implementors on a person-to-person basis. The particular innovation under study appeared to be an integral part of the organization, having developed from an approach to problem solving that used parent groups, steering committees, and advisory councils effectively. Critical advocates who played key roles fell into two categories: conceptualizers and implementors. These advocates were high-level administrators, middle managers, and those outside the school organization. Support from the top was judged to be most crucial.

In summary, the organizational structures that have been described here as creative, though shortlived in some cases, represent the most ambitious attempts to set into operation a progressive theory of special education organization. In each of the examples, planners have sought ways to balance the strengths of special identity against the merits of integration in order to maximize educational benefits for all students. The success of the Madison system, whatever the contributing factors or its future endurance, stands as an example for emulation.

SUMMARY

If conclusions can be drawn from this discussion of organizational principles and the examples to be found in recent practice, it should be clear that we believe that special education assumes a broad role in the leadership of school system functions. Individualization of instruction, essential for students with special learning needs, can and should be expanded to all students. Much of the needed instructional service must be carried out within the mainstream, but teachers need assistance in the rapid assimilation and application of information as well as alternative ways to meet the multiple and diverse needs of the students.

The complexity of the task is indisputable. The educational system has been too fragmented and unorganized to meet the challenge. The problem of students who are failing in regular programs has resulted in duplication of remedial, compensatory, vocational, and special education efforts. The regular staff has been alternately threatened by and disappointed with the delivery of alternative programs for students with special needs. To confront the problem, there is a need for planning and evaluation, personnel training, and research and development. Special educators should play a major role in developing and implementing these functions. But this cannot be done without attention to organizational relationships.

Special education should be reorganized as an integral support system for all children. This must begin with reinforcing the school's responsibility to serve all children. Initially, the shared or centralized responsibility of special education demands a change in role and function. If the schools are responsible for serving all children in the least restrictive environment, school administrators must assume the responsibility to organize, operate, and evaluate all programs for all children at the district or building level. Special educators should then plan, organize, and evaluate their contribution as a support system to the regular administrative and instructional staff. The organization should help special education to

1. Provide support and assistance to regular education personnel to help them teach and organize instructional services for handicapped students and others with special needs
2. Establish direct services that allow for the unique learning and behavioral needs of students in the least restrictive environment
3. Set up a building-based team effort of parents, students, and professionals for the planning and placement of handicapped students
4. Initiate alternative settings and services at the building and district levels
5. Provide for evaluation of students' progress and decision points for exiting from various programs and services
6. Enable professional staff development to increase teacher and administrator competencies
7. Develop a field-based action research program that tests the application of basic learning principles to instruction, behavior management, and mental health of students, parents, and professionals
8. Negotiate and obtain external participation of other state and community agencies for the support of instructional programs, mental health services for children, and social welfare services for parents and children
9. Provide direct consultative services to parents and students to assist them in becoming better participants in the educational planning process
10. Apply criteria derived from considerations of process and least restrictive environment to all individual educational planning and placement alternatives developed at the building or district levels.

Achievement of these objectives calls for an organizational structure in which special education leadership operates on two levels and permits dual authority within parts of the subsystem. In policy matters, the special education administrator must participate in all aspects of the system. At the management level, the locus of operation should not be limited to particular special programs; authority must be shared with the mainstream personnel. While it takes much more than an organization chart to achieve this, and informal relationships, personalities, and idiosyncracies will play a part, the concept must be legitimized and officially endorsed if it is to occur at all.

ILLUSTRATIVE CASE

The school district serving the city of Soda Water Springs is of moderate size, enrolling about 25,000 students. With the election of a new school board majority and the appointment of a new superintendent last spring, the time seemed ripe for a serious look at the administrative organizational structure. As one of the key surviving central office administrators from the "old regime," Dr. Pat Karkowski, Assistant Superintendent for Instruction, has been asked to chair a process for studying alternative approaches to organizing the district and for advising the superintendent and the board as to whether the existing structure should be maintained or a new one adopted.

Pat has been advised that a free hand should be exercised, with little regard for incumbent personnel, as job descriptions for existing slots, impending retirements, and slack in the personnel budget provide sufficient "wiggle room" to permit change if it is warranted. As the new boss put it, "If a change is needed, we should do it before the honeymoon ends!"

Furthermore, the political activity and public discussion that culminated in the election of the new board, makes it clear that perceptions in the community regarding various special programs, including those for the handicapped, are "hot topics." The management of relationships between the regular and special programs must, therefore, be addressed in whatever is recommended. Recognizing the volatility of the situation, Pat has decided to "diffuse the risk" and enlist a broad-based committee to participate in the study and develop recommendations. This Organization Advisory Committee includes teachers and principals representing each level in the system, some central office directors, supervisors, and consultants and an equal number of parents and other concerned citizens. This committee is rather large, but it seems to be getting things done, and Pat's handling of the process has allowed the membership to feel truly enfranchised.

To help the committee understand what is currently in place, the organization chart was reviewed and analyzed, with particular attention to the structure for various special programs. It was noted that about 2,000 students are identified as handicapped and are served with a variety of programs encompassing a wide range from part-time attention by itinerant or resource room teachers to full-time placement in residential settings outside the public schools' domain. All these programs are under the authority of a Division of Special Education, headed by a director. The staff employed for these programs report through a line structure of departments to the division director. The management of services procured outside the system is also the responsibility of this Director. This responsibility includes all fiscal affairs from budget development to final accounting. The authority and program relationships in this system are illustrated in the chart (Figure 4-5) with certain portions elaborated to focus on the details of the special education programs.

The supervisors in the special education departments of Part-Time Programs and Full-Time Programs provide both technical assistance and evaluation and supervision of the staff employed in those programs. They are expected to have curriculum and instruction expertise in special education and program management capability. The director of the Division of Special Education oversees all programs and is responsible for relationships between these programs and clients, both inside the system (regular teachers, principals, and other division directors) and outside (parents, community agencies, and taxpayers).

It was also noted that approximately 1,000 other students who are *not* identified as handicapped receive a variety of *indirect* special services in the system every year. These services by psychologists and other consultant staff include pupil assessment, consultation with the regular classroom teachers, and counseling for parents and students who have difficulties in school but either have *not yet* been confirmed as handicapped or have been determined to have special needs too minor to warrant a handicapped classification.

The Organization Advisory Committee did its homework, studying the existing structure, examining current practices in a number of other districts of similar size, and even consulting some books on organization theory. Therefore, Dr. Karkowski was confident that the product of the committee's deliberations could be passed on to the superintendent and board for consideration with high credibility.

The recommended new structure for Soda Water Springs called for pulling together all special services (handicapped, psychological, health, and social services) into one division headed by an assistant superintendent, an added position at that level. This position would exercise a line relationship to a small group of support service administrators who direct a staff of consultant and technical assistance personnel. Through these positions, the assistant superintendent for special services would have a staff relationship to the larger number of personnel who provide direct service to students in the schools. The line authority for all direct service personnel assigned to schools would rest with the regular administrators of those buildings. The chart depicting these recommendations (Figure 4-6) does not include details of the Business Division, since no changes were involved there. Both charts illustrate the distinction between line authority roles and staff consultant (supervisor/specialist) roles in regular curriculum, special education, and support service departments.

In forwarding the committee recommendation to the boss, Pat recognized that in deciding between the existing structure and the new proposed one, the board would have to consider a number of policy questions. For example,

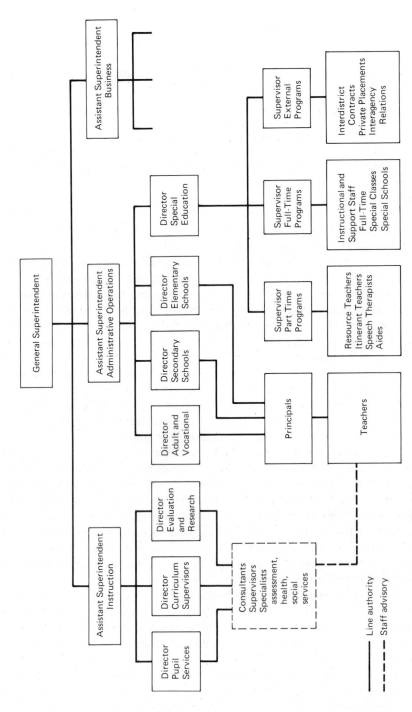

FIGURE 4-5 Organization Chart, Soda Water Springs.

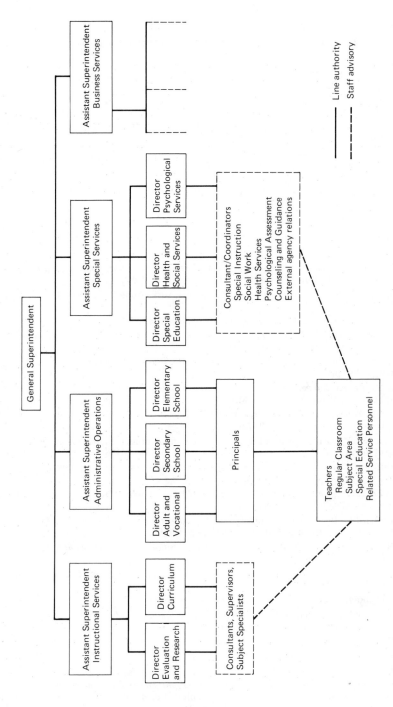

FIGURE 4-6 Proposed Organization Chart, Soda Water Springs.

General Superintendent

Assistant Superintendent Instructional Services

Assistant Superintendent Administrative Operations

Assistant Superintendent Special Services

Assistant Superintendent Business Services

Director Evaluation and Research

Director Curriculum

Director Adult and Vocational

Director Secondary School

Director Elementary School

Director Special Education

Director Health and Social Services

Director Psychological Services

Consultants, Supervisors, Subject Specialists

Principals

Teachers
Regular Classroom
Subject Area
Special Education
Related Service Personnel

Consultant/Coordinators
Special Instruction
Social Work
Health Services
Psychological Assessment
Counseling and Guidance
External agency relations

——— Line authority

- - - - Staff advisory

What underlying values are implied by each structure?

What assumptions and perceptions about special education does each structure suggest?

What benefits to the consumers of services does each plan promise?

What benefits to system personnel can be expected from each?

What does each structure sacrifice?

What are the long-term effects that can be predicted of one structure contrasted to the other?

What are the significant fiscal considerations, in terms of numbers and levels of positions or other service costs?

What measures can be devised to determine successful implementation?

NOTES

[1]Edgar L. Morphet, Roe L. Johns, and Theodore L. Reller, *Educational Organization and Administration,* 4th ed. (Englewood Cliffs, NJ: Prentice-Hall, 1982), p. 65.

[2]Daniel E. Griffiths, *Administrative Theory* (New York: Appleton-Century-Crofts, 1959), pp. 89-91.

[3]Morphet, Johns, and Reller, *Educational Organization*, p. 63.

[4]Rae M. Levis, *The Education Service Agency-Where Next?* (Arlington, Va.: American Association of School Administrators, 1983).

[5]Stephens Associates, *Education Service Agencies: Status and Trends* (Burtonsville, Md.: The Author, 1979), pp. 1-2.

[6]*St. Louis Developmental Disabilities Treatment Center Parents' Association* v. *Mallory*, U.S. District Court, Western District of Missouri, Central Division, 1980.

[7]Karl E. Weick, "Educational Organizations as Loosely Coupled Systems," *Administrative Science Quarterly*, 21, no. 1 (March 1976), pp. 1-19.

[8]Frank M. Hodgson, "Special Education—Facts and Attitudes," *Exceptional Children*, 30 (1964), pp. 196-201.

[9]Clifford E. Howe, *Administration of Special Education* (Denver: Love, 1981), pp. 54-55.

[10]John W. Kohl and Thomas D. Marro, *A Normative Study of the Administrative Position in Special Education*, Grant No. OEG-0-70-2467 [607] (Washington, DC: U.S. Office of Education, The Pennsylvania State University, 1971).

[11]Leonard C. Burrello and Daniel D. Sage, *Leadership and Change in Special Education* (Englewood Cliffs, NJ: Prentice-Hall, Inc., 1979), pp. 88-102.

[12]Boston Public Schools, *Administrative Reorganization of the Department of Special Services*, 1976.

[13]Boston Public Schools, *Superintendent's Circular*, no. 154 (Boston: The Schools, April 27, 1977).

[14]Burrello and Sage, *Leadership and Change*, pp. 88-90.

[15]Madison Metropolitan School District, *A Plan to Maintain and Improve Effective Schools in the 1980s* (Madison, Wisc.: The District, August 1982).

[16]Ibid., pp. 9-13.

[17]Ibid., pp. 24-25.

[18]Ibid., p. 26.

[19]Geraldine T. Muoio, *A Case Study of Innovation: The Integration of Severely Handicapped Children into Typical Public Schools* (Unpublished doctoral dissertation, Syracuse University, 1983).

CHAPTER 5
ISSUES
IN FISCAL POLICY

The financing of special education has sometimes been viewed as an issue separate from the rest of educational finance. This view has, of course, been sustained to the degree that the delivery of services and the organizational mechanisms for such delivery have been segregated from the general educational enterprise and identified with other social service systems. The factors regarding the status of special education and its relationship to the larger system, which have been discussed in the preceding chapters, are also manifested in financial relationships and policies. Therefore, to understand fiscal issues in special education, we must look first at the broad scope of educational fiscal policy as a whole.

It would be inappropriate to attempt even a cursory coverage of educational finance in this chapter. However, there are a few underlying concepts from the literature and common understandings of educational finance that apply to issues of support of the special education delivery system. It is also clear that as the philosophic and conceptual base has developed in recent years for the increased integration of special and general education, certain issues that had been seen as primarily applicable to special education interests also have significant implications for general educational fiscal policy.

The authors are indebted to Eileen F. McCarthy for her contribution to this chapter.

Therefore, this chapter will deal initially with a few of these more relevant linking concepts that constitute basic principles for educational fiscal policy. After establishing the considerations for optimal policy in general, we will discuss some specifics regarding the evolution of special education support systems, particularly those dealing with sources of revenue, and the considerations in distribution of revenue. Finally, we will examine recent developments in state-level special education fiscal policy in regard to resource distribution and the merits of the various methods currently utilized.

In a later chapter on fiscal management, we will examine some of the data on expenditure history and its implications for operational decisions on programming. At that point, we will also consider some of the developing approaches to analysis of resource requirements and implications for future planning.

BASIC CONCEPTS

Since 1970 there has been a dramatic acceleration of interest and activity around the general issue of educational finance policy reform. In a manner paralleling the progressive thrust in policy development in special education, judicial, legislative, and regulatory activity throughout the United States has focused on rationalizing and improving upon the existing policies for the support of public education. This activity has emphasized varying objectives and even more varying mechanisms for pursuit of those objectives. This variety is a function of political, economic, and general social forces, some of which parallel those forces that have brought about other (nonfiscal) changes in special education policy.

It is generally recognized that three strongly held values influence public policy in the American culture. *"Equality, efficiency,* and *liberty* are viewed by an overwhelming majority as conditions that government should maximize."[1] It is quite obvious that these three abstract goals are antithetical and that exclusive pursuit of one is at the expense of the others. Priorities among the three are a matter of ideological preferences. Persons concerned with educational policy are continually faced with the dynamic equilibrium among these values, "with the balance at any particular point being fixed as a consequence of a complicated series of political and economic compromises."[2]

As with all other issues in educational policy, government at the state level is the major locus of influence. It is generally accepted that "in financing public schools, states traditionally have been concerned with adequate provision of educational adequacy, efficiency, and equality, in roughly that order."[3] In spite of extensive controversy, debate, and discussion in the policy literature, accompanied by the adoption of fiscal policies by states that purport to address the concern for *adequacy, efficiency,* and/or *equity,* the terms have not been appropriately defined, but left to rather vague interpretation.[4]

It is also evident that the definition of *liberty,* or freedom of choice is also subject to varying interpretations. We intend to delineate these concepts and present illustrations of how they are manifested in special education policy.

Adequacy in School Finance

In the literature of educational finance, adequacy has usually been defined as the provision of learning services sufficient to meet a goal. Since goals have tended to be poorly specified, the question of "how much is enough" has been difficult to answer. Chambers and Parrish state that "since there is no social consensus as to the specific outcomes that should result from public education and the technological relationships between educational resources and outcomes are not well understood, it is our contention that the issue of adequacy in educational provision cannot be objectively resolved."[5]

Certain goals are sufficiently concrete and universally accepted that adequacy in respect to them is readily recognized. There is little argument that lack of access to a school constitutes an inadequacy. Similarly, a certain amount of time over which schooling is available (hours, days, years) has also become *somewhat* standardized. Such measures of resource input to adequate education are easily accepted. But when questions arise as to the number of students per teacher or the amount of support services in a school, the standard of adequacy is much more debatable and is generally resolved in the interplay of political-economic forces, with no one claiming an absolute answer to the question "How much is enough." However, the focus on resource input does permit a calculation of total expenditure per student, which can be compared from one time or place to another and thereby provide a type of global indicator of *relative* adequacy. It is assumed that (other things being equal) a greater expenditure in one educational system than another can be associated with a higher likelihood of positive outcomes. It should be noted that *outcome* remains the true standard for which resource input is only an available, more measurable proxy. While measures of attainment, achievement test scores, and similar standardized assessment instruments have long been accorded some status as indicators of general educational system performance, the specific concentration on minimum competency testing as a graduation requirement in nearly half the states (by 1982) is indicative of an increased focus on outcomes.

The concept is complicated significantly, however, when major variances in pupil needs are introduced. From both the input and outcome perspective, it is recognized that handicapped students (and others having special needs) must be considered in accordance with a different standard. While most states have acknowledged the difference in the form of resource input allocation (often in terms of weights or ratio indices purported to be objectively determined), the magnitude of the resource differentials are to a large extent a reflection of values and political compromises rather than objective reality regarding pupil need. From the outcome side, a different standard of adequacy is reflected in the adjustments to competency testing procedures that are designed for certain handicapped students in some states. Furthermore, as Martha McCarthy has suggested, the whole concept of the individualized educational program (IEP) constitutes a different threshold of adequacy in programs for the handicapped, as compared with the general school population."Whereas the basic education program usually is considered sufficient if it satisfies minimum input requirements, programs for the handicapped must be *appropriate* to address the students' educational (and perhaps noneducational) needs."[6] She points out that the courts have in many cases acknowledged that the resources called for to provide an appropriate education for the handicapped may necessitate a sacrifice in services for the rest of the school system.

It should be noted that such considerations are focused only on the resource input side of the definition of adequacy. The courts, as well as other policymakers, have tended to steer clear of the specification of outcomes, especially where a high degree of pupil variance is anticipated, until recently. In the case of *Rowley*,[7] as discussed in Chapter 2, the crux of the issue was the determination of what constituted an adequate amount of service to meet the legal requirement of an appropriate education. The services (a sign language interpreter in the classroom) called for in the IEP carried obvious fiscal implications for this and similar cases, which the school system argued were not necessary. The ruling of the U.S. Supreme Court, in favor of the school system, was based to a large extent on the finding that the child was making average progress in school without the additional service. This decision reflected greater weight to *outcome* indicators that were objectively observable than to the less tangible projections of how much more Amy Rowley might be able to achieve if accorded the *full opportunity* to learn, which the additional services would provide.

In summary, it is clear that adequacy has been an imprecise, dynamic, and expanding standard. Despite numerous attempts to deal with the concept in laws, regulations, court rulings, and policy statements, definitions remain ambiguous. As additional responsibilities are assumed by public education, additional commitments of resources are necessary. Changing expectations of both consumers, school professionals, and society at large cause the minimum foundation of fiscal support to be constantly shifting. More critically, the interaction with concepts of efficiency and equity must also be considered.

Efficiency in School Finance

Economic efficiency is generally seen as attaining the maximum units of output for each unit of input. In American education the focus on efficiency has varied greatly over time. At the turn of the century, significant attention was given to scientific management, in which attempts were made to reduce schooling to a series of principles that could enhance learning and reduce costs. The era of "cheaper by the dozen," time and motion studies, and efficiency experts in the schools has been well documented.[8] Again in the 1960s, the "accountability movement" that accompanied the rapid upsurge in federal social programs and the competition for the available resources generated a renewed interest in demonstrating efficiency.

Much of the time, however, other forces have apparently held greater influence over educational fiscal policy. Between 1940 and 1970, perpupil expenditures for U.S. public schools increased 500 percent (discounting inflation) and costs outstripped growth in gross national product, without discernible increases in output.[9] During the rapid growth period of the 1950s and 1960s, the need to accommodate the new population effectively eclipsed efficiency considerations. But declining enrollment, accompanied by high inflation, spurred an interest in the 1970s to use whatever mechanisms could hold the line on spending. Three types of measures are available and have been used by various states: (1) statutory limits on per-pupil revenues collected or expended, (2) tax rate limits, and (3) annual votes on local district budgets. These measures have been viewed as having limited effect of the achievement of true efficiency.

A somewhat more promising approach to efficiency can be seen in the various "technical-industrial" models that were applied to education as a part of the accountability movement of the late 1960s. The basic point of accountability is fixing responsibility for reaching specified educational goals, measuring precisely whether goals have been reached and, in some instances, calculating the costs of doing so. The models borrowed from military, industrial, and commercial institutions include such schemes as "management by objectives" (MBO), planning-programming-budgeting systems (PPBS), systems analysis, program evaluation and review technique (PERT), performance contracting, and production function analysis.[10] The utility of any of these models in the educational setting depends on the degree to which the goals of the system can be specified, the products measured, and the actual costs of various resource inputs compared.

Within special education, the adoption of the IEP as a major platform of service delivery policy exemplifies a type of accountability. It has not been seen as a vehicle for cost-effectiveness analysis, however, and its implementation has generated some concerns regarding its possible interpretation as a performance contract. Policy statements from the federal level have been necessary to establish that teachers could not be held legally liable for children's nonattainment of IEP goals. This limitation on the scope of accountability reflects the type of professional resistance to the idea of efficiency that has been found consistently in education. It is generally recognized that the fears of teachers regarding measurement of productivity are justified, given the existing ambiguity of the goals of schooling and the inadequacies in the art (or science) of measurement.

Perhaps the bottom line in professional reactions to accountability is the infringement upon professional autonomy. Recognition that teaching, at its best, is an individualized process places a high value on the exercise of discretion and professional judgment as to what the student's pace should be toward which goals. This factor tends to make most mechanisms for accountability difficult for the professional to accept. The situation is ameliorated considerably by the IEP, in which both goals and the methods of measurement of their attainment are agreed upon in advance, by all parties concerned. However, the general idea of evaluation schemes as a means to efficiency still generates professional resistance. "No matter how they show it, professional educators, though usually willing to agree that an enterprise as costly and as important as schooling must be subjected to measurement and evaluation, are generally reticent to approve any practical plan to do so."[11]

Equity in School Finance

The pursuit of "equality" as a societal value in America has usually translated into "equality of educational opportunity." Since virtually no one would argue that education should or could be absolutely equal for each individual, the variance in interpretations has revolved around the possible meanings of "equal opportunity."[12] In the most simple form, it could be interpreted as nothing more than *equal access* to whatever is established as the state supported minimum program or foundation of support. A more reasonable interpretation takes into consideration the varying characteristics of learners and uses the concept of *equal treatment* being possible only when the system provides unequal resources as a means of compensating for the unequal needs of various students. It is this concept, of course, that provides the rationale for special education, compensatory education, and a few other specially funded programs. Still another interpretation employs the idea of *equal outcome,* based on the assumption that school achievement is so crucial to "life chance" that the school must be responsible for bringing virtually every student to at least some level of desired performance. While this interpretation is generally recognized as beyond the reasonable reach of educational systems, either technically or fiscally, there are some elements of the idea that can be seen in the efforts to set minimum competency requirements and in the "standard raising" rhetoric of the various task forces and reports assessing education in America in 1982, 1983, and 1984.

The term "equity" has become the most accepted expression for the concept of equal educational opportunity, and in view of the variety of possible interpretations, elaborations of this term have been developed. Equity is recognized as having a number of dimensions. From the perspective of the student, equity can mean either the assurance of *equal dollars* per student or the assurance of enough dollars to provide *comparable programs,* given differing student needs and differing costs for services. But the concept of equity also can be viewed from the perspective of the taxpayer, in which the objective may be to pursue either an equal burden for the support of education or a comparable burden, given differences in wealth and certain other relevant factors.

Experts in educational finance have adopted the term *horizontal equity* to express the concept of "equal treatment of equals." This is of course most applicable where conditions place a high priority on reconciling existing differences in levels of fiscal support that have no rational basis. The term *vertical equity* is used to express the idea of "unequal treatment of unequals," which is most relevant in the determination of appropriate support for programs for students with varying special needs. However, both horizontal and vertical equity can also be applied to the taxpayer side, where variation in ability to support the educational system is the key consideration.

The major school finance reform efforts of the 1970s, which have extended to the present with little sign of abatement, had a predominant objective of equalizing differences in educational expenditure that result from differences in taxable wealth per student among a state's school districts. While the general principle of equalization, to adjust at the state level for differences in school districts' capacity for generating revenue, had been a part of most states' school finance policy since early in the century, its effect on achieving true equity remained fairly limited. The impetus for serious challenge of the status quo was a series of lawsuits in various states, that could be attributed to a rising consciousness regarding civil rights to "fair treatment."

The Serrano case[13] and the litigation in other states that followed it established the principle of "fiscal neutrality" that basically states that the support of public education must not be a function of local wealth but of the wealth of the state as a whole. But the focus on the school district and the taxpayer, rather than the varying needs of students, in the behavior of the courts and in the most common application of the principle of fiscal neutrality, is consistent with long-standing thinking regarding public support of education. The concept of vertical student educational equity, employing different treatment of children on the basis of their circumstantial needs, is not only of more recent origin but tends to be more difficult to pin down with sufficient clarity to satisfy policymakers.

On the other hand, the post-*Serrano* pursuit of fiscal neutrality for the taxpayer and for the school district as a whole has been the focus of litigation in many states:

> Between the late 1960s and the early 1980s court suits were brought in twenty-four states challenging the constitutionality of the states' systems for financing education. . . . Beyond this, new rounds of litigation are being undertaken, or contemplated, in four states in which the highest state court has already declared the system unconstitutional.[14]

It is clear that the development of practical responses to the objective of vertical equity (the unequal treatment of unequals) in general educational finance must to a large extent be attributed to the demonstration of significantly varying needs for resource inputs for handicapped students to receive a "fair share" of society's offerings. The differing needs of special populations that are now recognized and factored into most state fiscal policies include other groups, such as economically disadvantaged, native American, and bilingual students. The categorical grants, pupil weighting, or other revenue distribution mechanisms that will be described in some detail in a later section of this chapter were first utilized in the specialized (often isolated) programs for handicapped children. The underlying philosophy was perhaps best articulated in a statement by the National Legislative Conference Special Committee on School Finance:

> Equality does not mean equal treatment. The crucial value to be fostered by a system of public education is the opportunity to succeed, not the uniformity of success. While all are equal under the law, nature and other circumstances yield advantages to some, while handicapping others . . . Equal treatment of unequals does not produce equality. A concept of equal educational opportunity should reflect a sensitivity to the differences in costs and variations in needs of those to be educated.[15]

Liberty in School Finance

The prominence of the value of liberty in the American culture has usually been expressed as the freedom to choose. The dispersal of governmental authority across the three branches (judicial, legislative, and executive) and various levels (federal, state, and local) is believed to enhance the maintenance of liberty. It is readily recognized, however, that the pursuit of that value, perhaps most concretely manifested in the formation of many thousands of small local school districts, carries the high risk of both inefficiency and inequity.[16]

Freedom of choice in education has been an issue before the courts and in legislative proposals for most of this century. The arena of debate has primarily centered on the role of private versus public schools, as affected by governmental actions on compulsory education, regulation, and fiscal support. In recent decades the freedom of choice debate has turned toward the libertarian value of exercising a preference for a certain kind of educational program, whether in a public or privately operated institution and whether on religious or other qualitative attributes. The right to make such choices has been supported by the U.S. Supreme Court.

The financial support of such choice, however, has remained clearly constrained by the Constitution. The major proposals to overcome that barrier have been through mechanisms to cause public aid to go through the child or his or her family, rather than directly to the private school. These have focused on either of two plans—educational vouchers and tuition tax credits.

Educational Vouchers.   Levin has described the history of the concept of educational vouchers as a major mechanism for freedom of choice.[17] The first modern era proposal for the use of vouchers for the purchase of educational services was advanced by Milton Friedman in 1955.[18] This plan suggested a government supplied allocation that the parent could use to pay for a specified level of tuition at any approved school.

The best known implementation was a modified version, with the choices precluding any nonpublic alternatives, in the Alum Rock School District at San Jose, California. The most advanced developments in this field are probably incorporated in the "Initiative for Family Choice in Education" proposed in California by Coons and Sugarman.[19]

The relationship between voucher alternatives and key social dilemmas has been discussed by Levin. A major point is that most plans would appear to encourage "separation and stratification of students according to parental commitments and orientations and by tailoring curricula to appeal to and reinforce these parental concerns."[20] This would certainly have a negative effect on the generally desired preparation for democracy. It also appears that the expansion of choices and market responsiveness that the voucher idea provides would be much greater for upper income groups than for lower-income and minority populations, which in turn would lead to even greater class stratification and socialization than in present school systems. In summary, public support would be used to promote outcomes that conflict with important social purposes of schooling.

It should be noted that in spite of these negative considerations, a type of educational voucher system has been quite generally applied to a small minority of the school population for some time. Children with severely handicapping conditions whose needs have been perceived to be too complex to handle within the public system have been authorized in many states to receive financial aid to cover costs of attending private schools especially equipped for that purpose. The predominance of this alternative varies among states and regions of the country, but virtually every state had allowed for state or local funds to be expended for tuition to private schools, even before the advent of Public Law 94-142. The private school provision within that federal policy increased considerably the tendency in most states to utilize that option. The requirement that all costs of educational services be at *public expense,* prohibiting additional educational charges to be assessed on parents, takes care of some of the problems debated in other voucher proposals. The availability of public funds for private school placement is not routine, however; it requires initiative on the part of the parent or school district. It has been noted that a much greater likelihood exists that families of higher socioeconomic levels will pursue the necessary procedures to assure their children of such placements. Federal data indicate that the greatest proportion of due process hearings regarding services have been concerned with parental requests for private placements. State regulations generally include the exercise of controls at both the local and state level to prevent unjustified assignment and tuition grant payment of children to private schools. However, it seems evident that in an area of ambiguity of pupil need and agency capacity for service provision, the private alternative is given the benefit of the doubt. Again, this demonstrates the application of the freedom of choice value.

Tuition Tax Credits.   The appeal of family choice as a means of enhancing liberty in education has also found expression in federal and state tax policy. While proposals for tuition tax credits had been advanced by Senators Moynihan and Packwood in the late 1970s, the major thrust for this idea came as a part of the Reagan administration's offensive for educational reform in 1983. Jensen points out that the chief reservation regarding tuition tax credits, even among their advocates, rested on constitutionality. Since most private schools are sectarian, it was feared that such policy would involve the government in support of religious activities.[21] The U.S. Supreme Court has ruled on many questions regarding state aid to private schools over the years, and the "wall of separation" between church and state has provided the basis for its decisions.

The Supreme Court's decision in the Minnesota case of *Mueller* v. *Allen*[22] in June 1983 appears to be a significant departure. The ruling that a Minnesota law was constitutional, though providing a tax deduction for tuition, was based on the fact that it was available to all, regardless of whether the tuition (and certain other educational costs) is paid to public or private schools. It has been noted by those who strongly oppose such policy, particularly the American Federation of Teachers, that since public school students pay no tuition, and have minimal educational expenses, such provisions in fact are a benefit only to those attending private schools. For those who fear any additional erosion of the public school system, the price of such support of freedom of choice and libertarian values is simply too high.

Summary

The four major values that influence the development of general fiscal policy in education in the United States have been presented for the purpose of providing a backdrop against which to understand past and prevailing approaches to the support of special education services. The concepts of adequacy, efficiency, equity, and liberty have been discussed as they have acted upon educational policy, and in certain instances as they have been manifested in special education. These understandings should also serve as a platform for considering current and future developments in special education fiscal policy.

SPECIAL EDUCATION FINANCE

Policy development in both educational finance and special education service delivery has undergone intense scrutiny and a significant amount of change in the past decade or two. Both arenas of policy interest have experienced an acceleration of judicial system activity as well as legislative and regulatory consideration. It is not surprising that special education concepts have been found to be particularly relevant as general educational finance is debated or that basic fiscal issues become a central focus when overall special education policy is on the public agenda. McCarthy and Sage have noted that the concerns of educational finance have perennially focused on "determining (defining, identifying) (a) the total need for service, (b) the source and amount of total resources, and (c) an acceptable means of distribution between resources and needs."[23] The search for acceptability in this sense always involves a balance between the pragmatic press of political reality and the idealistic press for fairness, or equity. As we have suggested earlier in this chapter, the concept of *fiscal neutrality* has come into consideration strongly from the perspective of resource generation (the taxpayer) and is more recently being introduced into the student need side of the equation. While it has been generally recognized that services for certain (e.g., handicapped) children cost more per child than do regular education programs, and that the burden of meeting such costs should be spread broadly across governmental jurisdictions, the great variety of students needs has not been sufficiently addressed in existing financial formulas.

> Special education requires a focus on individual pupil needs; general education fiscal systems, based on average group needs, are insufficiently flexible. Furthermore, it can be assumed that existing special education fiscal systems do not provide adequately flexible programming and that there is a need to develop systems which do. Flexible programming can occur only when decisions are not dependent upon fiscal influences and appropriate resources are provided for each child's unique or unequal needs. That is, we must approximate fiscal neutrality in order to achieve true equity.[24]

Evolution of Policy

The history of special education fiscal policy, according to Weintraub and Higgins,[25] can be described as encompassing an evolution through three phases, as follows:

PHASE 1: THE BENEFACTOR ROLE

In this phase the state's support of special education was more in the realm of charitable activity. Services were funded when pressure was sufficient, but was random and permissive rather than mandatory, and there was little consistency in fiscal support among the states.

PHASE 2: THE PROGRAMMATIC ROLE

In this phase increased mandation occurred, and the states moved into the role of "buyer" of services. Standards were established on the programmatic nature of services for each disability group, and services expanded to the degree that the state provided fiscal support. The introduction of federal dollars also stimulated program development, and by 1971 all states had some provision for state aid to local special education services beyond that of general school aid, even though it was clearly insufficient to meet all needs.

PHASE 3: THE FACILITATOR ROLE

With the establishment of special education services as a right of all handicapped children, the state's primary role shifts to one of establishing and enforcing criteria for the delivery of services, while the onus of that delivery falls directly on the local school districts. While the level of the states' financial support has generally increased, its function has been facilitative more than directly programmatic, since the responsibility (and major financial obligation) belongs to the local district.

Criteria for Policy Development

Criteria on which to base special education finance policy have been drawn from a number of sources in the literature of general education finance as well as from that of special education. Key considerations that have been suggested are

1. Adequacy of funding in relation to need in terms of quantity and quality of services
2. Equity of fund distribution
3. Anticipated effects of service delivery in regard to quality of life and future economic benefits
4. Comprehensiveness of services and programming in relation to need
5. Control and coordination of services
6. Compatibility with regular education finance and service delivery
7. Efficiency[26]

While the specifics of each state's funding methods are varied, all of the distribution methods concerned with special education funding are based on the assumption that such support must rest on a broader base than that used for general education. To elaborate, whatever combination of local, state, and federal financial support exists for the education of the mainstream of the population, that portion of the population defined as having special needs will require heavier support from the less localized levels of government. The rationale for this assumption is that

1. Children with special needs, by definition, are a minority group existing as a small but significant proportion of the whole population.

2. The exact proportion will vary significantly from one subcategory of special education to another, and from one location to another, without regard to local economic ability to provide support.
3. The cost of educational services to meet these needs will be proportionately greater than the costs for children at large, based on an uncertain and varying ratio utilizing (a) geographic locale, (b) subcategory of special need, and (c) the particular patterns of service delivery employed.

Some specific factors that would seem to be of primary importance when in search of policies for optimal fiscal supports from the state for special education in local school systems can be identified from an analysis of relevant literature. These include consideration for variations in the nature of the population to be educated, their identified needs, the models of service delivery utilized, the governance structure under which the services are organized and operated, the resources available to the organizational unit, and the costs of given units of resources in particular localities. McCarthy and Sage have elaborated on each of these factors, as they impact upon financial distribution policies.[27]

Population Characteristics. Demographic data from a variety of sources make it clear that variations in population density, socioeconomic status, and cultural characteristics are associated with variations in need and/or demand for special education. While such factors may not create major differences in the incidence of severely handicapped students, the effect on the proportions of mildly handicapped who are identified as requiring services is pronounced. These relationships are not necessarily directly proportional. High-density population (urban central cities) as well as very sparsely populated deprived rural regions may both have higher needs for service than suburban areas. The size of a system (pupil enrollment) may interact with other factors such as efficiency of the delivery system and client sophistication to affect the demand for service. It has been well recognized that a magnet effect occurs where services are well developed, and this is particularly subject to consumer awareness. Overall, it is clear that fiscal support requirements are impacted by basic population characteristics.

General educational finance policy in most states has manifested awareness of (if not full accounting for) this source of variation. The concept of *municipal overburden,* which was a major point of the *Levittown* case in New York State, is to a large degree based on the empirical observation that urban centers have a disproportionate share of students with extraordinary needs as a function of economic disadvantage and handicapping conditions. Additional factors that are embedded in the municipal overburden concept will be discussed later in this chapter, but the issue of population characteristics is a central determiner of fiscal need.

Individual Needs. While population factors influence the needs of a community in the macro sense, the needs of individual students for special instruction and related services is a function of the process of developing the individualized educational program. The predominant special education funding systems throughout the states have tended to link varying amounts of extra state aid to varying categories of handicapping conditions, the assumption being that the cost differential between regular educational services and those for various handicapping conditions could be computed (on the average) and provide a basis for reasonable support. Early examples of studies of costs of special education, such as the 1970 effort by the National Educational Finance Project, approached the matter in this way.[28] This assumption was much more valid when special education services tended to be more standardized among all members of a group, but the introduction of the IEP, to the extent that its intent is realized, offers an opportunity and a mandate for much finer tuning of individual needs. This, in turn, should translate to more prescriptively determined services.

Service Delivery Options. The result of individualized educational program planning is expected to be a prescription for particular services, delivered in accordance with models designed to provide best for identified needs. A major consideration in such prescription is the degree of intensity of specialist personnel service contained in the IEP. It is recognized, however, that a similar level of labor intensity may be packaged in various ways and that these variations may have an effect upon the total fiscal support required. It should be noted that even if financial support formulas are devised to render the level of service fiscally neutral, making the decision as to placement and prescribed services independent of local cost considerations, accountability for expenditures must occur at some level of regulatory control. Within the realm of related services, even more than with special instruction, major cost variations can be expected as a result of fine distinctions in the decisions regarding the differences among appropriate, optimal, and ideal programs. This was the central issue in the *Rowley* case and will be a consideration in virtually all of the more complex instances of service needs. The most recent studies of special education costs, such as the Rand study reported in 1981 (which will be discussed in detail in Chapter 11), have attempted to address the multiple variations in service delivery options in ways that were not practicable in the earlier efforts.[29]

Governance Structures. The variety of organizational units that may assume responsibility for special education services have been described in Chapter 4. The relationship of those influences to fiscal support considerations is also significant. The need to draw low incidence students from a broad catchment area has been the rationale for the use of intermediate school districts, state-operated residential programs, and private schools as alternatives to the regular local school system. Economy of scale and the need to concentrate expertise for specialized services for thinly dispersed pupil needs has been a strong consideration. However, this has frequently had unforeseen fiscal impact.

> Different laws and regulations covering operation, and more important, the funding of such different organizational units have led not only to programmatic variation, but in some cases to rather clear fiscal incentives for choosing to place a pupil in one or the other alternative governance units. It may prove economically more viable for the local school system to send the pupil to an intermediate cooperative facility or to a private school than to provide the appropriate service locally. As long as equally appropriate services are obtained either way, there is no problem. However, it has been charged that placement decisions may be strongly influenced by the fiscal advantage of one type of unit over another. Where that is the case, the need to correct the funding scheme to more clearly achieve fiscal neutrality is obvious.[30]

The issue is particularly sensitive where the fiscal impact on the placement decision results in utilization of services in more restrictive environments than would be the case under purely neutral circumstances. A specific example of such a situation had been cited in New York, where for a long period of time the state support system for services delivered through boards of cooperative educational services, and through private placements yielded a smaller net cost to local school districts than to provide the service internally.

Resource Variation.   In addition to the variables discussed already, which tend to be focused on students and the relationships between them and the educational system provided, another major consideration is aggregate quantity of revenue producing wealth. This factor determines the capacity of the system to purchase all the resources for the general as well as the special education program, and must be included as a fiscal policy consideration in all funding schemes. The heavier cost impact of each handicapped child, as compared with other pupils in the system, and the need for flexibility in the support of special education accentuates the need for resource neutrality and taxpayer equity as a necessary, though not sufficient foundation for special education fiscal policy.

Resource variation can also be manifested in the availability of certain components that are necessary to an adequate program but are distinct from general wealth of the community. For example, the presence of appropriately trained personnel may vary, exclusive of general wealth, and constitute an important consideration in the total support system. Some communities may have to pay a premium to procure personnel who would be readily available elsewhere. This has been particularly noted in the case of certain related services personnel, such as occupational and physical therapists. Other less tangible resources, such as enriching community facilities, volunteer personnel, and university training program personnel, also may influence what a program can provide for a given cost.

Cost Variations. The calculation of differences in costs from one system to another, for standard units of resources, has been included in the development of general school finance schemes in many states. Much of this variation is a function of general consumer price indices or similar cost-of-living measures. This is probably most significant in salaries for teachers, but it also can be seen in costs of transportation, food service, maintenance, and so on and may be attributable either to labor union strength in a locality or to the value-related practice of simply paying higher salaries in hopes of attracting and keeping superior personnel. The totally accurate interpretation of the significance of some of these conditions may be difficult to achieve. It has been argued, for example, that while certain uncontrollable cost variations (such as cost of living) should be taken into consideration in a distribution formula so that the state could assist those localities having an extra heavy cost burden, the fact that a locality *chooses* to pay its teachers more to enhance quality is a matter that is locally controlled and should not require the fiscal involvement of the rest of the state. Similarly, urban centers may find the high cost of maintaining buildings in densely packed, high-vandalism areas inescapable; likewise, the tax burden for police, fire protection, and social welfare are all included in the concept of *municipal overburden.* However, the degree to which such factors should be included in a general state education fiscal policy continues to be a source of debate. The 1982 decision of New York State's highest court in *Levittown,* and the subsequent refusal of the U.S. Supreme Court to review the case, would seem to suggest that the municipal overburden argument is not compelling.[31]

Fiscal Policy Outcomes. A study of key policy influencers in New York State regarding the potency of the six variables described, which took place at the time of major political activity in the legislature, the regulatory bodies of the executive branch, and the state courts, specifically addressed the issue of how to secure an optimal special education fiscal policy for that state. Conclusions summarized by McCarthy[32] suggested that while perspectives on the importance of the six factors were greatly influenced by respondents' professional role, geographic location, and organizational affiliation, as well as by currently volatile political events, it was agreed that fiscal neutrality and least restrictive environment were inextricably related. Furthermore, the relationship between fiscal incentives and choices among various governance structures for service delivery constituted a significant source of nonneutrality in the state's existing policies. It was agreed that variations in needs and variations in resources were the most important considerations in the pursuit of an optimal policy and that these two components of equity were frequently in conflict with the press of political reality. It was also made very clear that in spite of all attempts to pursue fiscal policy rationally, and with due regard for all of the balancing variables, the bottom line tends to remain a political judgment of how many dollars can be captured from the total public budget at any given time.

Approaches to Funding Formulas

It is important to remember that in spite of pervasive federal involvement in special education in recent years, the fiscal support of the system remains chiefly a state and local function. With appropriations consistently falling short of congressional authorizations in the law, it can be anticipated that federal participation in the total funding structure could never reach 15 percent of the special education expenditures. Given this modest input from the federal level, the major consideration remains how the state should best distribute funds for partially or totally equalizing the cost differentials between regular and special education services in local school systems. Various approaches to making these distributions are used among the states. Descriptions and classifications of the approaches that most clearly capture current practices have been reported by Hartman[33] and by Moore, Walker, and Holland.[34]

Hartman indicates that six types of formulas are used to distribute state funds to aid local districts. Although this typology is useful for comparative purposes, the formulas are not mutually exclusive, and in actual practice many states utilize a mixture of approaches. The types may be classified as follows:

1. *Unit.* Funding is determined on the basis of units of service provided (e.g., instruction, administration, and transportation), with varying amounts allocated to support the unit. This may include salaries and all other operating expenses.
2. *Personnel.* Funding is focused only on the personnel costs of the unit of instruction provided and may be limited to salaries alone.
3. *Weight.* Funding is based on a count of pupils served, with a weighting factor (usually varying according to types of handicap) employed to differentiate from regular perpupil funding.
4. *Straight sum.* Funding is set at a fixed dollar amount per pupil, which may vary by type of handicap.
5. *Percentage.* Funding is based on a percentage of approved expenditures.
6. *Excess costs.* Funding is provided by reimbursement of expenditures that are in excess of those for regular pupils, either totally or in part (up to a ceiling).

Using a slightly different classification of funding types, Moore, Walker, and Holland indicate that in 1982, a weighting system was most frequently used, with pupil weighting the method in 15 states and weighted teacher or classroom unit in 10 states. A percentage approach based on actual expenditures was used in 15 states and a percentage of personnel salaries in 4 states. A flat grant per classroom or teacher unit was the method in 6 states. A flat grant per student (the distribution method from the federal level) was not used by any state.

In discussing the relative merits of the various funding methods, Hartman suggests that the six types can be grouped into three general categories, according to the main factor used for allocation. Under this scheme, the major types would be resource-based formulas, child-based formulas, and cost-based formulas. Some of the incentives and disincentives of each type can be anticipated.

Resource-Based Formulas.   Placing the emphasis on the resource supplied, such as the teacher or other personnel, rather than the pupil has the advantage of focusing on the source of the cost. It is less likely to cause overidentification of pupils (bounty hunting) since the link between childcount and dollars is indirect. In the many states where the basis for general support is the teacher unit, such an approach for special education has the advantage of compatibility with the total system. However, it tends to require considerable regulatory activity by the state to determine the quantity of units to authorize, the minimum and maximum allowances of pupils per teacher, and all other aspects of service delivery that are constituents of both costs and benefits. This also probably translates into local district accounting and reporting requirements, which can be burdensome.

To the extent that state regulation may be desirable (e.g., to reinforce selected programmatic alternatives), a resource-based approach can be quite effective. However, it can constrain local innovation. Furthermore, if the formula is based too specifically on the teacher or special class unit, it can discourage mainstreaming efforts that might otherwise occur. Given the variety of current and newly developing programming alternatives, the increasing variety of possible staffing approaches, and the wide geographically based range of salaries and other cost factors, a resource unit system providing a flat rate for each employed person will probably fall short of equitably compensating true service costs.

An advantage, however, may be the way in which the funding formula links to program and fiscal planning. "The planning sequence begins with the handicapped children to be served, moves to the determination of the type of appropriate programs and the number of units of each, and then automatically provides the total funding amount through the unit funding amounts and quantities of the various units."[35] Furthermore, such formulas provide a basis for tracking special education funds.

Child-Based Formulas.   Pupil unit formulas, whether straight sum or weighted, are most vulnerable to causing overclassification. However, in the many states that use pupil enrollment or attendance as the basis for general state aid, such a scheme for special education may be almost mandatory for reasons of compatibility and political acceptance. A straight sum or single weight for all handicaps probably carries the most potential for misuse, since it can encourage identification of borderline cases that will be relatively inexpensive to serve, yet will yield the same state support as those individuals having greater (and more expensive) needs. This also constitutes an incentive for underserving the more needy. If differential weights or dollar amounts are provided for certain programs, it can influence placement into programs that provide the most funds, regardless of need, thus confounding least restrictive environment considerations. If the differential weights are accurately adjusted so that state supports closely match real costs (that is, are fiscally neutral) and a sufficient number of levels of support are included, the funding approach can prove to be a definite facilitator of optimal programming. However, such precision is difficult to maintain as a matter of statewide policy and will most certainly require complex accounting procedures at both local and state levels to keep track of amounts of time spent by students in each type of program alternative. Such accounting and fine-tuning requirements may well prove politically lethal in most states.

Child-based formulas in general provide good accountability as to numbers of students served, although the expenditures per child are not as readily tracked. However, aggregate tracking of funds may be sufficient for most purposes. The variations in resources assigned to individuals must be accounted for if complete tracking of funds is an important consideration.

Cost-Based Formulas. Cost-based formulas are theoretically fiscally neutral if excess costs are *fully* reimbursable. However, fiscally prudent policymakers are rarely sufficiently trusting in the behavior of local practitioners to provide an unlimited ceiling on claimable expenditures. Percentage formulas that call for local system sharing of whatever expenditures are documented tend to be more acceptable in the compromises drawn between state and local obligations for program support. Reimbursement of excess costs up to an established ceiling per child or per instructional unit appears to be a reasonable method. All cost-based approaches have the advantage of minimizing the labeling of children and also permit maximum flexibility in programming alternatives, since the expenditures may not necessarily be tied to specific resources. They, therefore, have potential for enhancing program development and choice for each student. However, such formulas do carry fairly complex cost accounting requirements and approval procedures, constituting an administrative burden at both local and state levels. The greater the state share in the formula, the more stringent these are likely to be. Whether this factor outweighs the benefits of approximating fiscal neutrality is a matter that must be answered in the context of each state's specific political climate.

Viable Compromises. A general aim of special education fiscal policy cited earlier is the facilitation of programmatic flexibility, which demands that financial considerations do not overbalance the decision process in determining services for each student. This translates to fiscal neutrality from the perspective of both the service recipient (student) and the resource provider (taxpayer). In the search for optimal solutions, policy changes in various states in recent years have increasingly taken into consideration the recognition of differentiated levels of service intensity (and therefore costs) rather than the oversimplistic use of a single weight or rate, and yet also avoided the misconceived (pseudoprecise) focus on disability classifications. This has resulted in some schemes that are charged with employing too much accounting complexity (as in Florida) due to so many different weights associated with the varieties of classifications and programming options. It has also caused distress over the loss of familiar classifications and doubts about the fiscal neutrality of the assigned weights to the approved levels of service and options (as in New York). A significant strength in the New York policy is the combined use of an approved excess cost concept with a variable weighted pupil attendance unit based on intensity of service provided rather than disability classification. The adoption of that approach represents a sophisticated blending of concepts that capture at least some of the benefits of a more optimal plan, reduce focus on disability classifications, move a good way toward fiscal neutrality, yet walk the narrow line of political acceptability. It is probable that such compromises will continue to provide incremental reform in special education funding in many states.

SUMMARY

On the basis of observations of existing policies and practices among the states and the concepts cited throughout this chapter, certain considerations may be set forth as key criteria for state-level policymakers. Moore, Walker, and Holland cite the following as essential to optimal special education funding schemes:

> *Compatibility with other state funding policies and practices.* Approaches which do not differ significantly from existing general methods have much greater acceptance.
>
> *Rationality and simplicity.* Formulas which are easily understood, logical, and have straightforward relationships among the key policy elements have a clear advantage.
>
> *Ease of modification.* The ever changing rates of inflation, relative costs of resources, etc. make it important for funding formulas to be self adjusting or easily changed as circumstances require.
>
> *Minimized misclassification.* Formulas must avoid incentives which might influence classification on other than optimal programming choices.
>
> *Reinforcement of least restrictive placement choices.* To the extent possible, funding schemes should support other existing programming objectives.
>
> *Avoidance of stigmatizing labels.* The practice of basing funding on service options rather than disability classifications permits a reduced emphasis on labels.
>
> *Accommodation of varying student needs across districts.* Funding approaches should allow for the fact that different localities may experience quite different incidence rates of various types of students needing service.

Accommodation of cost variations. Costs of standard units of resources may vary considerably within a state, and formulas should permit allowance for these differences.

Adjustments for fiscal capacity. Since a major portion of special education finance remains a local responsibility, the wide range of capacity to support education in general must be considered in any funding formula.

Funding predictability. Funding formulas must make it possible to predict the total support needs, both at the local and the state level. Stability within the system is an important attribute for planning and assuring adequate support.

Containment of costs. The funding approach must assure that unforeseen circumstances will not overwhelm available resources. Ideally, the system should reinforce efficiently operated programs.

Minimized reports, record keeping, and state administration. Funding formulas are most acceptable and successful when they make minimum demands on administrative personnel at both local and state levels.[36]

It is noted that trade-offs are necessary. That is, while a simple formula is desirable, it is less likely to distinguish well among varying districts' needs. The more stability and cost containment that is assured, the less capability there is for accommodating the full range of costs.

Some general fiscal policy considerations that seem to be critical to flexible programming have been suggested by McCarthy and Sage as follows:

Since funding methods have a high capability for creating implicit incentives and disincentives for particular programming decisions, provisions should exist to make service options as "cost neutral" as possible. While it is recognized that fiscal neutrality in the pure sense can never be fully attained, it is important for policy influencers to consciously pursue neutrality as a major goal.

The achievement of fiscal neutrality should take into consideration the potential variations in levels of service, types of service models, and governance structures within which services are delivered. Each of these factors has impact both individually and interactively on the attainment of fiscal neutrality.

Since variations in need result from geographical population differences, distribution policies allowing for regional variations should be recognized.

Densely populated urban areas with a disproportionate number of special needs students might best be aided by a different formula than the rest of a state, using an "urban multiplier." The unique problem resulting from a particular geographic location should not constrain flexible programming.

A provision for variations in system costs for factors such as personnel and facilities, occurring as a result of geographic location, should be part of general school finance formulas.

Since it is the pattern of service delivery that most affects variations in costs, aid should be based on levels of services rather than the types of handicapping conditions or diagnostic label. This at least facilitates programming flexibility.

Since variations in resources are generally the result of the differences in property wealth among school districts, a different and more equitable measure of a district's wealth should be established, such as the inclusion of a personal income factor or a combination of both wealth and income. The complexity of the overall funding scheme should be minimized to enhance general political acceptability. Fiscal policy is subject to a wide variety of understandings and interpretations even among persons with considerable familiarity and sophistication with education policies and practices.[37]

It is evident that recent fiscal policy changes in a number of states have taken cognizance of these considerations, but it is equally clear that much room remains for continued development and reform. Another expression of the need for development can be seen in the congressional action in the establishment of a Commission on Financing of a Free and Appropriate Education for Special Needs Children, in 1982. This commission, with a membership of 20 experienced leaders drawn from professional organizations and federal, state, and local educational policymakers prepared a report directed to the Select Education Subcommittee on Education and Labor, which concluded with nine priority recommendations, as follows:

1. State and local education agencies (SEAs and LEAs) should establish more flexible and individualized options in the regular education program.
2. States should develop standards that define the financial responsibility of LEAs for the related services mandated by P.L. 94-142 and interagency agreements that ensure ready access to the full range of financial resources available under various state and federal health and human service programs for such mandated services. The Department of Education should enforce the requirements that exist under Section 504.
3. State and local education agencies should initiate interagency coordination at both the state and local levels to spread the financial burdens associated with low-incidence handicapping conditions and unusually expensive related services among cooperating agencies.
4. States should develop community-based residential programs in coordination with school district special education programs to avoid the high costs of unnecessary institutionalization.
5. State and local education agencies should initiate conflict resolution strategies to improve parent-school communication, encourage joint decisionmaking, and reduce unnecessary conflict-related expenses.
6. Congress and the Department of Education should target a portion of current discretionary resources to encourage SEAs and LEAs to use more effective administrative policies and practices.
7. The Congress should preserve the P.L. 94-142 statute without change because it is based on sound equity principles and is working well to ensure a free, appropriate public education for all handicapped school-age children.
8. The Congress should increase current P.L. 94-142 (Part B) appropriations, and both federal and state governments should allocate new funds to support critical intervention strategies for at-risk children below school age.
9. The federal government should fully fund the EHA discretionary program to support research, training, model development, and dissemination programs that together work to ensure that every handicapped child receives an appropriate education.[38]

It is clear that this commission placed great emphasis on the leadership role of the federal government to accomplish all that needs to be done at the state and local levels. It is likely that this expression is to some degree a reaction to the political climate of the time, in which the strongly articulated goal of the federal executive branch was to minimize its role in education policy. As a creation of the legislative branch, this commission could be expected to state the case for federal leadership as strongly as possible. Quite aside from partisan considerations, the recommendations do highlight some critical needs for resolution of fiscal policy problems.

ILLUSTRATIVE CASE

The legislature of the state of Equitania has for some time been in search of a fiscal policy that would assure that the distribution of funds from the state level to local school districts will be fair to everyone—the taxpayer (rich or poor) and the school child (regardless of varying need). For the general school programs, the state aid formula now provides about 50 percent of the average per pupil expenditure in districts of average wealth. In very poor districts the state share (aid ratio) can be as much as 90 percent (but not more), and in very wealthy districts the state share can shrink to (but not be less than) 10 percent. The total state aid to each district is calculated by multiplying the aid ratio times the average enrollment in the district during the second month of the school year times a figure equal to the previous year's statewide average per pupil expenditure. This formula seems to be fairly satisfactory for the average pupil.

It is not quite so clear what should be done to allow for variations in pupil need. At present, Equitania is operating under a procedure that allows districts to report the enrollment of all handicapped students in two different ways—first as part of the total general enrollment and then separately for an added allocation. This additional aid is calculated for each district on the basis of the average expenditure per handicapped student (in that district) minus the average expenditure for all students in the district. This "excess cost" for special education is then reimbursed by the state at the rate of 75 percent, regardless of the relative wealth of the district. This policy has seemingly facilitated the growth of special education programs in the state, allowing districts to spend whatever is required to deliver adequate service, with not too much strain on local budgets.

A state Task Force on Equity and Efficiency has been meeting during the past year, and one of the chief items on its agenda is the way in which the state formula handles variations in student needs. It has been noted in some of the testimony collected by the task force that the policy may be too liberal (thereby threatening efficiency) since there is no cap on what a district may spend and still get 75 percent of it from the state. Others complain that very wealthy districts, that rightfully receive only 10 to 15 percent state aid for their general school programs are not only spending imprudently for handicapped students, but also are labeling more kids to "clean up at the 75 percent rate." These charges are advanced mostly by the poorer districts who see present policy as inequitable, since it clearly benefits wealthy districts more than poorer ones. Fiscal conservatives on the task force have noted that there ought to be more stringent accounting requirements to differentiate between the programs provided and resources expended for students with severe problems and needs versus those with only minor variance from the average. Some parent advocates have agreed that given the lack of differentiation, districts are prone to focus on the "easy to serve" and give insufficient attention to the "tough cases."

A proposal for change in the special education funding formula has now been advanced by one subcommittee of the task force. This proposal calls for abandoning the 75 percent excess cost reimbursement aspect and applying the same state aid ratios (based on local district wealth) for special education as are used for the general support program. However, differentiation would be provided by having handicapped student enrollment counted with varying weights, depending on what type of service the child was receiving. The proposed weights and program specifications (expressed in comparison to regular students, who count as 1) are as follows:

SERVICE TYPE	PERSONNEL LOAD	WEIGHT
Full-time special class (mild)	Class enrollment limited to 15	2.0
Full-time special class (moderate)	Class enrollment limited to 10	3.0
Part-time resource room	Maximum load = 20; instructional groups limited to 4 pupils	7.5
Itinerant teacher/ therapist	Maximum load = 50; service groups limited to 3 pupils	10.0

All weighted enrollments will be calculated as "full-time equivalents." Pupils receiving part-time services will be counted at the higher weight only for that proportion of the day or week for which the special service is received and weighted as "1" while in regular school programs.

Reaction to the proposal has been mixed. Some observers note that while the change would excuse local districts from separate accounting for special education expenditures, it would add complications of pupil enrollment accounting. Others point out that while these weightings may allow for services delivered in groups of from 3 to 15, it does not provide for those cases that require individual instruction or various related services. Some specific questions addressed to the task force in the first public hearing on the proposal were the following:

How would the "weighted enrollment" concept (as opposed to the present "excess cost" concept) affect taxpayer equity?

Would poor and rich districts be differently impacted?

Would the proposed weights for various special education programs really provide "fiscal neutrality" in terms of pupils getting the services they need?

How could the formula be extended to include students who require even more intensive services? What weight would be appropriate for one-to-one instruction?

How would the change affect classification of children as handicapped?

How would total statewide expenditures for special education services be affected?

Enrollment count is taken only in October of each year. How could pupils whose special education services change later in the year be accounted for appropriately?

In preparation for the next public hearing, task force members are hoping to have some answers ready. Are answers possible? What should they be?

NOTES

[1]Walter I. Garms, James W. Guthrie, and Lawrence C. Pierce, *School Finance: The Economics and Politics of Public Education* (Englewood Cliffs, NJ: Prentice-Hall, 1978), p. 18.

[2]Ibid., p. 19.

[3]Ibid., p. 184.

[4]Jay G. Chambers and Thomas B. Parrish, *Adequacy and Equity in State School Finance and Planning: A Resource Cost Model Approach* (Stanford, Calif.: Institute for Research on Educational Finance and Governance, 1983), p. i.

[5]Jay G. Chambers and Thomas B. Parrish, *The Issue of Adequacy in the Financing of Public Education: How Much is Enough?* (Stanford, Calif.: Institute for Research on Educational Finance and Governance, 1982), p. 1.

[6]Martha M. McCarthy, "Adequacy in Educational Programs: A Legal Perspective," in *Perspectives in State School Support Programs,* eds. K. Forbis Jordan and Nelda H. Cambron-McCabe (Cambridge, Mass.: Ballinger, 1981), p. 334.

[7]*Board of Education of Hendrick Hudson Central School District* v. *Rowley* 50 U.S.L.W. 4925, 4932 (U.S. June 28, 1982).

[8]Raymond Callahan, *The Cult of Efficiency* (Chicago: University of Chicago Press, 1962).

[9]Garms, Guthrie, and Pierce, *School Finance,* p. 25.

[10]Ibid., p. 249.

[11]Ibid., p. 260.

[12]Ibid., pp. 21-24.

[13]*Serrano* v. *Priest,* 5 Cal. 3d 584, 96 Cal. Rptr. 601, 487 P. 2d 1241 (1971); subsequent opinion, 135 Cal. Rptr. 345, 557 P. 2d 929 (Dec. 30, 1976).

[14]Tyll van Geel, "The Courts and School Finance Reform," in *The Changing Politics of School Finance,* eds. Nelda H. Cambron-McCabe and Allan Odden (Cambridge, Mass.: Ballinger, 1982), p. 71.

[15]Anthony Morley et al., *A Legislator's Guide to School Finance* (Denver: Education Commission of the States, 1973), p. x.

[16]Garms, Guthrie, and Pierce, *School Finance,* pp. 30-31.

[17]Henry M. Levin, "Educational Vouchers and Social Policy," in *School Finance Policies and Practices,* ed. James W. Guthrie (Cambridge, Mass.: Ballinger, 1980), pp. 235-263.

[18]Milton Friedman, "The Role of Government in Education," in *Economics and the Public Interest,* ed. Robert A. Solo (New Brunswick, N.J.: Rutgers University Press, 1955).

[19]John E. Coons and Stephen D. Sugarman, *Education by Choice* (Berkeley: University of California Press, 1978).

[20]Levin, "Educational Vouchers," p. 250.

[21]Donald N. Jensen, *Tuition Tax Credits: Has the Supreme Court Cleared the Way?* (Stanford, Calif.: Institute for Research on Educational Finance and Governance, 1983), p. 2.

[22]*Mueller* v. *Allen,* _____ U.S. _____, 103 S.Ct. 3062 (1983).

[23]Eileen F. McCarthy and Daniel D. Sage, "State Special Education Fiscal Policy: The Quest for Equity," *Exceptional Children,* 48 (Feb. 1982), 414.

[24]Ibid., p. 415.

[25]Frederick J. Weintraub and Scottie Higgins, *Planning State Fiscal Policies to Meet Local Needs* (Reston, Va.: The Council for Exceptional Children, 1982), pp. 2-5.

[26]Charles D. Bernstein, William T. Hartman, and Rudolph S. Marshall, "Major Policy Issues in Financing Special Education," *Journal of Educational Finance,* 1 (1976), 299-316.

[27]McCarthy and Sage, "State Special Education," pp. 416-417.

[28]Richard A. Rossmiller, James Hale, and Lloyd Frohreich, *Educational Programs for Exceptional Children: Resource Configurations and Costs,* National Educational Finance Project Study No. 2 (Madison: Department of Educational Administration, University of Wisconsin, 1970).

[29]J. S. Kakalik, W. S. Furry, M. A. Thomas, and M. F. Carney, *The Cost of Special Education,* Rand Note N-1792-ED (Santa Monica, Calif.: The Rand Corporation, 1981).

[30]McCarthy and Sage, "State Special Education," p. 417.

[31]Education Week, August 18, 1982, p. 17.

[32]Eileen F. McCarthy, *Policy Considerations for State Special Education Funding Systems* (Doctoral dissertation, Syracuse University, 1980).

[33]William T. Hartman, *Policy Effects of Special Education Funding Formulas* (Stanford, Calif.: Institute for Research on Educational Finance and Governance, 1980), pp. 6-23.

[34]Mary T. Moore, Lisa J. Walker, and Richard P. Holland, *Finetuning Special Education Finance: A Guide for State Policymakers* (Washington, D.C.: Education Policy Research Institute of Educational Testing Service, 1982), pp. 78-98.

[35]Hartman, *Policy Effects of Special Education Funding,* p. 16.

[36]Moore, Walker, and Holland, *Finetuning Special Education Finance,* pp. 84-88.

[37]McCarthy and Sage, "State Special Education," pp. 418-419.

[38]*The Report of the Commission on the Financing of a Free and Appropriate Education for Special Needs Children* (Washington, D.C.: The Commission, March 1983), pp. 1-2.

CHAPTER 6
CRITICAL SUCCESS
FACTORS
IN LEADERSHIP

In Chapters 1 through 5 we have discussed the major forces that facilitate and restrain change and movement in special education within the total school system. Perhaps the most potent of these forces has been the zeal of special educators who lobbied for recognition of the rights of handicapped children in the 1970s. The expertise of these special educators and their emotional involvement with the cause of handicapped children have led quite naturally to a desire to maintain control over the programs to which that drive has given life.

With the passage of Public Law 94-142, the rights of children and the mandated provision for service have been established. Continuing that progress will require a coalition of educational management, teachers unions, and other members of the educational community to resolve the apparent conflict between the doctrine of least restrictive alternative and the delivery of specialized technical services.

The leadership challenge facing special education in the 1970s and early 1980s focused on demonstrating the need for services for the exceptional student and securing state and federal safeguards that ensure a right to an education and treatment. The management issues were (1) gaining access to those services if they already existed or (2) developing new services in sufficient quantity to meet the needs identified. Operational procedures covering referral, assessment, and placement of eligible students occupied the time of the chief administrative officer in special education and many supportive and instructional staff members. The factors facilitating and hindering these two goals are presented in Figure 6-1.[1]

CURRENT CIRCUMSTANCE
IN SPECIAL EDUCATION LEADERSHIP

The current trends and issues facing special education leadership personnel are embedded in the past but are magnified by current fiscal constraints. While special education continues to grow in numbers of children served and resources expended in many of the states (although at a slower rate than the period from 1970 to 1980), regular education has suffered its most significant decline in terms of total students served by the public schools. This trend is projected to continue well into the early 1990s. This growth-decline imbalance

FIGURE 6-1.   Summary of Driving and Restraining Forces Influencing the Realization of Free, Appropriate, Public Education for the Handicapped. *Source*: Leonard C. Burrello and Daniel D. Sage, *Leadership and Change in Special Education* (Englewood Cliffs, N.J.: Prentice-Hall, 1979), p. 67.

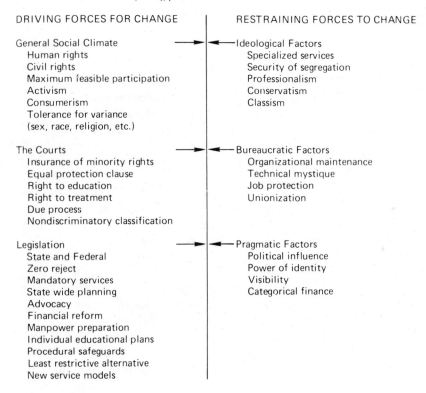

DRIVING FORCES FOR CHANGE	RESTRAINING FORCES TO CHANGE
General Social Climate	Ideological Factors
Human rights	Specialized services
Civil rights	Security of segregation
Maximum feasible participation	Professionalism
Activism	Conservatism
Consumerism	Classism
Tolerance for variance	
(sex, race, religion, etc.)	
The Courts	Bureaucratic Factors
Insurance of minority rights	Organizational maintenance
Equal protection clause	Technical mystique
Right to education	Job protection
Right to treatment	Unionization
Due process	
Nondiscriminatory classification	
Legislation	Pragmatic Factors
State and Federal	Political influence
Zero reject	Power of identity
Mandatory services	Visibility
State wide planning	Categorical finance
Advocacy	
Financial reform	
Manpower preparation	
Individual educational plans	
Procedural safeguards	
Least restrictive alternative	
New service models	

has put more strain on the regular versus special education relationship. Local administrators want more control over special education funding and expenditures. Special educators may actually get fewer dollars than they are entitled to from all sources of potential income—local, state, and federal. They are also being asked to control existing costs and expenditures.

To compound the problem, regular teachers are referring more students, especially in the learning disability category, to special education teachers to help alleviate the pressure to raise student performance in the regular classroom. This pressure, well documented in the Office of Special Education's annual reports to Congress, increases the difficulty that special educators have in negotiating the placement of students back into the mainstream.

Increased fiscal constraints, declining regular student populations, and reduced options for placing disabled students into regular mainstreamed classrooms combine to create a major leadership challenge to provide appropriate specialized services to the 10 percent of students receiving special services. In short, the current challenge is to strive for quality by providing appropriate special education programs at the most reasonable cost.

Quality and cost are accompanied by new public scrutiny to demonstrate that special education is beneficial. Are special educators setting high expectations for the students in their programs? Do disabled students ever leave special education once they are referred and placed? If, and when, they leave, how well do they perform in the regular program? Do they get diplomas and graduate? Are graduates succeeding in postsecondary education programs? When they leave school, are they prepared for the world of work? What is the postschool adjustment rate and employability of graduates of special education programs? Are severely handicapped students being prepared to enter competitive or sheltered employment or none at all? Maximizing student performance and postschool adjustment of exceptional students are the twin imperatives for serious observers of special education to consider in the near future. The planning and preparation must begin now.

CRITICAL SUCCESS FACTORS
OF SPECIAL EDUCATION ADMINISTRATORS

Information Systems Analog

Burrello and Johnson have undertaken a series of research studies to determine, through the eyes of special education administrators, both personal and organization factors that are critical for their success in the 1980s.[2] John Rockart developed the concept of critical success factors (CSFs) to enhance understanding of the world of the information specialist in major corporations, public institutions, and human service agencies.[3] He was particularly concerned with the notion of what must go right for the information executive to succeed in a changing world of information use, control, and support. He identified a set of factors that typifies the information specialist executive and a set of variations from the set of generic factors. We provide a review of Rockart's research because we believe his work with information systems specialists is a fitting analog to the role of the specialist in special education management.

Both groups of managers—information systems executives and special education administrators—were employed because of their technical skills to develop and operate (at least initially) centralized services for relatively few mainstream users. They responded to the needs of top management first because these managers have always been more preoccupied with building and sustaining their own sphere of influence in the corporate world or in the world of central office politics. While significant differences do exist between information systems executives and special education administrators, their similarities are striking.

Rockart's factors for the information specialist were

Service. Efficient and effective services rendered as perceived by the end user and the corporate executive.

Communication. Establishment of two-way communication patterns between endusers of the services provided and corporate leadership.

Information system human resources. Changing system services functions from centralized to decentralized; end user demands a more managerially competent, yet technically literate, consultant who supports line and staff managers to become self-sufficient by learning how to build and operate their own systems.

Repositioning the information system's function. Technically this means providing end users with new sets of tools, techniques, and processes that allow them to access and use information in new ways; organizationally, it means moving from a line relationship to a staff orientation to support end users rather than direct hardware and systems development personnel; and psychologically, information systems must be moved out of "an automated accounting and paperwork image" to a group committed to integrating information as well as people to make decisions rather than crunching data.[4]

To summarize, Rockart identified four characteristics that he feels differentiates information system executives. They are: (1) the maturity and size of the organization, (2) the service versus supportive orientation of the I/S departments, (3) the human, organizational, and financial resources available, and finally, (4) the "world view" of the key leader in the information system's executive suite. The leader's grasp of the direction of his or her field and place in the company as a whole are key determinants of the differences in the generic set of critical factors influencing success on the job.

Specific Critical Success Factors

Burrello and Johnson conducted in-depth interviews with 15 local and cooperative special education directors in a Midwestern state to determine what must go right for them to be considered a success as an administrator of a special education organization.[5] Directors were also asked to identify those factors that ensured success for a special education organization. They were also asked what program effectiveness meant to them and ways to measure their concept of program effectiveness. The interview data were recorded onto 3'' by 5'' cards and were sorted to reduce redundancies. Sixty-six individual statements emerged from the first sort. Each of the researchers then sorted the data independently to identify themes. Twenty-nine items evolved from the independent sorting, categorizing, and discussion. All but 6 items were eventually selected unanimously. These 29 items were classified into personal and organization CSFs, grouped into six generic categories and then placed in a pilot survey rating instrument. The pilot survey was administered to a group of 22 urban administrators and supervisors in an Eastern state. On the basis of their responses, 2 items were excluded and a third added. Twenty-eight items were reorganized into the final instrument.

The experimental form of the survey was mailed to 80 additional administrators. The respondents were asked to answer each of the 28 stems in terms of their agreement as to its significance on a 5 point Likert-type rating scale from "strongly agree" (1) to "strongly disagree" (5). Respondents were also asked to rank from most important to least important only those items they strongly agreed with. Eighty-eight percent of the surveys were returned and subjected to analysis.

Table 6-1 displays the results of rating and ranking of the 28 CSFs that emerged from the initial set of interviews and the pilot test sample. Of the 28 items, 13 were rated strongly agree or agree. The 13 are placed in ranked order. Items 23 and 21 tied in sixth place. Only 4 of the those 13 items were considered personal CSFs as compared with 9 organizational CSFs.

Special Education Managerial CSFs

Four themes emerge from the in-depth interviews, the categorization of the individual statements from the sample, and analysis of the rating and ranking of the 28 items that were placed in the survey instrument.

The quality of direct services to the clients of the special education program is the underlying theme of the highest-rated and ranked items in the survey. Changes in individual students in special education and returning students to their peer group in regular classes are twin measures of program effectiveness for the different student populations that special educators have to manage.

Directing, developing, and supporting staff to set realistic goals and meet expected outcomes for themselves and their students are a close second as components of program effectiveness.

The third theme concerns the perspective of special education within the total school district and community. Special education administrators believe that to be successful as leaders they must adopt the big-picture perspective and

TABLE 6-1   SPECIAL EDUCATION MANAGERIAL CSFs

CATEGORY	TYPE OF CSF
DETERMINING PROGRAM EFFECTIVENESS	
1. Special education must demonstrate that it is providing instructionally effective programs and services that promote student growth in three areas: academic, behavioral, and social.	Organizational
2. Special education must be perceived as a part of the entire school corporation and participate in the regular education process in such areas as personnel development.	Organizational
HUMAN RESOURCE MANAGEMENT	
3. Special education administrators must see themselves as supportive persons to teachers.	Personal
DETERMINING PROGRAM EFFECTIVENESS	
4. Special education programs must make effective changes in students as evidenced by students returning to regular classrooms and in their social and emotional adjustment.	Organizational
HUMAN RESOURCE MANAGEMENT	
5. Special education staff must be realistic and meet goals and expected outcomes.	Organizational
PLANNING AND DECISION-MAKING	
6. Special education administrators must build trust through the accurate use of data.	Personal
7. Special education must develop procedures that are reasonable and consistently followed.	Organizational
COMMUNITY RELATIONS	
8. Special education must project a positive image.	Personal
9. Special education administrators must get support from the community and upper management.	Organizational
10. Special education personnel should work to make parents of exceptional children feel included and acknowledge that good things are happening for students.	Organizational
MANAGING HUMAN RESOURCES	
11. Special education administrators must be perceived as being fair by staff while working on their behalf.	Personal
PLANNING AND DECISION-MAKING	
12. Special education administrators should communicate with principals on short- and long-range planning and changes.	Organizational
LEADERSHIP	
13. Special education administrators must make decisions that consider the broad view (entire picture) and in a timely way that involves input from key stakeholders.	Organizational

convince upper management that they are concerned and know their role in the total school community.

The fourth theme, while supportive of the first and third theme, is also distinct from them. The community relations theme related to program effectiveness and enhancing student performance underscores the findings from the effective schools research that parent involvement is meaningful and in substantive ways is positively related to higher student performance.[6]

Parental involvement also relates to the third theme in that the positioning of special education in the school district is supported by the power and influence that special education administrators gain through their interaction within the school community. The correlation between community support and positioning within the school district hierarchy is highly related to the level of respect for the special education leader and influence within the superintendent's cabinet. A balance between external and internal support, while difficult to achieve and maintain, must be accomplished as a factor in organizational leadership.

A Generic Set of CSFs
for Special Education Managers

"Providing a quality service at a reasonable price" was an often-heard expression in the interviews with special education directors. The concept of CSFs can be used as a means to focus on increasing individual student performance and providing a range of services to meet the diversity of individual needs of exceptional students. The measurement devices that special education administrators used, however, ranged from counting complaints and due process hearings to periodic surveys of parent perceptions of service quality. We recommend four types of service measures: first, measures of efficiency such as time to process a referral versus; second, measures of effectiveness or the ratio of referrals to placements. Each measure should be selected with a view toward state and federal compliance requirements. In addition, professional standards of best practices should influence consumer and upper management perception of the quality of services provided regardless of the method of evaluation employed. Finally, the issue of cost should be separated in terms of what is intrinsically meritorious and what is considered worthy in the local context.

Actually, the concepts of merit and worth are germane to each of the measures just outlined. They deserve special mention because they are, in Guba and Lincoln's view, pluralistic phenomena and different judges at different times arrive at substantially different judgments.[7] Judgments of worth, however, are subject to wider variability since they are more contextually bound. We have adapted an example of Guba and Lincoln to illustrate the dilemma of estimating worth and merit in educational settings.

Consider an evaluation of a curriculum and its appropriateness for special populations. It might be judged by professors of education for *merit* on its simplicity, straightforward form, targeted scope, lack of convoluted writing, and degree of integration, that is, the extent to which all its substantive and formal components are properly articulated "or fit." But it is judged for *worth* by special education teachers as to the extent to which it provides a model for student learning, is appropriate to the needs and aspirations teachers and parents have for the students it is to serve, is free from any bias, and is teachable by the average member of the school faculty. (We provide more discussion on evaluation in Chapter 12.)

A second phrase that resonated through the interviews was "establishing two-way communication between management and the school-community." The role of the special education administrator includes that of educator of top management and community patrons to illustrate how special education services can impact students and regular programs in a positive manner. For severely handicapped students, the issue surrounding their placement in regular school buildings versus segregated settings demands enlightened special education leadership to dispel much misunderstanding as to which severely handicapped students can be integrated, with what degree of student to student interaction, and at what cost.

Clearly, the task of communicating orally and in written form to the range of constitutencies that impinge on the special education administrator is formidable. After serving a year as the acting director of special education, a director of curriculum in the Berkeley School District in California remarked, "I'd rather be a principal of two Berkeley high schools simultaneously than be the director of special education here." Managing internal and external constitutencies is a major leadership function to which we devote attention in Chapter 9.

A third paraphrase from the interviews was that: "Maintaining highly spirited staff who are interpersonally as well as technically competent to share their expertise with colleagues and parents is critical to our success."

Selecting, supporting, and maintaining a quality staff was high on the agenda of the sample of directors. Yet the pressures to do more with less (for example, to see and consult with more teachers who want to refer marginal learners because they are under the gun to show more gains in student performance) causes special educators to grow weary. Finding occasions for staff exchanges, better supervision, professional incentives, and development opportunities requires imaginative leadership. Negotiating directly with principals to gain their spirited support and acknowledgment of the special education presence in their buildings will go a long way with the special education staff. Developing building-based teams to support all teachers in need will integrate the special education staff and provide support for all teachers. Many strategies and tactics presented in Chapter 7 are related to managing human resources in special education more effectively.

Differences in CSFs

As our research continues to evolve, it may be possible to make finer distinctions between groups of administrators and their rating and ranking of CSFs. For the present, Rockart has suggested that the stage of organizational development and the particular department's position within the organization is perhaps the most important reason for differences in CSFs across information specialist executives.[8]

We would speculate that special education administrators with longevity within local school districts as compared with those in intermediate or cooperative units would rank CSFs differently over time. The latter group is more exposed to changes in local leadership and loosely coupled arrangements that allow a great deal of freedom to move in and out of their cooperative arrangements.

The size of the district or intermediate unit as well as the maturity of the organization and the positioning of the special education administrator interact to increase its complexity and what the administrator feels that he or she must respond to in order to be perceived as successful.

Another variable that effects administrative behavior in special education is the changing expectations that state and federal government representatives can bring to bear on special education planning and implementation. Redefining expectations leads to changes in CSFs. For example, the minimum competency movement is exerting pressure on special educators to seek inclusion or exclusion from state and local testing provisions. Maryland, Florida, and New York are three states requiring special education student to be included in statewide testing programs. While not widespread, this state-level expectation will cause significant changes in curricular emphasis across the country if this trend continues. We continue to discuss this issue in Chapter 8.

Another example of rising expectations at the federal level suggests more scrutiny of the postschool adjustment and employability of exceptional students. Current federal initiatives on the relationship of special education to vocational education and transitional programming from the school to the world of work and independent living are clearly on the agenda of many local special education administrators.

THE FUTURE AND CRITICAL SUCCESS FACTORS

The following factors are those that we consider most significant to the future agenda for special education; that is, as specialized student services, special education should include

1. An interagency consortium of educators, public and mental health, and social services agencies committed to the identification of infants and families of high-risk children who need early intervention to prevent the lasting debilitating effects of poor learning conditions.
2. A preschool program that focuses on family intervention and parent training as well as stimulating high-risk children.
3. An educational assessment process that focuses on students and teachers in need of assistance to prevent the labeling of children as deviant.

4. Building-level teams that can develop services at that level for all children with special needs as opposed to district teams developing segregated programs. These teams provide the occasion for both general and special education personnel to share in joint problem solving to assist suspected students with special needs.

5. A specified contract for students placed in educational alternatives to the regular education program.

6. A supportive service staff that cooperatively works together to develop a continuum service. Services within a variety of environments and settings and conditions can provide for the wide range of students, professionals, and parents.

7. A commitment to professional development of staff in pursuit of quality performance.

8. Deliberate efforts to involve parents in decision making and to train them to be more effective partners with professionals in the education of their children who have complex and often confounding problems.

9. A data-based action research model, with intervention and evaluation built into an evolutionary process, with a feedback cycle, leading to a more efficient planning and instructional process.[9]

We believe that special education can contribute to the education of all special needs students by expanding its commitment to an empirical search for what works in individual classrooms and schools. This knowledge and skill can be most effectively transmitted through the use of existing consultant and resource teachers. On a daily basis, these helping teachers can support regular classroom teachers in the direct application of learning gathered from research and practice in special education.

Rising public expectations, combined with special educators' own commitment to harness electronic technology, will further the service agenda of special education as experimental education for all.[10] Technological applications already exist to help in the design of computer support systems for individual student planning and the monitoring of instructional progress. In Chapter 10 we describe some of these applications.

SUMMARY

The push for free and appropriate education for all children in the least restrictive environment implies the need for innovation within the public schools. The current separation of special education from other related services to students in the public schools is arbitrary and artificial, and an action research response to students and teachers alike who need support to increase performance is lacking.

To increase the system's capacity to respond to teachers and these students, a repositioning of special education and other supportive services is necessary. We have proposed that the special education leadership role initially become a linking role between special education and other central office services to these clients.

This repositioning involves a commitment to be responsive and to share the responsibility and the resources needed to implement such a program. It also involves a commitment to support quality special education teaching personnel in their sharing of our field's accumulated knowledge and skills in the education of exceptional learners. This will demand staff reorientation and consultation. Finally, it involves accepting and embracing error. Michael has argued that professionals in human services will have to accept the instability and value-laden conflicts that permeate our current circumstances.[11] Special education administrators can negotiate their circumstances best by applying learning principles in an action research context, by urging their teachers and staff to demonstrate and model excellent teaching behavior, and by illustrating individual student growth through an ongoing evaluation process.

NOTES

[1]Leonard C. Burrello and Daniel D. Sage, *Leadership and Change in Special Education* (Englewood Cliffs, N.J.: Prentice-Hall, 1979), pp. 66-68.

[2]Leonard C. Burrello and Vernon A. Johnson, "Critical Success Factors in Managing Special Education," unpublished paper (Fall 1984).

[3]John F. Rockart, "The Changing Role of the Information Systems Executive: A Critical Success Factor Perspective," *Sloan Management Review* (Fall 1982), pp. 3-13.

[4]Ibid., pp. 7-8.

[5]Burrello and Johnson, "Critical Success Factors," p. 2.

[6]Larry Cuban, "Transforming the Frog into a Prince: Effective Schools Research, Policy, and Practice at the District Level," *Harvard Educational Review,* 54, no. 2 (May 1984), 129-151.

[7]Egon Guba and Yvonna Lincoln, *Effective Evaluation: Improving the Usefulness of Evaluation Results Through Responsive and Naturalistic Methods* (San Francisco: Jossey-Bass, 1981), pp. 39-41.

[8]Rockart, "The Changing Role of the Information System Executive," p. 9.

[9]Leonard C. Burrello, Michael L. Tracy, and Edward W. Schultz, "Special Education as Experimental Education: A New Conceptualization," *Exceptional Children,* 40 (Sept. 1973), 29-34.

[10]Burrello and Sage, *Leadership and Change,* pp. 181-182.

[11]Donald Michael, *On Learning to Plan and Planning to Learn* (San Francisco: Jossey-Bass, 1973).

CHAPTER 7
HUMAN RESOURCE MANAGEMENT

Personnel matters constitute one of the most frequently discussed topics in educational management. Much has been written that can be applied to the practice of personnel management in educational settings. Likewise, in special education, the topic of personnel development has received the greatest attention in the literature on personnel management.[1]

We have been discussing issues that we view as the most pressing management concerns facing special education leaders in the public schools. All the issues are mediated by human performance. The status of education personnel in the eyes of the national community, both in the administrative and the teaching ranks, challenges educational leadership to attract and maintain a highly skilled and committed cadre of personnel to career opportunities in the public service of education. This is the first major resource management issue, which we believe will continue to challenge management in the foreseeable future.

The second major issue is the actual management of what we call *shared* human resources. Teachers and related service personnel in special education programs find themselves often reporting to more than one designated ad-

---

The authors are indebted to David Zadnik who did the research, review, and study of current evaluation practices in special education.

ministrator. They may be hired by one administrator, supervised by a second, and evaluated by still a third. We present our analysis of these potential role conflicts through a review of the decision-making authority in local school systems.

The third major issue in human resources management is embedded in the first two, relating to the process of personnel development. As we indicated earlier, much has been written about technical assistance in its various forms—supervision, consultation, and training to name three. We discuss each and how they are interrelated at the district and building level in the paragraphs that follow.

The fourth issue is one of personnel evaluation, which is often confused with supervision. The role and responsibility conflict has been well documented. It is our position that the controversy around these two issues is misplaced and that a school system led by enlightened management will foster a climate of professional behavior that emphasizes self-improvement. Creating a climate that supports teachers and others to search for excellence is the major task of leadership. The solution lies not in trying to do one thing 1,000 percent better but to do a thousand things 1 percent better. The story portrayed by Peters and Waterman is supportive of recent research on effective schools.[2] Furthermore, these schools, as reported by Cuban, do more than one thing well. The fact is that they put many things together, which results in a synergistic reaction.[3] As we look at the human resource component, we should heed the advice of Peters and Waterman to consider all the parts that make the educational enterprise as the secret to school improvement. Focusing on any one is insufficient. It is for these reasons that we start with a most generic factor, creating the climate for quality and personnel development.

Throughout this chapter we share our observations and conversations with administrators across the country who have tried with much success many of the suggestions we now offer. We hope that these recommendations will serve well in meeting the continuing challenge: maximizing human potential.

CREATING A CLIMATE
IN SEARCH OF EXCELLENCE

In our opinion, the public schools are threatened by the public's image of the schools as a holding pen—a place between preschool and adolescence where the youth of the nation spend many hours negotiating the minimum with their teachers. Their dialogue sounds like, "You don't hassel me and I won't hassel you." "Let's just get through the day, and it will be easier for both of us." This negotiation toward the mediocrity is repeated daily in our schools, beginning sometime in the fifth grade or the first part of middle school.

Just as pervasive is the view that teaching and teachers are second-class professionals and special educators are nationally subsidized missionaries who perform with the proverbial patience of Job, God's work with those less fortunate. Some teachers have apparently internalized this notion. Lortie describes teachers as isolated, parochial, and powerless—as a semiprofession that has difficulty defending itself against the external pressure and outside influences.[4]

The renewed public interest in education, fueled by the host of conflicting national reports and disparate political commitments to public education, spurred 38 states to initiate reforms ranging from minimum competency testing to class size legislation for the early elementary grades. And according to the Phi Delta Kappan-sponsored Gallup Poll in 1984,[5] for the first time in eight years, the schools received a positive grade. As a result, however, teachers and administrators concerned with higher expectations being set for their behavior and that of their students are not inclined to share their classrooms with special students integrated into regular classes or gifted students in need of still greater challenges.

With this scenario, creating a climate in search of excellence may seem to be an impossible task. On the contrary, the climate only begins to develop by enlightened leadership, as "when persons with certain motives and purpose mobilize, in competition or conflict with others, institutional, political, psychological, and other resources so as to arouse, engage, and satisfy the motives of followers."[6]

This type of leadership is transcending rather than transforming. Transcending leadership "binds leader and follower together in a mutual and continuing pursuit of a higher purpose" instead of bartering individual purposes as in transformational leadership. In the latter form, leadership is a bargaining process that binds the leader with the followers only when both have something to gain.[7]

Making people (in this case, teachers) the most important asset of our educational system is the key. Peters and Waterman present a dramatic case in their portrayal of Rene McPherson of Dana Corporation.[8] McPherson suggested that the starting point for making changes and focusing on results begins with top management: "Personal productivity of the top managers is a vital symbol." But he argues nobody is told how to do it. If there is a "how," in his view, it's the people at the bottom of the organization. He describes this belief in this way:

> Until we believe that the *expert* in any particular job is the person performing it, we shall forever limit the potential of that person, in terms of both his own contribution to the organization and his own personal development. Consider a manufacturing setting: within their 25-square-foot area, no one knows more about how to operate a machine, maximize its output, improve its quality, optimize the material flow and keep it operating efficiently than do the machine operators, material handlers, and maintenance people responsible for it. Nobody.!

He adds:

That is, when I am in your 25 square feet of space, I'd better listen to you![9]

The implications are clear. To value teachers is to respect their professional capacity to manage their instructional environments. If they are unable to demonstrate positive results, the leader should provide support. If they are still unable to perform after a reasonable period of time, then there is a need to consider transferring positions, changing to another position or leave teaching altogether. We must communicate to teachers that they have responsibility for their own behavior. By increasing their own sense of responsibility, the organization gains more commitment and energy for its goals.[10]

Top management can begin to model for the professional staff and, indeed, for all those they manage to invest in their own personal improvement. Likewise, management should encourage and create the occasion for staff members to share their own improvement plans with their peers so that each can use the other as a resource to reach their own goals. Each member should identify annual plans and activities for personal and professional improvement within the area of responsibility. Where their plans require the consent of others, it must be obtained and noted. Both parties then become party to the improvement activity and annual evaluation of progress.

In the case of top management and building-level leaders, plan evaluation should include assessing staff perception of their contribution to facilitating staff performance and support for personal and professional changes leading to personal excellence and school improvement. Verifying leadership behavior as facilitating should include the creation of a positive working environment and specific references to how managerial behavior leads to increasing student growth. Peer assessment, where appropriate, should also be conducted to provide feedback on managerial behavior as a member of the district's management team. Establishing and creating mature personnel teams within and between staff groups is an important criterion to assess in managers. Assessing managerial modeling behavior should be a key dimension of the evaluation. Each evaluation should occur with one's own supervisor or other designated feedback person.

Building-level teams are an excellent vehicle for special education district personnel to support both building-level leadership and the staff itself. Through building-level teams, the district office is able to create an occasion for group problem solving on referred or placed students, to discuss the nature and frequency of services needed to support the student or teachers as needed, and to become a means of staff development. Each of these arrangements seeks to foster building-level ownership for special education and to extend the range of services to include the needs of the regular staff in managing disabled students in their classes. It provides an opportunity for sharing the human resources indigenous to the building and those being offered from the district special education offices in a more efficient manner. Stokes has reviewed six types of building team arrangements and underscores the need for building leadership involvement and support as well as the need to carefully introduce and assist in the initial stage of team development. Modeling with a core group of three to six persons is recommended before introducing the concept to the entire staff.[11]

Developing and maintaining a district pool of resources to support innovative ideas and individual and team progress through an awards program gives visibility and provides incentives for individual and group behavior. A closing awards ceremony that celebrates student accomplishments as well as those of community agencies and volunteers, coupled with a staff awards presentation acknowledging the contribution of high flyers and building-based teams, showcase the staff and help to build the spirit. Peer and supervisor assessments should be combined in determining award winners.

MANAGING SHARED HUMAN RESOURCES

The search for excellence then begins with transcending leadership that helps to create occasions for personal expression of growth and ways to inspire the school community. Frequent face-to-face conversation is essential to move staff in the direction desired.

The personnel function in special education permeates all managerial functions. It goes far beyond the line authority to hire and fire. Table 7-1 shows the key subfunctions that make up personnel management. The grid also allows for an assessment of the special education administrator's decisionmaking authority in contrast to that of personnel directors and building administrators. We have limited our contrasting authority to four of Tannenbaum and Schmidt's 7-point continuum of power and influence between managers and nonmanagers.[12] The desired decisionmaking authority of the special education administrator is contrasted to what it actually is in most settings. It is important to keep in mind that in systems with 15,000 or more students, personnel directors usually play a key role in personnel position establishment and actual presentation to the superintendent and the board for final approval. Most other functions are shared with building-level administrators, with final approval in some cases resting with the building principal.

Betz has suggested that the overall relationship between the special education and the building administrator be separated into systemwide management issues and daily operations issues. Each should have individually delegated responsibilities to perform within their own jurisdiction, but each should also share responsibilities for selected functions such as the selection and assignment of staff. Some examples of individually delegated responsibilities of the principal include student discipline, staff scheduling, coordi-

TABLE 7-1   Personnel Functions in Terms of Desired (D) and Actual (A) Decision-Making Responsibilities of Special Education Administrators and Others

PERSONNEL FUNCTIONS	INDIVIDUALLY DELEGATED		JOINT		CONSULTATIVE ADVISING	INFORMATION GIVING ONLY
	D/\A		D/\A		D/\A	D/\A
Identification/ Justification	x	x			x*	x
Defining essential personnel characteristics needed	x	x		x*		x
Develop recruitment materials and conduct recruitment	x*		x	x		x
Selecting personnel			x	x		
Assigning personnel			x	x		
Supervising personnel			x		x	
Evaluating personnel			x		x	
Terminating personnel			x		x	
Training personnel	x		x			

x* - size of district may cause this relationship to occur

nation of related service personnel, and allocating building resources. Betz has even found some issues where neither group of administrators was sure what to do. Their dilemma involved due process hearings, a situation that may have changed in ensuing years.[13]

An example of the consultative or advising authority relationship might occur in the principal's jurisdictional area of student discipline. When a case involving a disabled student arises, principals may seek the advice of the director to determine if the student's disability contributed to the student's observed behavior and, therefore, might warrant a case conference before disciplinary action is undertaken.

The director of special education may provide information, rather than advise or actually be involved in a decision, with a facilities planner before a series of school closings hits the community. The closings may or may not affect the special education programs of the district, but having the district-level consideration may save the board and superintendent much embarrassment before going public and suffering from lack of information in response to patron queries about the effect of closing on their handicapped youngsters. We have seen situations in which directors, because of their position in the district, do not have access to the planning or the decision-making situation, that is, their immediate supervisors failed to involve them or solicit their views before a decision was made. This oversight may demand careful scrutiny to see if a pattern of exclusion exists. In Chapter 9, we return to this discussion of managing internal constituencies and the role a director often takes versus other internal or external parties.

The research on supervision clearly suggests that role ambiguity and conflict occurs when communication between principals and the central office breaks down. The shared nature of the appointments, the technical mystique surrounding special education, as well as the availability of supervisors demand careful attention and much discussion. Testing for participation in decisions in vague situations is a good practice. Owens suggests the three-way test of decision making: (1) relevance—whom will it affect; (2) expertise—who has the know how to solve the problem or prevent it; and (3) jurisdiction—who is responsible for making the decision, whose turf is affected.[14]

In managing human resources, making explicit the role responsibilities in the general sense described by Betz is useful, but not always possible. Dealing with exigencies that arise, using Owens's three-way test of decision making, may be of some help but not always practical when the phenomena are unknown. Making explicit one's values, however, is both possible and practical, and it gives others the freedom to act without fear of sanction. A set of values that aids in the negotiating of responsibilities between regular and special education administrators and supervisors are presented below:

1. A commitment to improve individualizing services to all students in need by increasing the predictability and management of those behaviors that would improve those services
2. Developing a shared vision of what is desired
3. Developing an interdependency among regular and special education staff committed to make the shared vision a reality
4. Encouraging innovation and risk taking where change is seen as a process of growing better rather than as a process of making the sick well
5. Encouraging individual responsibility for behavior and decision making to occur at the level closest to where the service is being provided.

These values anticipate a set of behaviors that foster shared ownership of special education. They require collaboration rather than competition. They challenge us to assume responsibility for our own behavior rather than project our lack of courage to risk or our predisposition to blame others. These values form the basis of an open negotiation and the possibility to become transcending leaders.

PERSONNEL DEVELOPMENT

There are three major forms of personnel development that we cover: (1) in-service training or continuing education, (2) supervision, and (3) the consultation and networking of staff resources.

The Inservice Training Context

In reviewing the state of the art, Cruickshank et al. delineated four general trends in inservice education:

1. A movement from a compensatory to a complementary view of the function of inservice
2. Progression from a discrete to a continuous view of inservice, thus blurring the line between preservice and inservice
3. Shift from relatively simple to more complex inservice programs that cover a wider range of material and respond to a more diverse audience
4. Movement from circumscribed control by either the public schools or institutions of higher education to collaborative governance mechanisms, including teacher involvement[15]

Inservice education and personnel development is changing within a broader educational environment that includes the following forces described by Burrello and Byers.[16]

1. *Declining student enrollments.* The phenomenon of fewer students has been translated into reduced need for expanding school faculties. In this way, the potential impact of new ideas brought by new faculty members has been reduced. Inservice education, therefore, is increasingly viewed as a vehicle for revitalizing current faculty with fresh ideas and new learnings from recent research. This fact more than others perhaps reinforces the need to "blur the line" between preservice and inservice education as the emphasis shifts to a lifelong learning perspective.
2. *Fewer staff openings.* Declining enrollments in schools also means that school faculty tend to remain in their positions for longer periods of time. In the past, schools relied on high turnover rates to assist in the implementation of school change. As many new teachers were employed each fall, new procedures or programs could be implemented rather smoothly, necessitating merely overcoming the resistance of relatively few of the "old guard." Now this annual reshuffling of teachers occurs only at a minimal level. Inservice education for a stable faculty is seen as a necessary vehicle for both professional renewal and school change such as that mandated by P.L. 94-142. These stable faculties need leadership, resources, and support to respond to changing educational mandates that require them to take on new roles and responsibilities (e.g., regular teachers serving handicapped children in their classrooms).
3. *Few persons seeking teaching as a career.* Increasingly men and women, and teachers in particular, are choosing other careers for both economic and professional reasons. For those who stay, a long-term career orientation toward teaching further reduces teacher turnover. In addition, teachers' attitudes toward continuing professional development are changing as teaching is viewed not as a temporary job but as a lifelong career. As professionals, teachers feel a need for renewal and growth to avoid becoming stale.
4. *Organized teachers.* As the teaching force in a school becomes more stable, teachers' unions have become stronger and have focused not only on job-related issues (salaries, benefits, work conditions) but also on professional development issues such as public school responsibility for inservice programs, released time

for inservice, and incentives for participation. The local bargaining unit is becoming a more vocal advocate for a wide variety of teachers' needs. In addition, the governance of inservice educational and professional development is becoming a collaborative function rather than an individual or an administrative/board responsibility. P.L. 94-142 mandates collaboration in the development of the state's comprehensive system of personnel development. Many school districts are finding this collaborative model is also applicable at the local level.

5. *Governance issues.* Procedural and political issues have been identified by a national study of inservice teacher education funded by both the National Center for Educational Statistics and the Teacher Corps. The study provides both a summary of the context of inservice education in general and suggests a future direction that deserves elaboration. The findings are summarized below:

There are two general structural problems with ISTE (Inservice Teacher Education). First the vast varieties of possible training options need to be interfaced closely with teacher needs and general thrusts of school districts. Theory based approaches to education need to be followed up by clinical training which is largely mediated by teachers themselves. Second, the vast problems of time in which to be trained and providing training close to the work site have obviously not been solved at all.

ISTE, in short, is a cornucopia of problems crying for alternative solutions. No single approach to the governance, structure, substance, or process of ISTE is likely to solve very many of its problems. We, obviously, should enter a period of experimentation with alternatives—alternatives which make inservice education more relevant to the teacher and which experiment with various forms of governance, kinds of interfaces, alternative trainers, modes of directive, and self-directed teacher education.[17]

6. *Results orientation.* Taxpayers are increasingly demanding that schools be held accountable from both a fiscal and cost-effective standpoint and also, more important, from an educational standpoint, for the services they provide. The "back to basics" and "minimum competency" movements of the consumers of educational services are two efforts to hold educators more accountable for the performance of students. Individual education planning for handicapped children under P.L. 94-142 has been attacked by teachers, administrators, and board members concerned that they might be held liable if a child failed to achieve prescribed and negotiated objectives. Although such liability is not the intent of the law, school personnel can be held accountable if the services prescribed in the IEP are not provided.

Within this general context, educators now must take a closer look at the function of inservice education for school personnel to meet both institutional renewal and professional development needs of providing educational services to all children.

Institutional Renewal

As discussed, schools as organizations have utilized inservice education programs to respond to needs identified by leadership both within and outside the organization. A particular inservice education program may be developed in response to a variety of forces within the general framework of institutional renewal. The framework involves three phases: (1) external mandates for change, (2) a problem-solving focus, and (3) adoption and implementation of innovations.

Personal Development

Teachers and others in education have more personal reasons to participate in inservice education programs that go beyond the external pressure for institutional renewal.

Dan Lortie provides an analysis of the professional dimensions of teaching, particularly in comparison with other professions. He notes the relatively short preparation or preservice training required of teachers and the underdeveloped reward system for professional growth activities once teaching has begun. Education does not have a strong history of valuing continuing education for professional development.[18]

Within the broad context of individual professional development, inservice education may respond to several needs.

1. *Personal Enrichment* —Inservice may offer the opportunity for self confrontation, introspection, and analysis. Examining values and basic issues in human relationships may help teachers grow as people, thus enhancing their mental health and personal vitality. The focus of this kind of inservice is removed from the daily life of teachers in the classroom but its impact may be felt indirectly in higher morale and increased commitment to the profession and its tasks and to the students. Inservice for this purpose emphasizes increasing personal effectiveness rather than acquiring specific professional skills. Inservice to fulfill these needs is usually self-selected and mostly self-directed.

2. *Professional Renewal* —Inservice may provide opportunities to keep abreast of new professional developments in education and related fields. Participants may learn about recent research and innovations and their application to practice. Teachers are motivated to develop a desired level of competency, to achieve ''a sense of excellence'' and a''sense of efficacy'' in what they do. Commenting on the Rand Study, Ryor found a key variable in school change efforts is the teachers' sense of efficacy, that what they do in the classroom does make a difference.[19] As professionals, teachers continually strive to improve skills and expand knowledge. Inservice to meet these general professional needs may not be directly related to the daily teaching role. Such inservice, by exposing teachers to new ideas, may stimulate them to develop new skills or areas of competence in their daily work.

3. *Career Development* —Inservice may actually provide skill training that allows teachers to expand their professional competencies and responsibilities. Though direct application of their learnings to their present position may be difficult, such inservice may provide the training necessary to move up the career ladder to other leadership positions within education.

4. *Improving Professional Performance* —Actually this focus on professional performance overlaps with institutional renewal activities such as responding to external mandates, new innovations and building based planning and problem solving. Inservice to improve professional performance is directly related to teachers' daily classroom roles but not mandated by school administration, laws or other forces external to the individual teacher. Teachers participate in these

inservice programs because they want to improve their own professional expertise and on-the-job performance. These inservice activities are very directly tied to job related skills and knowledge that individual teachers identify as areas in which growth is needed.[20]

Teachers then may have a variety of motivations for participation in inservice training programs, ranging from very personal needs to more professionally related concerns. If inservice providers take the position that teachers, in general, want to do a good job and want to develop that sense of efficacy, then inservice for purely professional development of individual teachers may be a valuable vehicle for increasing teacher effectiveness and the quality of instruction. It is worth remembering in this context that "the desire to change, if it is to be consequential, must come from within."[21] Individual growth, however, must have institutional support if the learnings of inservice are to be applied in the classroom with students. The school must value and support professional growth for teachers but also foster a climate conducive to institutional growth and change as well. In being supportive of a *developmental* rather than a *deficit* model of change for individuals, the school environment will focus on strengths and match resources to facilitate growth in specified areas. An atmosphere in which renewal is a positive process for both the individuals and the organization will provide a supportive educational environment within which all can continue to learn.

Dilemmas for Personnel Development Planners

From this review of the context of inservice and the conflict and interaction between professional and organizational renewal orientations, a series of questions or dilemmas results.

The following is a restatement of these dilemmas as a series of organizational initiatives originally presented by Burrello and Walton that can be considered by inservice providers.[22]

Who Is Responsible and in Control of Inservice Education?   The dichotomy of professional development and institutional renewal confounds the development of a more comprehensive and, in the long run, more effective inservice education program. The dichotomy involves the dual role of the teacher as professional and as public employee. The question focuses on the issue of who is responsible for continuing education and development. On the one hand, as professionals, teachers are responsible for their own development and ongoing learning. Professionals from all fields are expected to assess their own strengths and weaknesses, develop a plan, and begin to move toward those goals in a self-renewal process. On the other hand, as public employees, teachers are expected to improve their skills and knowledge related to their specific work assignments. In a fundamental way then, their job descriptions and employers exert direct control over the content and process of these inservice education programs and become the driving force for change in practice, not the teachers' own personal needs and preferences.

Increasingly, the institution's responsibility for inservice education is being defined as encompassing only job-related inservice.[23] The implications of delivering training programs must be examined within the context of the school norms and program regularities that exist.[24] Generally, professionals have been instructed to seek professional growth opportunities on their own initiative with little institutional recognition of their efforts, much less rewards, financial assistance, or other support. School management and policymakers are reluctant to reduce classroom instructional time. Any invasion of the negotiated school day is met with resistance. On the other hand, while many teachers also share this view, after-school continuing education or specific skill training has traditionally been a poor alternative. This dilemma apparently is our present and immediate future reality.

What Constitutes Inservice Education?   Inservice education is generally judged to be a "frill" as opposed to an integral and essential activity. The stakeholders in education are far from in agreement on a definition or a focus for inservice. The lack of a universally accepted definition of the term "inservice" is best characterized by an observation of a practicing administrator; "Any time a group of teachers is assembled for a speech on a prescribed spring or fall day, call it inservice."

Who Values Inservice Education?   Part of the political confusion over the responsibility and definition of inservice is related to the value placed on inservice education. Fostering professional development for its own sake is not sufficient to garner community or administrative support for inservice education. Evaluating the effectiveness of inservice education on behavioral change of children alone is too threatening to educators and too difficult to assess.

How Can Inservice Be Evaluated?   This question cannot be addressed adequately until the earlier questions are resolved. Value, concept, focus, and responsibility for inservice education and professional development must be delineated before inservice interventions can be evaluated.

PERSONNEL PLANNING FOR EXCEPTIONAL CHILDREN

The context of inservice education and the dilemmas that flow from those contesting forces provide the backdrop for developing a comprehensive system of personnel development under P.L. 94-142. Special and regular education alike must attend to the prevailing values, norms, and organizational factors that affect both planning and gaining support from board members, administrators, and organized teachers.

First, planning a response to teacher needs for inservice surrounding handicapped children should acknowledge teachers' and administrators' own sense of efficacy in their professional roles. Their own underlying concepts of the meaning of handicaps, acceptance of deviance, sense of conformity, and standards for student behavior cannot be ignored, for they have a major impact on their capacities to work effectively with handicapped students. School personnel are caught in the dilemma of fostering basic skills and minimum competencies on the one hand and attending to individual differences of learners on the other. These conflicting expectations reduce the professional sense of efficacy. Handicapped children daily challenge basic assumptions of teaching and established routines, teacher-child interactions and classroom management. Enhancing the teachers' sense of efficacy within this conflict-ridden context is one key to successful staff development programs.

Second, while individual conflicts surface, the processes to identify, refer, examine, and plan individually for handicapped children within school organizations are changing. The general thrust of special education itself is still shaped and directed by a separatist, specialist mentality that militates against the concepts of least restrictive environment and individualized planning for children. Implicit in this comprehensive legislation is the need to reexamine special education's relationship to the general concept of the school as a dynamic social system. A series of questions might best illustrate the type of reexamination that is necessary. Who is responsible for handicapped children? Specialists? Regular teachers? Principals? Or all? Are they responsible for all or part of the child's program? When does their individual responsibility begin and end? What changes are necessary to establish regularities in the school to accommodate new behaviors?

Deno,[25, 26, 27] Reynolds,[28] and Burrello et al.[29] have since the early 1970s called for a conceptualization of special education as experimental education and as a support system within the general structure and framework of the public schools. This concept of special education will foster alternative definitions of personnel development and inservice education in particular. A new conceptual framework for special education is needed because the questions posed earlier cannot be dealt with in the roles, norms, and structures of regular and special education prevalent in school systems today.

Both professional self-renewal and institutional renewal inservice programs directed toward improved professional performance on the job demand approaches based upon best practices as suggested by Lawrence[30] and expanded on by Huston[31] and Jamison.[32] Training teachers and administrators to plan and educate handicapped children more appropriately demands translating theory into practice through clinical training or demonstration teaching that model techniques in actual practice. For example, the resource teacher model may be a vehicle to demonstrate special education practices that work in regular classrooms. If inservice education and training activities fail to provide opportunities for the transfer of theory and skills from lectures, simulations, and case studies into the teacher's classroom, little will be gained. Demonstration and practice are necessary for transfer and actual change in teacher behavior to occur. Special education service models must also be responsive to inservice best practices. Resource teacher and other specialists must expand their attention to include not only children who receive their instructional services but also regular class colleagues who can benefit from peer consultation. The National Diffusion Network "What Works" series has a host of model projects that are disseminated with support for school systems that choose to adapt the models to their own settings.

Model strategies alone, however, will not overcome the resistance to change noted earlier. Certainly, successful approaches will provide models for others to analyze, modify, and adapt to their own situations. Beyond developing and disseminating inservice models, a broader reconceptualization of education, schooling, and learning must be launched to achieve real and lasting change in public education. Change in the public perception and institutional definition of schooling is part of the solution to fostering both individual and organizational renewal with respect to educating all children, including those who are handicapped.

SUPERVISION AND EVALUATION

In the last section of this chapter, we discuss the relationship between personnel supervision and evaluation. In Chapter 12, we discuss program evaluation. The purpose and focus of personnel supervision and evaluation are similar—to increase personnel performance in the delivery of effective instruction. The strategy and ultimate use of the data generated are dissimilar. Supervision presupposes a helping relationship where the teacher or related staff member requests assistance, for example, in solving a student programming issue. Evaluation is, however, organizational directed and generally bound by policy negotiated by state and local districts.

Supervision culminates in the generation of alternatives for teachers and supervisors to select the most appropriate resolution to the programming issue. In contrast, evaluation is designed to determine the probationary or tenure status of the individual professional. Evaluation reports stipulate who is to receive additional assistance to bring their performance to a satisfactory level. Reevaluation is designed to assess if that satisfactory level has been achieved.

We suggested that personnel policies and leadership personnel should focus on creating a climate for personal and professional growth. This focus leads to a supportive environment for productive people who actually deliver service to students to pursue their own professional development needs. The organizational commitment to growth is essential in increasing the potential of educational human resources.

Clarifying the purpose, focus, and use of supervisory and evaluative judgments is the first step in bringing about the appropriate use of both functions. Second, the relationship of the practice to be observed and supported through supervision or evaluation should be based upon a synthesis of the data in teacher effectiveness and student learning. Zadnik analyzed the research on teacher effectiveness. His synthesis is outlined as follows:

> The research on teacher effectiveness has strong implications for building principals and other personnel responsible for supervising special education instruction staff. By using the outline provided below, supervisors can observe and monitor the critical behaviors that have proven empirically to be characteristic of effective teachers.

1. *Pre-Instruction Factors*
    Diagnosis
    - Accurately diagnoses and predicts cognitive performance levels of students.
    Content Decisions
    - Promotes extensive content coverage and high levels of student involvement.
    Time Allocation Decisions
    - Maintains high levels of allocated time for a particular content area of curriculum or lesson.
    Pacing Decisions
    - Determines the pace of instruction which is consistent with student ability levels.
    Grouping Decisions
    - Determines the effective group size and composition consistent with student ability and aptitude levels.
    - Selects relevant criteria to be used as a basis for group assignment.
    Activity Structure Decisions
    - Develops goals of instruction which are both clear and systematically organized.
    - Varies materials, lesson organization and structure for different purposes.
    Prescription Decisions
    - Prescribes instructional activities which match needs and skill levels of individual children.
    - Prescribes lessons which have continuity within and between them.
2. *During Instruction Factors*
    Engaged Time
    - Maintains high levels of engaged time for each lesson.
    - Maintains high levels of engaged time that is consistent with time allocated for a lesson.

- Demonstrates skill in predicting engaged time rates for individual students.

Time Management

- Systematically organizes and conducts instruction so there is little waiting time or management time.
- Controls, monitors, and evaluates the amount of allocated and engaged time per lesson.

Success Rates

- Consistently evaluates and if necessary modifies activities to insure individual student success.
- Presents learning activities which insure high levels of individual student success.

Monitoring

- Is active, moving from group to group, observing, providing cues, redirecting student attention and skill attempts.
- Enforces mild forms of punishment that are employed infrequently.
- Refocuses student back on task rather than enforcing punishment.

Structuring

- Provides clear information about the content that is to be learned and how to go about learning it.
- Reviews information, outlines content, emphasizes important points by providing learning cues and summarizes important information.
- Reviews content to clarify to students what is expected of them.
- Provides clear directions and communicates lesson goals and objectives to class.

Feedback

- Provides feedback that is immediate and task relevant.
- Provides reinforcement to students for correct answers and offers a rationale for incorrect answers.
- Provides frequent academic feedback to students which is nonevaluative.
- Praises students in terms of the work they produce.

Questioning

- Asks questions which are narrow, direct, and structured to enable students to understand the answer sought by the teacher.

3. *Climate Factors*

Environment

- Creates an orderly, safe, warm, learning environment that is task oriented, business-like yet simultaneously warm and convivial.
- Demonstrates sensitivity to students' needs.
- Begins and ends lessons on time.
- Effectively manages deviancy.

Expectations

- Communicates clear lesson expectations.
- Expects quality work and sets high but attainable lesson objectives.
- Creates environments that are characterized by low levels of student dependence on the teacher for directions or materials, etc.[33]

A supervisory model that contains the following criteria should enhance teacher and staff performance. The criteria are (1) a written purpose and focus statement, (2) that clearly outlines the use and application of supervisory reports, (3) that delineates the roles of school principal and special education supervisory personnel, and (4) that is based upon teacher effectiveness research. Model practices and procedures consistent with the purpose and focus of the supervising philosophy of the district complete a supervision program.

Supervisory Models

Various supervision models are presented in the literature and are being implemented currently in special education systems. One model that has received much acclaim in recent years is the clinical supervision model developed by Cogan and Goldhammer. Developed in the 1960s, "the model incorporates the concepts of collegiality, collaboration, skilled service, and ethical conduct." It focuses on the principles of integrity and individuality in teachers. The supervisor's role is to encourage, explore, and collaborate rather than coerce and demand. "Clinical supervision presupposes the professionalism of the teacher. This democratic human resources ethos is still generally accepted in most circles as the best supervision approach."[34]

Clinical supervision has entered the 1980s as an emerging and attractive subject. Yet, understanding it is not easy. Krajewski[35] outlined at least seven concepts or conceptual elements that can be derived from clinical supervision literature and practice. These concepts derived from clinical supervision are the following:

1. It is a *deliberate intervention into the instructional process.* The intervention is in terms of the supervisor observing a teacher's lesson, analyzing the lesson data, reporting aspects of it to the teacher, and then cooperatively building a sequential plan for teacher improvement. It is deliberate in the fact that the supervisor plans improvement. It is deliberate in the fact that the supervisor plans with the teacher the lesson to be observed, what teaching behaviors are to be observed, what instruments will be used in the observations, and what roles both supervisor and teacher will assume throughout the process.

2. It creates *productive tension for both teacher and supervisor.* In clinical supervision, supervisor tension may be more pronounced than teacher tension. Skills of analysis of teaching, rapport nurturance, adult psychology, observation instrumentation, and time management are all assumed by the supervisor.

3. It requires *supervisor knowledge and training.* To reduce the tension, supervisors must develop knowledge of instructional skills. Without the skills, they cannot fulfill their expected roles. Without training, they will not acquire the needed skills. Clinical supervision does not demand that every supervisor must be an expert or master teacher. Rather, it assumes that the supervisor be able to collect data objectively in an observed lesson on a specific teaching skill focus.

4. It is a *technology for improving instruction.* Clinical supervision is both technology and use of technology, with objectivity being the key. Emphasis on objectivity reduces the criticism that supervisors' instructional improvement efforts are subjective in nature and intent.

5. *Objectivity in clinical supervision is goal oriented, systematic yet flexible.* Improvement of instruction must be goal oriented. Clinical supervision must be effected in a systematic fashion, yet ensure flexibility to meet individual teacher needs.

6. *It requires mutual trust and rapport nurturance.* Rapport is the binding element for clinical supervision. Without the maintenance of a harmonious working relationship guided by mutual trust, the process is doomed.

7. *Rapport fosters role delineation.* In clinical supervision, role delineation is a must. Both teacher and supervisor must know, understand, and accept their own and each other's role. The supervisor must also ensure that understanding and acceptance exist equally with both neophyte and experienced teachers.[36]

Cogan identifies eight phases in the clinical supervision process:

1. Establishing the supervisory relationship, which builds a relationship of support and trust

2. Planning lessons and units with the teacher by determining lesson objectives, teaching styles, and assessment practices

3. Planning the observation strategy, discussing data to be collected and methodology to be used

4. Observing the lesson

5. Analyzing the observational data to identify teacher behavioral patterns and techniques

6. Planning the post-observation conference strategy

7. Implementing the post-observation conference and discussing the analysis

8. Recycling the process and determining future opportunities for growth.[37]

The research on the effectiveness of clinical supervision has been mixed. In a recent article, McFaul and Cooper question the model's utility in the context of the school workplace. They argue that using clinical supervision for "evaluation purposes is untenable. Its purpose was to help teachers, not to judge them and those two actions were deemed incompatible."[38] Glatthorn,[39] however, in his review of the research identifies some key research findings.

1. Teachers tend to favor a supervisor who is close and supportive.[40]

2. Most teachers and administrators agree with the basic assumptions of clinical supervision.[41]

3. Teachers seem to prefer clinical supervision to traditional supervision and believe that the techniques of clinical supervision are worthwhile.[42]

4. Clinical supervision can change a teacher's behavior in the direction desired.[43,44]

5. Supervisors using a clinical approach seem more open and accepting in postobservation conferences than those using traditional approaches.[45]

Numerous variations of this supervision model/concept have been practiced in the field. One worthy of consideration is a popular approach known as scientific supervision. Scientific supervision concentrates on teaching practices. Hunter's model prescribes a model of teaching characterized by the following components.

1. Diagnosis—identify a general objective and assess students present attainment in relation to it.
2. Specific objectives—select specific objectives for the lesson.
3. Anticipatory set—focus attention, review lessons, and develop readiness for the lesson.
4. Perceived purpose—clarify the objective for the pupils, explain its importance, and clarify it to previous lessons.
5. Learning opportunities—choose learning opportunities that will help learners achieve objectives.
6. Modeling—provide verbal and visual examples of what is expected to be learned.
7. Check for understanding—determine the degree of objectives achieved by students.
8. Guided practice—guide students' practice of learning, and monitor their performance.
9. Independent practice—provide opportunities for students to practice new skills.[46]

The Hunter model has received a tremendous amount of attention over the past few years. Two reasons can be cited as for its popularity. For one, its focus[47] is on the competencies of the teacher. These competencies parallel direct instruction practices. Second, its constructs are supported by research conducted on teacher effectiveness, which have been mentioned previously. Critics of the model, however, indicate that it presents only one model of teaching, which fails to account for the diversity in academic situations and student academic levels.

In another approach, Glatthorn[48] advocates for a differentiated system of supervision. He argues that due to teachers' growth needs, learning styles, and time constraints, supervision should be individualized according to each teachers' current level of development. In differentiated supervision the teacher decides among four choices:

1. Clinical supervision
2. Cooperative professional development—peer supervision
3. Self-directed development
4. Administrative monitoring—monitoring conducted by administrator, making brief unannounced visits to ensure staff are carrying out activities in a professional manner.

Synthesizing Effective Supervisory Practices

Whatever model or approach is used in a district to supervise special education staff, an effective supervision process will contain certain variables. Research literature identifies these variables, which are listed below as criterion statements. These statements will serve as benchmarks for measuring current supervisory practices.

1. The supervision process should be a systematic and carefully planned program that assists teachers in growing professionally. This program should be a written form of policies and procedures that serve as guidelines for the process.
2. Supervision should be provided by someone who has been trained and has had experience in the skills of planning, observing, conferring, and evaluating.
3. Supervision should be a shared accountability, multiple step process that clearly delineates role functions and requirements for supervisor and supervisee.
4. There should be a written statement of purpose or philosophy of supervision that delineates the tenets or beliefs of the process.
5. Organizational and instructional expectations should be clearly delineated, disseminated, and clarified with each professional.
6. The supervision process steps should include
   a. A preobservation conference that contains the following components:
      (1) Setting of teacher goals
      (2) Reclarification of supervisor/supervisee roles
      (3) Establishment of observation time, lesson objectives, and so on
   b. Formal, periodic observation where descriptive information regarding the lesson is documented.
   c. A postobservation conference
      (1) Where the supervisor provides descriptive feedback on the observation and teacher performance
      (2) Where plans for teacher renewal are established
   d. The design and delivery of technical assistance that facilitates teacher renewal
   e. A recycling of steps a-d throughout the school year
   f. Provisions for a formal summative evaluation that should be in written form and shared with each staff member
   g. Provisions for self-appraisal
   h. Participation by affected staff in the design of the supervision processes
   i. Participation by affected staff in the evaluation of supervisory instruments and processes, which evaluation should be conducted annually[49]

Analysis of Current Evaluation Instruments

Zadnik also conducted a survey of current supervisory and personnel practices as part of his CASE-supported research study. He found 46 districts willing to share their instructional personnel evaluation instruments currently in use. Of the 46, 37 had rating scales while 9 were openended. The first analysis focused on identifying the characteristics of the instruments currently in use. Procedurally, instruments were scanned before beginning a more systematic content analysis of all of the instruments. Scanning revealed, as in the Wood and Pohland[50] study, that items were more heavily weighted toward assessing teachers in terms of their multiple roles rather than the aspects of classroom management and instruction. The researcher used their category scheme to analyze the characteristics of the sample instruments. The categories were

1. *Personal characteristics*—such as flexibility, enthusiasm, responsibility, patience
2. *Instructional role*—preparation of lesson plans, student-teacher rapport, evaluating student progress
3. *Administrator/manager role*—such as classroom management, IEP management, record keeping
4. *Professional role*—professional growth and development
5. *Social role*—interpersonal relations with staff and community
6. *Organizational membership role*—conformity to organizational rules and expectations

The distribution of the 1,085 items contained in the 37 instruments are delineated in Figure 7-1.

The second analysis of evaluation instruments was conducted to answer the question, Are teacher effectiveness competencies present on performance evaluation instruments and if so, to what extent are they? The researcher, again, scanned the rating scales, concentrating on the categories of teachers in their instructional role and in their administrator/manager role. The results of the analysis are depicted in Table 7-2. The review of the research on teacher effectiveness conducted by Zadnik yielded an item pool of 17 variables categorized under the heading of preinstruction, during instruction, and climate factors that were associated with effective teachers. These variables are out-

FIGURE 7-1   Distribution by Category of Items in Rating Scale Instruments.

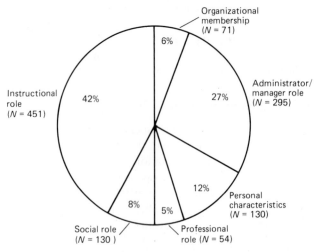

Percentages based on N = 1,085

TABLE 7-2 **The Extent of Exemplary Instructional Practices Present in 37 Personnel Evaluation Instruments**

INSTRUCTIONAL ROLE	NOT PRESENT	PRESENT	RATINGS			
			VERY WEAK	WEAK	STRONG	VERY STRONG
1. Preinstructional variables						
a. Diagnosis	13	24	6	8	8	2
b. Content decisions	15	22	7	8	5	2
c. Time allocation decisions	22	15	5	5	5	0
d. Pacing decisions	21	16	4	5	6	1
e. Grouping decisions	19	18	4	7	5	2
f. Activity structure decisions	15	22	6	5	9	2
g. Prescription	13	24	7	7	8	2
2. During instruction variables						
a. Engaged time	28	9	2	5	2	0
b. Time management	17	20	5	8	5	2
c. Success rates	17	20	4	10	4	2
d. Monitoring	15	22	6	6	8	2
e. Pacing	18	19	5	7	5	2
f. Structuring	18	19	3	8	16	2
g. Feedback	15	22	5	8	7	2
h. Questioning	12	25	3	11	8	3
3. Climate factors						
a. Environment	10	27	6	12	8	1
b. Expectations	7	30	5	12	10	3

Source: David Zadnick, "Instructional Effectiveness and Supervisory Practices in Special Education," CASE Dissemination Series (Bloomington, Ind.: CASE Inc., 1984), p. 47.

lined on the left side of the table. The right side of the table delineates the number of instruments in which the variables were present or not present. If teacher effectiveness variables were present on the instrument, the researcher would rank these variables on a scale from very weak to very strong.

The analysis revealed that teacher effectiveness variables appeared on 56 percent of the instruments. Where these variables were present in the instruments, over 60 percent were ranked by the researcher as weak or very weak with the remaining 39 percent rated as strong or very strong. Only 8 percent of the variables present in the instruments were considered to be very robust or strong. The variables that were identified as the lowest criteria for monitoring teacher performance were engaged time and allocated time. Both variables are two of the three significant aspects of academic learning time that are considered to be a major determinant of teacher effectiveness.[51]

SUMMARY

The research on teacher effectiveness and supervision practices provides a strong foundation for deriving implications for administrative management of special education programs. It is clear that school effectiveness research identifies the school administrator responsible for managing the instructional program as the key determinant in achieving a level of school effectiveness. This, in turn, contributes to increased levels of student achievement. Integrating teacher and school effectiveness variables provides a clear framework for school officials in managing and supervising the instructional process. For example, what we have learned from the research on teacher effectiveness is that teachers who allocate more time for instruction are likely to be more effective than teachers who allocate less time. From a management perspective, it is, therefore, necessary to determine management practices that could be initiated to increase the effectiveness of teachers regarding time allocation and other aspects of the instructional process.

The current high level of interest in instruction, heightened by the American public's concern about the quality of instruction in American schools, leads to issues of teacher authority and control of instruction. Typically, the administrative control exercised in a school building has been termed "loosely coupled." The research on school effectiveness suggests that student achievement is enhanced when the administrator is a strong instructional leader. However, teachers have had considerable autonomy with regard to decisions about classroom instruction. The effort to maximize student learning may clearly necessitate greater administrative control over classroom functions. This consequently may cause teachers to feel threatened about the extent and use of outside authority within their classrooms. Supervisors must be highly sensitive to exercising the right amount of control that avoids alienating teachers from the supervisory process yet achieves intended supervisory objectives.

It is advisable then for administrators to approach the supervision of instruction from the perspective that directives and suggestions about improvement are possible. However, they must clearly understand their role in the process and exercise that role accordingly. The control over instruction is best managed by the teacher.

The more administrators perceive their role in controlling instruction as highly directive and prescriptive, the more they limit the potential of a teacher's personal and professional development.

Within the latter view, teachers as professionals are considered to be responsible for their own behavior. Supervision now becomes an expert support system. Here, the teacher is encouraged to seek out consultation that is self-directed and nonprescriptive. The teacher, as client, seeks out assistance and remains in control of accepting and rejecting the advice and information. The supervisor is facilitative, approaching classroom and program improvement in a collaborative spirit with the teacher. The role of the supervisor is primarily catalytic. We return to Peters and Waterman and their corresponding notion that those who deliver the service know best:

> We let everybody do their job on the basis of what they need, what they say they'll do, and what the results are. And we gave them enough time to do it. We had better start admitting that the most important people in an organization are those who actually provide a service or make and add value to the product, not those who administer the activity.[52]

To summarize, the supervisor's ability to supervise instruction effectively is contingent upon the development and maintenance of personal and professional skills. The administrator who is responsible for supervision and evaluation must become knowledgeable about what to look for in observing instructional practices in special classrooms. Improvement of administrator skills is more likely to occur if districts offer administrative inservice programs on supervision and evaluation, and administrators clearly understand their unique role in the process. Where there are other supervisors (dual supervision) involved in the process, clear limits and role requirements must be established. Administrators must be fair in observing practices and accept variations in teacher behavior. Last, the process must be built upon trust that is continuously communicated by each party.

NOTES

[1]Judy Smith-Davis, Phillip Burke, and Margaret Noel, "Personnel to Educate the Handicapped in America: From a Programmed Viewpoint" (College Park: Institute for the Study of Exceptional Children and Youth, University of Maryland, 1984).

[2]Thomas J. Peters, and Robert H. Waterman Jr., *In Search of Excellence: Lessons from America's Best-Run Companies* (New York: Harper & Row, 1982).

[3]Larry Cuban, "Transforming the Frog into a Prince: Effective Schools Research, Policy, and Practice at the District Level," *Harvard Educational Review*, 54, no. 2 (May 1984), 129-151.

[4]Dan C. Lortie, *School Teacher* (Chicago: University of Chicago Press, 1975).

[5]George Gallup, *The Gallup Poll* (Bloomington, Ind.: Phi Delta Kappan, 1984).

[6]James MacGregor Burns, *Leadership* (New York: Harper & Row, 1978), p. 18.

[7]Ibid., p. 20.

[8]Peters and Waterman, *In Search of Excellence,* p. 245.

[9]Ibid., p. 250.

[10]Arnold S. Tannenbaum, *Control in Organizations* (New York: McGraw-Hill, 1968).

[11]Shari Stokes, *School-Based Staff Support Teams: A Blueprint for Action* (Reston, Va.: Council for Exceptional Children, 1982).

[12]Robert Tannenbaum and Warren H. Schmidt, "How to Choose a Leadership Pattern," *Harvard Business Review,* 51 (May-June 1973), 107.

[13]Monte Betz, *"The Development of Building Principal Competence in the Administration of Programs for the Handicapped "* (Unpublished doctoral dissertation, Indiana University, 1977).

[14]Robert G. Owens and Edward Lewis, "Managing Participation in Organizational Decisions," *Group and Organizational Studies,* 1, (1976), 56-66.

[15]Donald R. Cruickshank, Christopher Lorish, and Linda Thompson, "What We Think We Know About Inservice Education," *Journal of Teacher Education* (January-February 1979), 30, no. 1, 27-32.

[16]Leonard C. Burrello and Kathy Byers, "The Context and Need for Inservice Education for All Educators" (Reno, Nev.: Counterpoint Publications, 1982).

[17]Bruce R. Joyce, Kenneth R. Howey, and Sam J. Yarger, *Inservice Teacher Education Concepts Projects: Report I, Issues to Face* (Palo Alto, Calif.: Stanford Center for Research and Development in Teaching, June 1976), pp. 3 and 28.

[18]Lortie, *School Teacher,* p. 28.

[19]John Ryor, Albert Shanker, and J. J. Sandefur, "Three Perspectives on Inservice Education," *Journal of Teacher Education,* 30, no. 1, (January-February 1979), 13-19.

[20]Burrello and Byers, "The Context and Need,"

[21]Louis Rubin, ed., *The In-Service Education of Teachers* (Boston: Allyn & Bacon, 1978).

[22]Leonard C. Burrello and Ronald Walton, "Developing Organizational Support for Quality Inservice in the Schools," *Viewpoints* (Spring 1980).

[23]Joyce, Howey, and Yarger, *Inservice Teacher Education Concepts Projects,* p. 15.

[24]Seymour Sarason, *The Culture of School and the Problem of Change* (Boston: Allyn & Bacon, 1972).

[25]E.N. Deno, ed., *Instructional Alternatives for Exceptional Children* (Reston, Va.: The Council for Exceptional Children, 1972).

[26]E.N. Deno, "The Project Advocate System: An Exceptional Child Leadership Training Institute on an E.P.D.A. Mission" (Washington, D.C.: National Technical Assistance Systems in Special Education, 1974).

[27]E.N. Deno, *Mainstreaming: Learning Disabled Emotionally Disturbed and Socially Maladjusted Children in Regular Classes* (Minneapolis: Leadership Training Institute/Special Education, University of Minnesota, 1976).

[28]M. C. Reynolds and M. D. Davis, *Exceptional Children in Regular Classrooms* (Reston, Va.: The Council for Exceptional Children, 1971).

[29]Leonard C. Burrello, Michael L. Tracy and Edward W. Schultz, "Special Education as Experimental Education: A New Conceptualization," *Exceptional Children* (September, 1973), pp. 29-34.

[30]G. Lawrence, *Patterns of Effective Inservice Education: A State of the Art Summary of Research on Materials and Procedures for Changing Behaviors in Inservice Teaching* (Tallahassee: Florida State Department of Education, 1974).

[31]Harry Huston, *Inservice Best Practices: The Learnings of General Education* (Bloomington, Ind.: National Inservice Network, 1979).

[32]Patricia J. Jamison, "The Development and Validation of a Conceptual Model and Quality Practices Designed to Guide the Planning, Implementation, and Evaluation of Inservice Education Programs," Unpublished doctoral dissertation, University of Maryland, 1981.

[33]David Zadnik, "Instructional Effectiveness and Supervisory Practices in Special Education," *CASE Dissemination Series* (Bloomington, Ind.: CASE Inc., 1984), pp. 32-52.

[34]Shirley A. McFaul and James M. Cooper, "Peer Clinical Supervision: Theory vs. Reality," *Educational Leadership,* 41, no. 7 (1984), 5.

[35]Robert Krajewski, "Clinical Supervision: A Conceptual Framework," *Journal of Research and Development in Education,* 15, no. 2 (1982), 41.

[36]Ibid., pp. 41-42.

[37]Morris L. Cogan, *Clinical Supervision,* pp. 10–12. Copyright © 1973 by Houghton Mifflin Company. Adapted by permission.

[38]McFaul and Cooper, "Peer Clinical Supervision," p. 9.

[39]Allan Glatthorn, *Differential Supervision* (Alexandria, Va.: Association for Supervision and Curriculum Development, 1984), pp. 8-9.

[40]B. Gordon, "Teachers Evaluate Supervisory Behavior in the Individual Conference," *Clearing House,* 49 (January 1976), pp. 251-258.

[41]R. E. Eaker, "An Analysis of the Clinical Supervision Process as Perceived by Selective Teachers and Administrators," Unpublished doctoral dissertation, University of Tennessee, 1972.

[42]C. A. Reavis, "A Test of the Clinical Supervision Model," *Journal of Educational Research,* 70 (July-August 1977), 311-315.

[43]N. B. Garman, "A Study of Clinical Supervision as a Resource of College Teachers of English," Unpublished doctoral dissertation, University of Pittsburgh, 1971.

[44]R. J. Krajewski, "Clinical Supervision: To Facilitate Teacher Self Improvement," *Journal of Research and Development in Education,* 9 (Winter 1976), 358-366.

[45]Reavis, "A Test of the Clinical Supervision Model," p. 312.

[46]Madeline Hunter and D. Russell, *Planning for Effective Instruction* (Los Angeles: University Elementary School, 1980).

[47]Glatthorn, *Differential Supervision,* p. 10.

[48]Ibid., pp. 2-6.

[49]Zadnik, "Instructional Effectiveness," pp. 45-48.

[50]Carolyn J. Wood and Paul A. Pohland, "Teacher Evaluation: The Myth and Realities," *Planning for the Evaluation of Teaching,* CEDR Monograph (Bloomington, Ind.: Phi Delta Kappa, 1979), pp. 73-82.

[51]Zadnik, "Instructional Effectiveness," pp. 45-48.

[52]Peters and Waterman, *In Search of Excellence,* p. 250.

CHAPTER 8
CURRICULUM
INTEGRATION
AND DEVELOPMENT

Special education, the education of exceptional children and youth, has grown rapidly during the past two decades, both in numbers served and resources expended. Such strides have not been without significant growing pains. In responding to the plight of exceptional students floundering in or excluded from regular classrooms, educators created a specialized service delivery system and a set of curricula that were both more supportive and more restrictive. Now, after a decade since the passage of Public Law 94-142, newly gained knowledge, experience, values, and resources have returned the focus to the merging of general and special education, and an important question persists: How should the curriculum for these students be planned? As an integral part of the curriculum for all students or different from the curriculum for those considered as "normal" nonhandicapped students?[1]

This chapter presents a position for exploring several dimensions of the major questions and a set of alternative solutions for solving the problem. The remainder of the chapter provides arguments to illustrate contrasting views and emphasis in measuring student progress through the curriculum. The chapter ends with a series of implications for administrators to use in their

The authors are indebted to Edith Beatty, Michael Cahill, and Daniel Cline for their contribution to this chapter.

own practices in furthering the instructional quality of special educators and the relevance of learning experiences for exceptional students. We hope that the material presented in this chapter will assist administrators responsible for curriculum planning to formulate arguments and strategies to support their own positions.

DEFINING THE CURRICULUM
AND ITS RELATIONSHIP TO INSTRUCTION

The Curriculum Myth

Should the curriculum for exceptional or handicapped students be the same as or different from the curriculum for nonhandicapped students?

Before answering such a question, one should first pause to ask at least the following questions:

How does one define "curriculum"?

Are "same as" and "different from" the only two choices or are they points along a continuum of responses?

Is instruction a concept related to or apart from the definition of curriculum?

Can we really talk about "handicapped students" and "nonhandicapped students" as two sets of individuals distinctly different from one another?

Further development of these major questions should point to implications for addressing the development of the curriculum in regular and special education.

A seemingly obvious but necessary consideration may be whether or not a curriculum exists for nonhandicapped students at the local school district level. In many districts across the country, there is something of a "curriculum myth," that is, that a unified, coordinated course of study, complete with a philosophy, goals, and an evaluation scheme exists. The myth further suggests that there is an articulation between grade levels and that all key stakeholders understand its implementation. More typically, the curriculum is a set of courses based on standards that closely reflect the graduation requirements of the state agency. An inquirer may, in some instances, collect differing responses depending on whether the respondent is a central office administrator or a fifth grade teacher. In short, there is ambiguity and confusion in terms.

Curriculum and Instruction

Curriculum is often viewed as a part of instruction, teaching, and learning, not as a distinctive concept independent of the other three. MacDonald explains, "at the present it is well to recognize that there is no consistently clear distinction in use of much educational terminology." He offers a set of definitions. The curriculum system consists of persons who are a part of a social system that evolves in a curriculum, that is, a plan of action. Mac-Donald agrees that the boundary between curriculum and instruction is the key. He says, "they are essentially two separate action contexts, one (curriculum) producing plans for further action; and the other (instruction) putting plans into action."[2] Using a system perspective, he suggests that the "professionally oriented behavior of individual personality systems, called teachers by society, makes up the acts of teaching." Learning is the "phenomena or behavior that is noted in the performance of the student."[3] Teaching and learning make up the components of the instructional system. The instructional system is a social system, not a personality system. It is the action context within which formal teaching and learning behaviors take place.

Since each system is bounded, as Figure 8-1 illustrates, it excludes the possibility of any of the four areas being included in any other space. MacDonald observes, "traditionally, the tendency has been to include instruction within curriculum, and teaching and learning within the instructional setting. This position is impossible to defend from a systems position."[4]

In summary, then, "teaching is defined as the behavior of the teacher, learning as the change in learner behavior, instruction as the pupil-teacher

FIGURE 8-1   Action Space of Four Systems: Curriculum, Instruction, Teaching, Learning. Source: James B. MacDonald and Robert R. Leeper, eds, *Theories of Instruction* (Washington, D.C.: Association for Supervision and Curriculum Development, 1965), p. 4.

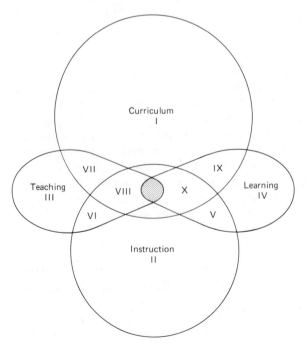

interaction situation and curriculum as those planning endeavors which take place prior to instruction."[5]

In Figure 8-2, Overly specifies the relationship among the four concepts and their relationships to one another in an enlarged system analysis of curriculum, instruction, teaching, and learning. Overly's diagram is a more detailed illustration of how the output of the curriculum system leads to the specification of input into the instructional system. The output of the curriculum system affects both teacher and student alike and, conversely, teaching acts and student performance, combined in his depiction of the instruction system.[6]

An important distinction needs to be made between the terms "curriculum" and "instruction." If we view the curriculum *per se* as the broader course of study, the expectations and values that a district holds for all students, and instruction as the act or practice of teaching students to become independent, then we could generalize that the same expectations hold for the handicapped learner. Even for the severely and profoundly disabled, in spite of their dependency, the curriculum ought to be more "same" and the instruction is the variable that may be more "different."

THE ROLE OF VALUES
IN CURRICULUM DEVELOPMENT

Cultural Determinism

Before moving to a discussion of sameness versus difference in curriculum development and the distinction between types of handicapped or exceptional students, a short description of the primary values that drive curriculum development is in order.

A primary purpose of education has been the transmission of knowledge across generations, transforming a human organism with potential for learning into a social being. This is accomplished as the customary ways of behaving, speaking, and thinking that have accumulated over time in various cultures are acquired and put into practice by the individual. Enculturation establishes the basis for coordinated group activity and is essential for group survival.

It is rare, however, even in technologically simple, small-scale societies, for an individual to learn all there is to know of his or her culture. This is true both because any cultural repertoire is large whereas the individual's capacity to cope with information is limited and selective and because certain individuals are systematically excluded from access to different kinds of knowledge on the basis of their status. Key questions to be asked of the educational process in any society include the following:

> What kinds of knowledge and behavior are shared by virtually all members of a society and are considered *essential* for membership?

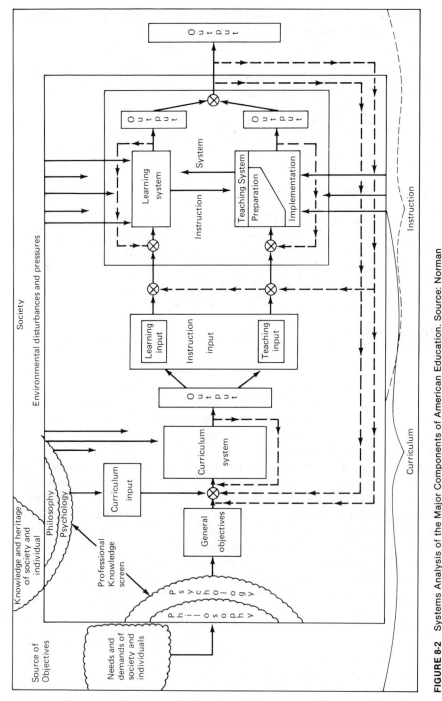

FIGURE 8-2 Systems Analysis of the Major Components of American Education. Source: Norman Overly, "The Development of a System for the Classification of Learner Behavior," Unpublished doctoral dissertation, Ohio State University, 1966.

What kinds of knowledge and behavior are shared by some but not all members of the society and therefore constitute *cultural alternatives?*

What are the criteria for determining what is *appropriate* for individuals within a society and who should learn certain types of knowledge and behavior?

In the United States the major part of each individual's knowledge and behavior falls in the category of "cultural alternatives." Biological and social factors have typically affected what alternatives are presented to whom and under what circumstances. The handicapped, as a class, have joined other historically suspect legal classifications into which students are grouped for learning, such as age, sex, race, measured ability, religious affiliation, and class status.

In classifying students as handicapped, questionable practices of assessment have had a profound impact on the labeling of individuals as retarded, emotionally disturbed, and so on for their education, however appropriately or inappropriately. Classically, education for the retarded, therefore, has historical roots in being "different" with such development by Itard, Seguin, and Montessori. According to Goldstein, the curriculum for the learning disabled was more often the "same" and without any kind of necessary modification.[7]

Minimally handicapped students, on the other hand, whose special learning problems were less apparent and not assessed were often found "in the back rows" of regular classrooms and/or were retained from year to year until they voluntarily dropped out. They experienced their education, never identified as being handicapped, with consequently fewer educational alternatives than they might have deserved. The more severely and profoundly handicapped students have either never been in school or were directed into special classes, separate facilities, or institutions outside of the public school system. As a result, they have often been denied access to educational alternatives and basic enculturating experiences provided for their nonhandicapped peers.

Much rethinking about exceptional student education was a necessary result of litigation and research around the following:

1. Lack of clear evidence showing superior educational achievement among handicapped students taught in special classes and institutions in comparison with those taught in a regular setting
2. Evidence of the harmful social effects of segregation on both sets of students in and out of the "mainstream"
3. Abuses of the special education system in that special programs became "dumping grounds" for behavior problem students and minorities as federal funding for the effort increased
4. Inappropriate discriminatory labeling and testing of children referred and placed in special education programs and the disproportionate numbers of minorities being placed in such classes, resulting in stereotypical behaviors and consequences difficult to "correct"

5. Questionable preconceptions about the abilities, disabilities, and learning styles of the learning disabled and the mentally handicapped in terms of learning potential versus limitations

6. Increased pressure on state and local school districts to be educationally and fiscally responsible for their handicapped population regardless of the handicapping condition or the burden of cost

7. Equal educational opportunity in terms of civil rights, access to programs and facilities, and so on.

Martin argued that P. L. 94-142, the Education for All Handicapped Children Act of 1975, affirmed the rights of the handicapped to a free, appropriate, public education in the least restrictive environment and mandated that IEPs (individualized education programs) for all handicapped students would ensure such rights. With this act, handicapped and nonhandicapped learners would be considered more alike than different and should be so treated in public school.[8]

Klein, Pasch, and Frew believe that special education leadership personnel had an opportunity early to seize the initiative to bring the best from regular and special education together to improve the learning experiences for all children.[9] To date, despite these aspirations, some attempts and few successes can be reported.

A Continuum of Contrasting Cultural Values

Underlying the points of view expressed over time on both the educational status of the handicapped and on what is an appropriate curriculum for handicapped learners are sets of values that might be found along a continuum of pluralistic values as "conservative/pragmatic" on one end and "experimental/egalitarian" on the other.

Some examples of views representing such a values conflict that affect decisions regarding our major curriculum questions are the following:

CONSERVATIVE/PRAGMATIC

Learning capabilities or aptitudes of individuals are largely beyond the capacity of education to change.

Individuals within a society are better able to serve in appropriate roles when tested, labeled, and grouped homogeneously in cost-effective educational and occupational training.

EXPERIMENTAL/EGALITARIAN

Learning capabilities or aptitudes are malleable, dynamic and can be significantly changed by education.

All students must have access to as full a range of educational opportunities as possible for as long as possible because

judgments of aptitude are premature when used early to determine long-range placements

means of measuring aptitude are biased and inadequate

categories underlying such placements have been poorly devised

advances in instructional technology

CONSERVATIVE/PRAGMATIC	EXPERIMENTAL/EGALITARIAN
	may unlock learner potential previously unsuspected.
Human and fiscal resources should be concentrated in improved education for non-dependent persons such that they are then better able to contribute to the improvement of life and society as a whole. This is more cost-effective in that gains are more measurable.	Resources invested in improved education of dependent persons will likely reduce their dependency for a lifetime. Personal and economic benefits accrue for all members of a society in the long run by increasing the number of contributing members and reducing the life-long economic burden of such alternatives as institutionalization.
Individual's responsibilities are to serve and to adapt to society as a whole.	Society's institutions must adjust to facilitate the full educational development of the individual. A society so reformed will benefit from a vastly increased reservoir of human resources.

As will be discussed later in this chapter, there are some obvious ramifications for educating students from this values conflict. While holding high expectations for all students, one must certainly allow for vast individual differences.

As an illustration of the value continuum just presented, three colleagues at Syracuse University published a debate over educating mentally retarded students. Winschel, Ensher, and Blatt argue for an emphasis on different sides of the continuum. Winschel, who proposes that the emphasis in the curriculum should be on "learning to learn," states that educators ought to be advocates for the eradication of retardation. He identifies four cognitive skills that handicapped learners must develop: listening, remembering, reflective behavior, and problem solving. Strategies for developing these skills have been more evident in the research than in practice. Faith in the "malleability of intelligence" demands that these foundation skills be learned even at the expense of the mastery of normalizing skills.[10] Ensher, who stresses a "learning to do" approach, argues that "growth in adaptive behavior in order to achieve the least dependent position possible within school, home, and society" is clearly the purpose of education and that training insufficiently grounded in the practical may be a disservice to the moderately and severely handicapped.[11]

"Learning to be" is the position Blatt advocates; he calls for an "infusion of creative thinking" into the field as well as a willingness to experiment with new and unorthodox methods and materials. For Blatt, both teaching and learning are parts of an ongoing process. "Always, the core is to be, to know who one is and thus to stand for something... the aim always being the comprehension of oneself in a larger context." A curriculum focus leading to increased self-confidence appears to be the primary contribution of Blatt's view.[12]

Burrello, Tracy, and Schultz believe a key issue in this debate, as in the value conflict, is that the consequences of being handicapped are as much the result of a technological failure to transmit knowledge and skills as they are persistent limitations of the individual versus the view that deficits are innate and mostly unrelenting and that, pragmatically speaking, gains are too marginal and too costly to attain through publicly supported educational programs and/or services.[13]

Frew comes close to providing a basis for a synthesis of these value systems in his attempt to bring together regular and special education through curriculum analysis and design.[14] All learning is developmental. His Functional Life Curriculum joins the learning of functional skills to the acquisition of such basic skills as reading, writing, and arithmetic in "the major areas of human activity—sociocultural, economic, political, and personal development."

> The old excuse that we are unsure of the overall potential for achievement will no longer work. The time has come to determine what to teach systematically and to continue instructional sequences as long as the student is learning and applying them appropriately.[15]

The kind of thinking exemplified in his Functional Life Curriculum, together with the movement toward an individualized educational program, suggest that the old distinctions among "academic," "career," "vocational," and "remedial" may be breaking down. By analogy with our perception of children's learning styles, we may come to see these types of curricula as occupying a continuum. They shade into and penetrate one another. Such a view would imply major changes in the way teachers are trained, in the way specialty areas are carved out, and in the way curriculum decisions are made from the top administrative level to the classroom.

If the education of the exceptional student will contribute anything of both immediate and lasting value to education in general, it is the process dimension of curricular decisionmaking, the individual education program planning process. By imposing such a structure, the IEP process allows educators to identify the needs of handicapped students and systematically formulate methods and stipulate resources needed for meeting those needs. It is a tool by which the "whole child" can be reviewed. If all children were able to benefit from such a process, a "whole curriculum" would need to be created as well. In this way, a curriculum could be designed to occupy a continuum with no absolute beginnings or endings and much room for expansion in many directions.

DEVELOPMENT OF STRATEGIES
FOR AN INTEGRATED CURRICULUM

While it is impossible to project all the circumstances around curriculum development or reform movements, we have attempted to describe responses to two general sets of conditions. The first is one where the special education leadership is attempting to build linkages into an already existing curriculum; the second is one where a curriculum reform movement is underway.

Condition No.1: Integrating
into an Existing Special Education Curriculum

Part of the curriculum myth is that the curriculum for all nonhandicapped students is the same, if one is in place. If there is such a curriculum in place, special educators can respond, "show us your curriculum and we'll answer the question of whether it ought to be the same or different for handicapped students." Is "the curriculum" a philosophy statement, for example, is it a course of study which provides for every individual to reach her or his full potential as a learner within the individual school and/or community? Is it the expected teaching curricula or the actual curricula teachers teach within? Is there a textbook series for each defined subject area? Are they used? Is there a continuum of skills for which there is a certain level of minimal competency? Are there criterion-referenced test items for the outcomes suggested? What are the characteristics of the learners who are succeeding in meeting established outcomes? How are they performing, to what degree of success? On the local level, it is a necessary antecedent for the curriculum planner to look at the existing curriculum. The more defined the existing course of study, the more explicit the framework the special educator has with which to work. The less structured the existing curriculum is, the more one can be opportunistic in redefining curriculum needs of handicapped students as part of the regular school statement.

Regardless of the degree of structure, the special education curriculum planner will need to create opportunities for the special education staff to review the curriculum, on a building-by-building basis, its milestones, and criterion-referenced test items if they exist by strand, by course, or grade level.

The special education faculty should validate that the curriculum under review is the one they observe and have to contend with as they attempt to integrate their work with mainstreamed students in regular classrooms with or without significant regular teacher participation. After such a review, the special education faculty should build a set of program descriptions to display how their students fit into the general education curriculum structure, identify critical success indicators, and develop criterion-referenced tests for disabled students moving within special education and between special education and regular education classrooms.

The special education faculty should next begin to build a linkage curriculum that describes the scope and sequences of the content and process linkups. An electronic information processing system should also be developed to document "typical progress" of student's groups by learner characteristics within specified time frames. These data, combined with a description of the instructional strategies used with specific students, represent the beginning of the instructional support system we will describe in Chapter 10. Both the linkage curriculum and the instructional support system can be automated to reduce teacher and/or administrative information processing demands and serve as a means to chart students' progress for all to view. In this way, the microcomputer can be a helpful tool in teacher as well as administrative decision making in the areas of curriculum and instruction.

While this is the first necessary condition for integration and linkage, it is insufficient because the curriculum lacks goals and outcomes for students below a mental age of 5 or 6. Special educators, early childhood specialists, and developmental psychologists need to develop a set of goals and outcomes to guide instruction from birth on, anticipating that few assumptions can be made about learner priorities or deficits for the severely/profoundly disabled student. These "special developers" also need to focus attention on the parent or guardian as primary caregiver, interacting with that child or student. Training programs as well as the curriculum, alternative instructional strategies, criterion-referenced assessment procedures, and a test-retest evaluation strategy are needed to create a necessary and sufficient system of curriculum and instruction. In Figure 8-3, we depict a continuum of curriculum integration between special education programs to the regular curriculum and the degree of special assistance students need as they move through the curriculum from preschool to adulthood.

The K-12 sequence of learning outcomes is primarily cognitively based and is placed in academic strands covering language, math, science, and social studies. Regular teachers need little instructional assistance to meet learner outcomes embedded in the regular curriculum. Special education teachers, however, must identify alternative learner outcomes, consider different measurement criteria, and use a variety of instrumental approaches to teach effectively to the special learning needs of exceptional students. The degree of curricular integration is of less concern as learner needs change. The curriculum actually expands to become more inclusive of affective and psychomotor domains in contrast to a more narrowly defined K-12 curriculum. The two areas of concern are the nature of instruction and the increasing level of support students need to achieve desired learner outcomes. These two concerns interact with the different structures and teachers that make up the regular and special education learning environments.

IEP: An Analog

The individual education planning process is analogous to curriculum planning for the individual student rather than classes of students. A broad set of goals must first be developed. In Figure 8-4, Overly's system analysis of the curriculum component of his earlier portrayal of the education system highlights the series of decisions an IEP planning team should confront to determine if the learner is indeed handicapped and how do his or her characteristics interact with the curriculum for *all* nonhandicapped students. The nature of the goals becomes the basis of a series of other curricular issues, knowledge, inquiry, and the scope and sequences of information desired. This

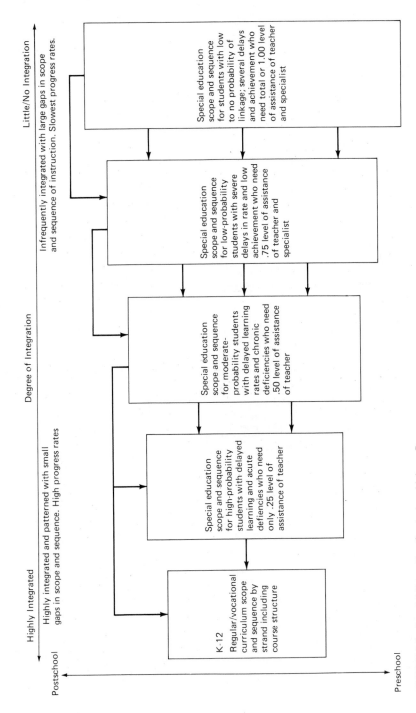

FIGURE 8-3 Special Education Curriculum Linkage Process.

Little/No Integration

Infrequently integrated with large gaps in scope and sequence of instruction. Slowest progress rates.

Degree of Integration

Highly Integrated

Highly integrated and patterned with small gaps in scope and sequence. High progress rates

Postschool

Preschool

Special education scope and sequence for students with low to no probability of linkage; several delays and achievement who need total or 1.00 level of assistance of teacher and specialist

Special education scope and sequence for low-probability students with severe delays in rate and low achievement who need .75 level of assistance of teacher and specialist

Special education scope and sequence for moderate-probability students with delayed learning rates and chronic deficiencies who need .50 level of assistance of teacher

Special education scope and sequence for high-probability students with delayed learning and acute deficiencies who need only .25 level of assistance of teacher

K-12
Regular/vocational curriculum scope and sequence by strand including course structure

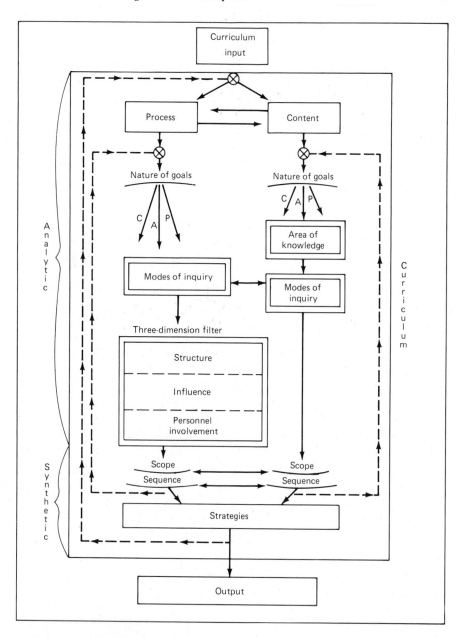

FIGURE 8-4   A Systems Analysis of the Curriculum: A subsystem of the educational system. Source: Norman Overly, "The Development of a System for the Classification of Learner Behavior," Unpublished doctoral dissertation, Ohio State University, 1966.

output becomes the primary input into the instructional system that binds the teacher-learner interaction.

The curricular related task as Overly's diagram suggests is analytic in reference to the IEP. The multidisciplinary committee should reaffirm what goals and values in the curriculum for *all* students pertain to the individual student. The teacher and other supportive staff, such as speech therapists, should then concern themselves with the synthetic task of determining how those selected curricular values and goals are best implemented. As students move into and exit from special education service domains, the regular teaching staff is needed to reassess those original curricular decisions and design still other instructional sequences to assist reentry in their curricular decision making.

Condition No. 2: Curriculum Reform
Is Underway or Nonexistent

We have been making the case that the principles and procedures used to develop, implement, and monitor the curriculum for handicapped students are essentially the same as those in the regular education curriculum. Factors that need consideration are:

The primary trainer or caregiver to the student
The scope and sequence of the curriculum and accompanying milestones
The handicapped students' abilities and disabilities
The environment(s) in which the curriculum is offered
Special technology that may enable special education students to learn the content presented

Administrators responsible for a curriculum for students receiving special education services have a major and important charge: They can be satisfied to be confined by existing curricular models for regular education students and make the necessary modifications *or* they can take a more proactive stance and work with the regular education counterpart(s) to design a fuller and more comprehensive curriculum adaptable for any individual student within the local agency. We have recommended using MacDonald's reconceptualist view of a dual dialectic as a model for reasons cited earlier.

In addition, one should look at the research on school improvement and "effective schools" that is currently an important topic for most curricular planners across the country today.[16,17] In reviewing some of the indicators of effective schools, a number of factors must be considered. Therefore, factors such as positive school climate, strong leadership roles of principals, parent and citizen involvement in the school's operation, recognition of teachers as adult learners, emphasis on evaluation and feedback, and high expectations placed on students for learning offer a springboard for some quality indicators of joint curricular planning for regular and special education. Edmonds also adds a new dimension for excellence, namely, the challenge of improving learning for all students regardless of socioeconomic level. The implication for us here is also improvement regardless of handicapping condition.

Strategies and major considerations for curricular reform and designing new systems should include, but not be limited to, the following questions, organized around five major areas: (1) communication, (2) school climate, (3) staff development, (4) curriculum dimensions, and (5) nature of instruction.

1. Communication
   - What are the existing structures in the LEA for planning for change and improvement of the curriculum?
   - How can the special education administrator best convince the administrative team that such planning and development will benefit the education of all students, handicapped and non-handicapped?
   - How can the community, both parents and citizens, be involved so that they both support the curriculum budget *and* the equal opportunities for handicapped students?

2. School climate
   - Do the people in the schools really view handicapped people as valuable and celebrate the differences rather than lament the obstacles?
   - How can those responsible for curricular development assess climate as a major factor?
   - What is the status of awareness of the handicapped learner and his/her role in the local school setting?
   - What are the expectations of teachers on the part of administrators and board members? What are the expectations of students on the part of teachers and other providers?
   - What is the existing relationship between regular and special education?

3. Staff development
   - What is the level of support for staff looking at curricular change and growth, and for implementing such new strategies?
   - How does the administration value the necessary ongoing development and education of staff as their roles change significantly?
   - What is the financial commitment to improve a staff which in most school systems nationwide is diminishing rather than replenishing?

4. Curriculum dimensions
   - What are the quality indicators by which any curriculum might be judged? And what are some additional indicators needed to evaluate a curriculum which expands to meet the needs of handicapped students?
   - What are state and local mandates and guidelines regarding the curriculum? Are the standards measured by traditional credits or units? By competency statements evaluated locally? By minimal competency testing either statewide or locally designed?
   - What is the function of the school? What is the purpose of the high school diploma?
   - Does the curriculum necessarily begin and end at discrete points or is it a continuum of skills adjusted and expanded for the entrance and exit of different individuals?

- What are the criteria for grade to grade promotion as well as for graduation?
- Is there a difference between a high school diploma and a certificate of attendance or a "special education diploma"?
- Are the graduation requirements such for handicapped students that non-handicapped student with special problems or needs may be discriminated against?
- Does the curriculum allow for a wide variety of options and goals as well as movement within and across strands, grade levels, and courses of study?
- Does the curriculum hold relevant and appropriate offerings for the students' real lives?
- Is there ongoing and adequate assessment and evaluation for all students such that individuals' education is appropriate and growth is measurable or describable?

5. Nature of instruction
   - Are there varying instructional methods and techniques to accommodate the various learning styles and modes of disabled children; such as attention to time on task, use of task analysis, and teaching through different sensory modes apparent?
   - Is the curriculum content appropriate, relevant, and instruction success-oriented for mentally handicapped students?
   - Are there planned activities to allow for the transfer of training to specific environments inside the school and outside?
   - Are there attempts made to survey the environments and communities handicapped students enter after school to determine if any unique characteristics should be included in the curriculum?
   - Are regular education teachers encouraged to consult with specialists to make their classrooms more accessible and programs consequently more attainable?
   - Do we allow for enough movement such that a student is able to succeed in a less restrictive placement after some years in a self-contained classroom.[18]

In working together to create one curriculum that provides for individual differences, it is hoped that administrators will address some of the common problems of communication among audiences, coordination across levels, and the needs of borderline or nonhandicapped students such as "slow learners" who often fall between the cracks of receiving special education services or not and develop a curriculum more flexible and yet dynamic enough to address the function of the educational offerings to all students.

Specific examples of amplification of the aforementioned considerations to be inclusive of handicapped or disabled students are the following:

Extending a continuum of skills to include an earlier set of developmental skills such as gross motor development, feeding, toileting skills, and language development that many handicapped and nonhandicapped students arrive in kindergarten already having acquired

Extending the continuum to include prevocational and vocational skills that are a necessary element in the education of many students in order for them to become successfully independent in the adult community, skills that many non-handicapped students typically postpone until postsecondary education

Expanding the curriculum to include supplemental related services such as speech, psychological, occupational, and physical therapy when such services are needed to benefit or enhance the student's educational program

Substituting such skills as adaptive physical education for regular physical education for physically handicapped students

Providing supplemental Braille and large-print books, auditory trainers, and speech communicators as adaptive vehicles to communication for sensory or neurologically impaired students who were formerly educated separately

Supplementing cognitive retraining programs in computer-based education for cognitively and/or neurologically impaired students who with some bypassing of impaired learning functions by appropriate software can learn the same concepts found in the regular curriculum

These suggestions are intended to help generate still others to consider as one develops a district's staff's potential to make the curriculum more inclusive of handicapped learners. While we have not discussed the private sector, it is clear that one should consider nonschool environments as key teaching and learning stations and, furthermore, consider ways in which to involve local business and commercial leaders to revisit the curriculum. Through such interaction, both parties have much to gain.

NOTES

[1]Edith Beatty, Leonard C. Burrello, Daniel N. Cline, and Michael Cahill, *Issues in Curriculum Development for Special Education* (Bloomington, Ind.: Council of Administrators of Special Education, March 1983).

[2]James B. MacDonald and Robert R. Leeper, eds., *Theories of Instruction* (Washington, D.C.: Association for Supervision and Curriculum Development, 1965), pp. 3-14.

[3]Ibid., p. 3.

[4]Ibid., p. 4.

[5]Ibid., p. 5.

[6]Norman Overly, "The Development of a System for the Classification of Learner Behavior Possibilities," Unpublished doctoral dissertation, Ohio State University, 1966.

[7]Herbert Goldstein, *The Social Learning Curriculum* (Columbus: Charles E. Merrill, 1974).

[8]Edwin W. Martin, "An End to Dichotomous Constructs: A Reconceptualization of Teacher Education," *Journal of Teacher Education,* 25, No.3 (1974), 217-220.

[9]Nancy K. Klein, Marvin Pasch, and Thomas W. Frew, *Curriculum Analysis and Design for Retarded Learners* (Columbus: Charles E. Merrill, 1979).

[10]James F. Winschel, Gail N. Ensher, and Burton Blatt, "Curriculum Strategies for the Mentally Retarded: An Argument in Three Parts," *Education and Training for the Mentally Retarded* 12, No.1 (1979), 26-31.

[11]Ibid., p. 28.

[12]Ibid., p. 30.

[13]Leonard Burrello, Michael Tracy, and Edward Schultz, "Special Education as Experimental Education," *Exceptional Children* (September 1973), pp. 29-34.

[14]Klein, Pasch, and Frew, *Curriculum Analysis and Design for Retarded Learners,* pp. 140-150.

[15]Thomas Frew, personal interview, June 1981.

[16]Ronald Edmonds, "Programs of School Improvement: 1982 Overview" Paper presented at NIE Conference, Michigan State University, 1982.

[17]Larry Cuban, "Transforming the Frog into a Prince: Effective Schools Research, Policy, and Practice at the District Level," *Harvard Educational Review,* 54, No.2 (May 1984), 129-151.

[18]Beatty, Burrello, Cline, and Cahill, "Issues in Curriculum Development for Special Education," pp. 22-28.

CHAPTER 9
CONSTITUENCY
MANAGEMENT

The significant advancements in service policies regarding special education that occurred state by state during the 1970s and early 1980s have undoubtedly altered the type of support needed for such programs. Once access to the school door was assured, a great deal of obvious patron participation was reduced. However, the deluge of national studies and reports on the status of education in the United States, and the data on particular areas of neglect of presumably mandatory provisions, including evidence of gross local variations, suggest that the need for constituent involvement continues. In this chapter, we will highlight the continuing need for an active special educator leadership role in constituency involvement and its implications for program development and maintenance.

Special education leadership personnel, like their counterparts in the rest of the education establishment, are acutely aware of the declining number of community members who have children in schools. The need to demonstrate successful and meaningful educational programs for exceptional students, which lead to more productive and less dependent community members, is critical to continued community support.

The process of administration can be viewed as the management of the various constituencies that make up the social environment of the organization being administered. This view places emphasis on the human relations dimension rather than on the various functions and processes of administration. Different types of organizations can be expected to have different types of persons and groups who relate to and influence the work of the organization. In Chapter 3 we discussed the process of informal power and influence, as it tends to be exercised in relation to special education services. In that context we noted the relevance of consumer groups, professional groups, and social advocacy groups as important sources of informal influence on the system and therefore, on the day-to-day activities of the special education administrator.

However, it should be clear that the nature of these relationships need not be "one way" and that administrators should not function as the passive recipients of whatever influence such groups happen to wield, or as purely reactive agents. Constituency management, on the contrary, implies a process by which the administrator uses knowledge regarding the interests and characteristics of all such constituencies in a *proactive* way to further the welfare of both the organization and those to whom it is dedicated.

A TAXONOMY OF CONSTITUENCY GROUPS

As organizations, public social service agencies (including education) certainly have a set of constituencies that are different from those of other organizations. Special education service agencies can probably be characterized as having particularly varied and potent constituencies. A taxonomy of the relevant groups may be useful to the administrator in analyzing their nature and needs and in planning for their effective management.

One could start from almost any point in classifying the types of constituencies, but certain distinct differentiating attributes stand out clearly. One such dimension includes the "insider-outsider" attribute. Whether an individual or group is inside the organization or outside it makes a significant difference in the manner by which influence is exercised, which, in turn, translates into appropriate managerial behavior. In a similar way, the "generalist-specialist" dimension, the "lay-professional" dimension, the "teacher-administrator" dimension, "instruction-related service" dimension, and the "consumer-provider" dimension can each be identified and analyzed in terms of their implications for constituency management. To capture all of the examples of such a multidimensional model graphically would require a mode of representation beyond the printed page, but a limited schematic diagram may be helpful in illustrating the variables most relevant to the special education administrator. Figure 9-1 is such an illustration.

It should be noted that the choice as to how to classify certain individuals or groups may be arguable. We have considered the local school district, as a legal entity complete with staff and policymakers, to constitute the organization. As such, the groups inside the organization include both professionals, paraprofessionals and laypersons. They include both specialists (those with

ORGANIZATIONAL INSIDERS

	LAY/PARA-PROFESSIONALS	PROFESSIONALS	
	PERSONNEL	GENERALIST	SPECIALIST
Instructional services	Teacher aides	Regular classroom teachers Library-media specialists	Special education teachers Chapter 1 teachers
Related services	Therapy aides	Nurses Social workers Physicians	Psychologists Physical therapists Occupational therapists Speech therapists
Support services	Bus drivers Custodians Food service Secretaries	Principals Curriculum supervisors Business managers	Supervisors Consultants
Policymaking bodies	School board members	Central administrators	

ORGANIZATIONAL OUTSIDERS

	LAYPERSONS	PROFESSIONALS	
		GENERALIST	SPECIALIST
Service providers	Concerned taxpayers Citizens advisory committees	Health agency personnel Social agency personnel Private practitioners	Psycho-educational clinicians Private school personnel University personnel State-operated program personnel State educational agency personnel Regional service agency personnel
Service consumers	Special education parents General education parents		
Policymaking bodies	Legislators State boards Courts	State education agency administrators	State advisory committees

FIGURE 9-1 A Taxonomy of Constituency Groups Relating to the Special Education Administrator.

technical expertise and/or interest in the special needs of handicapped children) and generalists who are involved with all school children. Furthermore, these can be broken down into those who are primarily concerned with instruction versus those who are associated with supportive or related services.

Those outside the organization also include professionals and laypersons in a variety of capacities more or less directly concerned with the special education program. Examples of significant constituency relationships to be handled can be cited, with particular attention to the very different role that the administrator must play with different groups.

TYPES OF ROLES FOR THE SPECIAL EDUCATION ADMINISTRATOR

In an earlier work, we hypothesized five major roles for the current-day special education administrator. These role dimensions have been described as follows:

Advocate.   The special education director may serve as an agent through which services are obtained. Utilizing legal processes and protections, the rights of the client are placed ahead of the interests of the school system when the director is playing this role.

Facilitator-Trainer.   The special education director may be responsible for staff development, providing orientation and technical assistance to both specialists and generalists on issues relating to special service delivery.

Policy Planner.   The special education director may be concerned with the determination of systemic interrelationships affecting special education programs: the development, adoption, and implementation of policies concerning identification of needs, resources, models of organization, and delivery strategies.

Monitor-Evaluator.   The special education director may be responsible for investigating the degree to which others are carrying out their responsibilities, program objectives are being achieved, and individual clients are receiving guaranteed appropriate services.

Program Manager.   The special education director may be directly involved with operational supervision and administration of services. While the degree of management involvement is likely to differ with the varying delivery systems required to meet the full range of severity of student need, the demand for technical management skills is predominant.[1]

The manner in which these varying roles are manifested in the relationships with various groups can be seen as we consider each type of constituency within the proposed taxonomy.

INSIDER CONSTITUENCIES

Among the insider groups, different managerial behaviors are demanded for at least three different types of constituencies. It is difficult to determine which of these may be the more important or the more frequently encountered. It depends on the prevailing situation within the organization, its health, the status of special education program development, and the maturity of the personnel employed. Some of the most prominent groups include the following:

Instructional Services Personnel

With special education teachers and teacher aides, the administrator must be concerned, at a minimum, with monitoring and evaluating the work of these specialists, and with their inservice development. Involvement may also include initial personnel selection, assignment, and retention decisions as well. Although the legal responsibility for evaluating these personnel may be shared with other administrators, primarily building principals, it should be anticipated that the special education administrator will possess the necessary expertise to augment whatever the generalist administrator may do in staff development and evaluation. Since personnel employment contracts must address the question of evaluation and retention decisions (including that of special education personnel) and such personnel may tend to feel that a special educator can better understand the nature of their work, the special education director may be found in a competitive position with the building principal where the interests of special instructional staff are concerned. Depending on the maturity of the special education system and the organization as a whole, relationships with these instructional staff members may take on an advocacy character, where the director must work to support and sell the program and its personnel to the remainder of the school. In a more mature organization, where basic acceptance is established, the issue may be more concerned with qualitative evaluation and the application of specific interventions to improve existing services. In either case, the special instructional personnel make up a key group for which management is essential.

While regular classroom teachers, as a group, would not be considered a part of the special education administrator's constituency, they do have a particular significance for the successful integration of special services within the total system. For this reason, the administrator's role with this group must emphasize advocacy and staff development through inservice training and technical assistance consultation. Where teacher unions or other employee organizations have taken a strong stand on the need for training and other procedures to assure the welfare of their membership in the face of special education policy changes, the administrator may be placed in a position of negotiating between employee groups having partly similar, but significantly differing, interests.

Related Services Personnel

The distinction between specialists and generalists within related services personnel is somewhat arbitrary, since some personnel, such as school psychologists and school social workers tend to be involved with the school population in general, but clearly are disproportionately involved with the subgroup that constitutes the special education population. Others, such as occupational and physical therapist, special education supervisory, and consultant personnel have an unequivocally specialist identity. Each of these subgroups constitutes a comparatively small number of individuals within the organization and is sufficiently specialized frequently to feel isolated and poorly represented where its members' interests are concerned. These personnel can easily feel that their work is being supervised and evaluated by administrators who are unqualified to judge them. In certain instances, this has become an issue for personnel contract negotiation. The special education administrator may qualify as the "least inappropriate" administrator in the organization and fall heir to the task of relating to this group as monitor, evaluator, advocate, and staff development facilitator. In any event, the interests of this group are sufficiently crucial to the successful operation of the special education program that the administrator must maintain a high level of awareness of their practices and problems.

Support Services Personnel

The professional generalists and nonprofessional support personnel in the organization, on the other hand, would not be considered a part of the special education administrator's constituency. However, in certain instances, such individuals and groups can be extremely crucial to successful program operation. The most critical group is probably the building principals', whether formally organized as a negotiating group or not. As approximate peers on the organizational hierarchy with the special education director, and as a group that shares (or competes for) authority over special education personnel and operational management, building principals must be understood and accounted for in the internal organizational relationships. In these relationships, the special education administrator may function primarily as a staff development facilitator, providing technical assistance (or inservice training) to the principals. However, as fellow administrators sharing responsibility for program development and operation, a policy planning role and a monitor-evaluator role may also be negotiated between the special education director and the principals. In a similar way, but to a lesser extent, other central office supervisors and middle-management personnel may constitute a group with which the special education administrator must relate, primarily over matters of curriculum and resource allocation. Again, a policy planning role would seem to be predominant in these relationships.

Nonprofessional support personnel within the organization may also demand a particular type of management by the administrator. Personnel operating the transportation system can be expected to have crucial influence of the operation of a special education program. They, therefore, have a significant need for inservice training that can be provided by personnel with special education expertise. To a lesser (but still significant) degree, custodians, secretaries, food service personnel, and other individuals who support the operation of the school system also must be considered when staff development facilitation and advocacy activity is exercised by the special education administrator.

Policymaking Bodies

The final group of organizational insiders that may be considered a constituency of concern to the special education program consists of both professionals and laypersons. The major personnel of the system's central administration and the school board, from one perspective, may be considered the most important constituency. It is this relatively small group that has the power to set policy and thereby determine the overall status of the special education program for the system. Although strongly influenced by external legal mandates and social pressures, this group still maintains the authority to shape many aspects of the program and therefore may be the group that the special education director must concentrate on most carefully yet assertively in the exercise of the advocacy and policy planning roles. The resource allocation control of policy groups alone makes communication and relationship maintenance with these groups of primary importance.

OUTSIDER CONSTITUENCIES

If the local school district is considered the major organizational unit for special education service delivery, then organizational outsiders consist of a wide variety of groups concerned with either the receipt or provision of service. These groups each call for particular relationship handling by the special education administrator, which can be portrayed as follows:

Service Providers

Since a major portion of the necessary special education services must be procured from professional agencies beyond the local school district, the satisfactory negotiation of relationships with these agencies is a crucial issue. As in the case of professionals inside the system, these agencies and the individuals working in them may be either generalists or specialists who are concerned exclusively with the needs of handicapped students. Furthermore, there is a variety of public and private units comprising the total service system. The optimal choice of whether a particular service for a given child should be provided by the local education agency (LEA) directly, or by a public regional agency, a state operated program, a university-affiliated facility, or a private school or clinic depends on communication and joint participation in total service planning. It should not be a matter of competition, but rather a complete examination of the particular needs of those to be served and the capacities of each unit of the service system. Interagency service agreements must be negotiated to implement plans in a manner that maximizes opportunity for the children and takes cognizance of cost-effectiveness considerations.

Certain agencies, such as general health and social service departments of local and state governments, have obligations and interests that cut across the total population and, therefore, cannot be expected to have the singular perspectives regarding the needs of handicapped students that are predominant in the thinking of the special education administrator. However, the crucial nature of certain related services for such children, and the probability that agencies outside the LEA may be responsible (or accessible) for support, lends major importance to harmonious and cooperative interaction for which the special education director may be the key facilitator.

Also falling within the general category of service provider, though in an entirely indirect sense, are the concerned taxpayers and citizens of the community whose votes are responsible for the authorization of local policies and funds. The presence of quasi-official advisory committees from time to time extends the potency of this school-community relationship. Efforts at enhancing partnerships between schools and business, as well as other elements of the community, may further accentuate the need for the administrator of special education to be able to explain and "sell" the merits of existing programs and demonstrate the need for change and improvement when called for. In all of these relationships with service providers outside the organization, the program advocate, policy planner, and general program manager role would seem to be centrally involved.

Service Consumers

In working with other constituencies, both inside and outside the organization, a major ally of the special education director may be the parents of handicapped children, individually or in organized groups. But a successful alliance depends upon the administrator being able to balance the interests and agendas of these consumers with those of the service providers and policymakers. The administrator can turn to this constituency when seeking advise, testing the viability of possible changes, and enlisting support. But the dependability of this kind of input can be assured only if the consumers have first been kept well informed and have been shown that their interests are taken seriously. There must be an established practice of involvement that is more than a mere token.

Service consumers may perceive the director in the LEA to be a true advocate for their needs, or they may only see another organization representative who is looking out for the financial welfare of the system or the comfort of its personnel. It may be necessary at times to raise to the surface the inherent value dilemmas that confront decisionmakers when the interests of one constituency are clearly different from (and often in conflict with) another's. Conflict can be used to make clear an important policy issue. However, the management of conflict—keeping it from blowing the lid off the system—is also a critical consideration.

In this respect, it must be recognized that the parents of children who are *not* in need of special education also constitute a group who have interests and that their interests may be perceived as being jeopardized by the growth of special education services. Competition for limited resources may very well set up a major challenge for the special education director to negotiate, in order to avoid having one (majority) consumer group placing constraints upon what another (minority) group wants and needs. The appearance of a higher level of "rights" provided to the parents of handicapped children through the instrument of the IEP and other procedural safeguards establishes parents who *do not* enjoy such advantages as a potentially opposing constituency. Dealing with this situation calls for a public information dissemination effort that can be considered an extension of the advocacy and trainer-facilitator role.

Policymaking Bodies

The major policymaking bodies outside the LEA include the state level legislatures, lay boards of education, state agency administrators, and courts. These forces must be understood, communicated with, and targeted for information regarding the needs of children and the goals of the special education service system. State advisory committees specifically authorized for the interests of handicapped children are an additional constituency that can and should serve as a mediating agent between special education administrators and the general policy groups. Such committees may transmit information in either direction and thereby exert influence between those who determine policy and those who execute the operations. Control of the agenda in these committees may have a significant impact on issues addressed and decisions made. Representation of special education administrator groups will usually be provided on such official state advisory committees, and it is important for the administrator to be familiar with these channels of communication and influence, whether through organized administrator associations or as a concerned individual. Aside from such committee activity, the opportunity to testify at open hearings convened by legislatures or by state boards of education is a frequent occurrence that local administrators must seize to promote their interests.

COMPARATIVE ROLE EXPECTATIONS

It can be assumed that perspectives regarding the role played by special education administrators may vary across key observers and participants within the local school district setting. An attempt to test the validity of our hypothesized roles was executed in a study by Anastasio,[2] in which a major question was the degree of consensus among and within groups of superintendents, principals, and directors regarding the role expectations for director of special education. In this study, a sample of 480 practitioners made up of an equal number superintendents, principals, and directors within New York State responded to an instrument that rated the degree to which each task (from a list of 43 items) was "essential to the role."

The results indicated very little between group variance, suggesting that each type of respondent had a largely similar view of the director's role, as presented by the task items on the instrument. Each group saw the facilitator-trainer role as least essential. Directors and principals saw the policy planner role as most essential, closely followed by the monitor-evaluator role. For superintendents, this order was reversed, but again by a very close margin.

Of perhaps greater significance in this study, a factor analysis of the instrument showed only three factors as clearly emerging and accounting for 87 percent of the total variance. The most clearly discerned factor, comprised of 12 items (accounting for 44.5 percent of the variance), included tasks most closely associated with *facilitator-trainer* activities. This would suggest that, although all types of respondents considered the facilitator-trainer role as originally defined by the instrument to be *least essential*, it was also the role that stood out most clearly when restructured by factor analysis to include a few additional tasks that had been originally assumed to belong to other categories.

A second factor, accounting for an additional 28.8 percent of the variance, encompassed 14 task items that readily fit the *policy planner* construct. While the first two factors were clearly similar to the theoretical constructs, the third factor to emerge was quite different and encompassed 11 items that had originally been identified with the monitor-evaluator, advocate, and policy planner constructs. Inspection of these items made clear that they addressed the issue of guaranteeing legal rights, that is, developing due process procedures, providing statements that guarantee the right of all handicapped children to a free and appropriate public education, and implementing legislation. Therefore, this new factor, accounting for another 13.7 percent of the variance, was labeled *legal rights guarantor*.

When the factor analysis was broken down for each respondent group separately, a somewhat different pattern emerged. While in the perceptions of directors themselves the facilitator-trainer factor was most prominent, and legal rights guarantor second, for superintendents this order was reversed. In addition, for principals' perceptions of the directors' role, the policy planner and legal rights guarantor factors appeared to merge, so that two new factors resulted. The most prominent of these, accounting for 45.8 percent of the variance, could be best described as an *external policy advocate* in that it emphasized tasks concerned with persons outside the system. The second factor, accounting for 25.2 percent of the variance, was labeled *internal procedural planner* since it focused on work within the system, setting up procedures for monitoring and guaranteeing safeguards and services.

The major finding of this study is the appearance of more commonality of expectations for the director among the three groups of personnel than had been anticipated. The clarity of the facilitator-trainer role reinforces previous observations regarding the technical specialist view of special education administrators. The emergence of the policy planner role as an important one in the perception of all respondents suggests a shift, or maturation, of the role from the technical, instructionally related one to a broader, more conceptually based, policy role. The apparent differences in perceptions or expectations, while not extreme, would seem to reflect the particular perspectives of the other administrators. Superintendents clearly saw the predominant role of the director as guaranteeing legal rights for the handicapped, and principals appeared to place emphasis on the external advocacy activity of the director.

The relationships between the special education director and the various constituencies are also affected by the view that other significant professionals hold of their own role in the special education system. In addition to the director, the principal is probably the major person whose role would seem to be centrally involved in administrative functions.

THE PRINCIPAL'S ROLE IN SPECIAL EDUCATION

The principal's responsibility for special education service delivery has been considered in a number of contexts. One of the most thorough analyses of the role of various personnel in administrative matters was presented in the manual developed by the Special Education Policies Project conducted by the Council for Exceptional Children.[3] This *SEAP Manual* was developed from information collected from a broad sample of administrators in LEAs and intermediate education agencies and resulted in a responsibility matrix that defined 27 operational and decision-making functions. The matrix assigned either primary or support levels of responsibility for each function to one or more of the 11 personnel who were presumed to be involved in special education, including building principals. In this matrix, principals were assigned a primary responsibility for 9 of the functions and support responsibility for

12 others, which constitutes an involvement in 78 percent of the functions. However, none of the functions was assigned *solely* to principals, suggesting that in the judgment of those contributing information to the matrix, principals should not exercise *exclusive* control over any of the functions. This judgment, therefore, implies that principals should abandon the traditional line authority in dealing with functions that take place within their buildings.

In view of these observations, Lietz and Towle report a study in which the opinion of elementary and secondary principals was solicited, regarding their role with special education.[4] The sample of 32 consisted of officers of large city school administrator associations and thereby represented a significant constituency. The principals ranked their real involvement and what they considered to be the ideal involvement in each of the functions, and these were compared with the level of involvement implied by the *SEAP Manual*. The results indicated that principals *desired* more responsibility than they *currently experienced* in 26 of the 27 functions listed in the *SEAP Manual*. Furthermore, they desired more responsibility than the *Manual* recommended in 10 of the 27 functions. There was general agreement between the principals and the special educators whose opinions constituted the source of the designations in the Manual, with respect to the principals' role in the five top ranked functions. However, the principals also suggested primary or support responsibilities for four functions for which the special educators had indicated no responsibility for the principal. Those functions included counseling, liaison with human service agencies, home visitation, and control of special education expenditures.

In summary, these respondents, who were principals themselves and also were leaders in principals' organizations, wanted principals to have more responsibility for planning, coordinating, and evaluating special education services and to maintain their current responsibilities for providing direct services to handicapped children, such as counseling, screening, and evaluating. It was noted that these preferences might be due to the tendency in most large systems for decisions about such matters to be made by superintendents, central office staff, and boards of education with little input from building-level administrators. Further, the staffing, programming, and procedural changes necessary to the implementation of new special education policies can be expected to have an unsettling effect at the building level, causing principals to feel that things are out of their control. It was, therefore, suggested that some increase in responsibilities for school principals appeared to be justified. However, it was also recognized that such increases might generate conflict between the specialists and general administrators. "Conversely, an opportunity to develop tighter interfacing among the staff's responsibilities for serving the handicapped could be created, depending on how well roles are understood and on the effectiveness of communication between the administrators and staff."[5]

The results of this study certainly emphasize the need for clear role definition for principals and for teamwork in facilitating the smooth sharing of responsibility. The need is particularly evident as we examine relationships among constituency groups, since principals are not only a major group with which the special education director must deal, but as such are key actors in all other constituency group interactions. That is, successful constituency group management for the director may well depend upon first managing successful interrelationships with principals.

NOTES

[1]Jean T. Anastasio and Daniel D. Sage, "Role Expectations for the Director of Special Education," Paper presented to the American Educational Research Association, New York City, March 1982.

[2]Jean T. Anastasio, "The Role of the Special Education Director: Expectations of Incumbents, Superintendents, and Principals" (unpublished doctoral dissertation, Syracuse University, 1981).

[3]Scottie Torres, *Special Education Administrative Policies Manual* (Reston, Va.: Council for Exceptional Children, 1977).

[4]Jeremy J. Lietz and Maxine Towle, "The Principal's Role in Special Education Services," *Educational Research Quarterly,* 4 (Fall 1979), 12–20.

[5]Ibid., p. 18.

CHAPTER 10
DECISION
SUPPORT SYSTEMS

Selection of technology as a prime management concern for special education leadership personnel has three bases. First is the amount of data involved in assessing, tracking, and placing eligible students into special services. Second is the consistent call for more and more data to support the management and continuation of programs and services to disabled students. Third, and equally compelling, is the need for information to help teachers become more instructionally effective in their classrooms and consultative activities with regular education personnel.

After a short status report on computer uses, we shall move to consider how these two needs—management and instructional decision making—can best be supported. Planning, implementing, and determining a set of policies to guide computer usage in these two areas concludes our discussion of the use of technology in special education.

THE STATUS OF TECHNOLOGY
IN SPECIAL EDUCATION

Management Uses

At the request of the Council of Administrators of Special Education (CASE), Burrello, Tracy, and Glassman in 1982 led a current use study of computer technology in special education. This study was commissioned to ascertain directions and the type of support needed to assist local school personnel in the design and use of technology for management purposes.[1]

The CASE study was based upon the responses from 348 managers from 48 states. A total of 163 replied that they were either actively using or designing computer management systems while over 185 were interested and wanted assistance in the design and selection of appropriate systems to meet their emerging needs.

An overwhelming majority of current users (94 percent) reported that they were using computer systems to control data flow, maintain records, and produce reports. A much smaller percentage (less than 20 percent) indicated other uses for planning and forecasting events, such as revenue from federal and state sources.

Descriptive information on the current status of students has been the primary output of computer systems requested and distributed by special education managers. The most frequently mentioned student data system was the individualized educational program (IEP), developed in response to teacher concerns about planning process demands. Paperwork and preparation time away from instruction are the chief complaints registered by teachers. Qualitative information, as suggested by Ragghianti and Miller, is now becoming more requested in response to queries about the cost of special education and quality of the programs being delivered, but there is little indication that these types of decisions are being supported by a computer mediated process. The type of quality information that will assist administrators in their response to questions of quality and cost of special education include

1. Relationship between student progress and type of placement, type of intervention, type and severity of the handicapped condition
2. Relationship of age of entry into special education and number of years of services needed, type of placement, and number of years in special education
3. Relationship between vocational education and level of independent living skills, job placement, and job success
4. Cost per unit of service and cost per time allotment for each service: staff time distribution for direct versus indirect services, staff time distribution by program area, comparison of expenditure breakdown for various programs[2]

Notably absent from these data is the need for measuring progress through any curriculum and/or basic competency structure. Apparently, few special education managers interact as end users within microcomputer environments in educational settings. We believe, however, that as more powerful software tools are being developed to assist and enhance managerial judgment at the middle-management level, this will change. Planning and monitoring applications will demand more managerial-level participation in modeling the variables that managers can best define.

The hardware and software being used were described and categorized by type and function. Hardware was increasingly moving to the microlevel, by nearly 2 to 1 in the CASE sample (N = 100), followed by mainframes (N = 57) and minicomputers (N = 25). Networking micros to mainframes and minis is apparently increasing. Few respondents hired computer service companies (N = 5).

In terms of software, single-purpose versus multipurpose use was the overwhelming choice of administrators in the sample. Software was either purchased off the shelf (68 percent) or developed (80 percent) by programmers to perform single functions like student tracking and federal program counting, producing psychological reports in a common format, and for other word processing applications. The multipurpose functions include business accounting and filing and statistical analysis packages.

Future software applications include assessment of students and scoring of tests, compliance monitoring, and expanded business functions such as inventory, billing for tuition, and revenue tracking.

To summarize the current status of use in special education management, administrators' responses were analyzed in terms of a series of six categories to evaluate their software development and purchase. These categories seem to underscore their current and future investment in computer technology:

Efficiency	Computer systems produce more information with fewer resources.
Control	Monitoring of programs and services is enhanced.
Accessibility	Information is readily available and quickly retrieved and redundancy is reduced.
Accuracy	Data can be updated easily to ensure current status.
Flexibility	System allows changing data elements without reinputing data as needs or requests for information change.
Speed	Produces reports in a timely fashion.

Administrators, however, remain cautious. Technical and managerial considerations demand close scrutiny while either building or expanding current capabilities. Both sets of considerations are listed here:

TECHNICAL CONSIDERATIONS	MANAGEMENT CONSIDERATIONS
Initial and expanding development time and costs	Staff resistance to change
Procedures for updating and insuring accuracy of information	Staff fear of technology itself
	Staff training needs
Dependability of equipment	Expectations for hardware
Availability of equipment	Expectations for software
Availability and utility of appropriate integrated software	Recruitment and retention of quality programmers

These considerations are influenced by public opinion and policy as well as by technological advancement. The special education leadership is planning today for tomorrow's instructional application(s) and networking multiuse groups who need a common student data base.

Instructional Uses

Clearly, instructional uses of computer technology are predominant in the minds of school boards, superintendents, and school patrons. The rush to computer-mediated instruction in special education has been no different. Hofmeister lists a number of applications related to and directly involved with individualized instruction. The current hardware and software applications include:

> Specialized pupil services, such as, vocational guidance and academic diagnostic and prescriptive activities
>
> Testing procedures, both individual and group, through optical scanning systems and individual "on-line" testing
>
> Computer-assisted instruction, including drill and practice, interactive video tutorial activities, simulation training, and academic gaming
>
> Computer literacy and science training, including computer language training and the technical skills involved in building and maintenance of computers
>
> Professional development and staff training through formal computer assisted instruction and informal experiences with computers[3]

Hofmeister goes on to say that instructional software, while expanding rapidly, has a long way to go:

> Special education pupils are often "special" because of their inability to learn easily from the haphazard structure of the environment. In order to teach concepts to special education populations, we need to have on hand a rich reservoir of examples and nonexamples of the concepts we are teaching. These examples and nonexamples need to be carefully assembled, carefully matched, and carefully managed. The management and selection of these examples and nonexamples is a complex task well suited to the memory capacities and interactive responsiveness of the computer.[4]

While there may be many benefits, little research on effects of microcomputer interaction and handicapped pupils has been reported. Some computer assisted instruction applications that have been reported include Carman and Kosberg,[5] Cartwright and Hall,[6] and Hasselbring.[7] Hofmeister cautions that six factors may hinder reaching the expectations that others hold. First, *computer access for handicapped pupils* may be thwarted by some who believe that the investment may bear little success. Second, for the many students with reading disabilities, *educational software* that presents most material in a textual form will cause problems. Third, the *mode of presentation* may also be inappropriate, in spite of computer developer claims to the contrary. Some pupils' needs will conflict with what computer software can do efficiently. Fourth, investment in the computer to *solve problems that are still undefined* will reduce our energy and the perceived value of the technology in other more relevant areas. Fifth, *physical individualization and social needs* may be neglected, and some move to provide computers at home may further isolate students who need peer and social interaction. Sixth and last, Hofmeister contends that the *instructional fragmentation* between the regular and special education curriculum frustrates mainstreaming efforts. We would add a seventh factor, *accountability efforts of special education administrators.*[8] The scope and sequence of curriculum content disrupts the communication between staff thereby hinders timely placement of student into regular programs. It also limits the opportunity to measure progress against special education student peers in regular programs.

Two exceptions to the foregoing have been reported by Bennett and Thormann. Bennett has reported the use of videodisk simulations with mentally retarded students that develops social skills.[9] Thormann reported that Oregon's 208 special units were beginning to use computers for drill and practice, academic gaming, and simulation training. Over 70 percent of the teachers sampled indicated that computer use was a motivating factor in significant gains in student self-esteem.[10]

To summarize, instructional applications hold great promise and many have already born fruit. The future, while bright, is filled with technical, social, and organizational problems that could hinder gains on behalf of handicapped students. The litany of pitfalls have been repeatedly identified. But research is well on the way to helping us move carefully and profitably to use technology in our instructional effort with the exceptional student.

BUILDING AN EDUCATIONAL DECISION SUPPORT SYSTEM

With this status report as a backdrop, we proceed to discuss management and instructional applications that are integrated into a model described by Burrello, Tracy and Bostrom, known as an educational decision support system (EDSS).[11]

The notion of a decision support system (DSS) was introduced in business literature as an alternative to management information systems (MIS). With the advent of microcomputers, the manager as enduser is more readily able to access and manipulate information for decision making. Remote, centralized data processing personnel were often unable to dissaggregate data in time to meet the needs of middle and upper management. MIS are better able to handle information for routine, structured, decision-making tasks. DSS were being developed to relate to more semistructured decision making tasks in the manager's everyday world. In this context, the concept of DSS was born.[12, 13, 14]

For our purposes here, we define a DSS as a set of microcomputer mediated systems designed by the enduser to support critical decisions of importance to them. An enduser can be a student, teacher, or administrator. DSS planners require extensive enduser participation in the design, development, and implementation of the system applications. The enduser is both creator and interactive user of the systems. The DSS should be highly flexible and facilitate the building of other applications through interaction. Ultimately, the utility of the system lies in its perceived value to the enduser and his or her capacity to leverage decisions of importance.

We believe that the introduction of DSS in educational organizations can provide an opportunity to restructure the schools to focus learning outcomes and the means to decentralize support to the individual teacher and building administrator. The focus of support is to assist the educational leader in the deployment of resources to support students and teachers. From the student-driven DSS, teachers and building level administrators can both better allocate their attention and efforts in the daily operations of the school and still provide the district leadership with the data they need to make annual tactical plans and long-range strategic plans to guide their boards of education into the future.

Student Decision Support Systems

The goal of public education is not only the acquisition of basic literacy but the development of skills that increase the decision-making and problem-solving behavior of the student. Academic, personal, and social experiences are combined with problem identification, resource identification and acquisition, problem-solving, and goal-seeking skills that are prerequisites to competency in an information society. A student driven decision support system allows the student to describe "what is" and "what might be," and determine the "what ifs" that affect the alternative futures that he or she may wish to pursue. The first type of decision support, therefore, is tied to supporting students in developing basic skills in decoding and encoding information.

The student support system is also to assist students in their goal-seeking behavior. This type of support is designed to help students formulate outcomes and set realistic criteria to measure their own progress. Another application of student support is to assist students as they engage in problem solving in their current and future settings. The emerging technology also enlarges the student learner's world view and facilitates the individual student's access to and application of information to personal, social, and other problem solving contexts, such as maintaining personal finances and planning the use of leisure time. In the future, information can be accessed electronically by the student by plugging into commercial data banks.

Networking within interactive information systems also allows student-to-student interactions as well as teacher-to-student interactions. Again, networking enables the horizontal link to occur and restructures the hierarchical relationship among the school, family, and student. The networking begins by creating a self-help oriented environment driven by the individual student's decision support system. Networking will reduce the threat of depersonalization by actually providing a unique occasion to link learner to learner, thus creating another opportunity to support technical skill training in a human network of interaction: "In the networking environment, rewards come by empowering others, not by climbing over them."[15]

Instructional Decision Support Systems

While an individual student-driven system serves as the basis of a restructured educational system, other supportive systems are needed for teachers, administrators, and policymakers. The second of these in the cascade of technical support systems has its focus on instruction. The instructional decision support system (IDSS) includes our current knowledge base of best practices in the instruction of basic skills, problem identification, problem specification, designing and selecting decision rules, accessing and using data banks, goal setting, and creating models of student learning and selecting learning interventions.

This type of decision support system will enable teachers to depict, through a modeling process, the individual student learning style and use this data to match and adapt instructional approaches to individual learner needs, select instructional resources to reinforce learnings, and provide evaluation milestones for feedback on student performance. These types of electronic support systems are known as expert systems. Prototypes exist in medical diagnosis.

The instructional decision support system would be open ended to allow for additional inputs and the sharing of teacher-to-teacher ideas and approaches to facilitating student growth. It should be tied to an emerging expert system that would assist teachers in matching resources to individual student learning styles. An added benefit, we believe, is that a technology of teaching should emerge that will better define the teaching profession as a unique discipline with a distinct contribution to make to the community at large. "The technology of the computer allows us to have a distinct and individually tailored arrangement with each of thousands of teachers and students."[16]

In addition, the technology could be used to support teacher-to-teacher interactions and accumulate teacher suggestions on selected learner problems. Colleagues reviewing an electronic bulletin board could send (via electronic mail) their suggestions to the colleague in need. These electronic communication systems also serve as a modeling device that help cooperating parties to interact more effectively and use one another as resources.

Curricular Decision Support System

The curricular decision support system is a dynamic data base that links the schools with the external world. This data base would also be open ended and facilitate the updating of usable knowledge. Its overseers would look to other data banks that expand the range of instructional offerings available to students at any one time.

The curriculum decision support system serves as a window for school patrons, state and local government, and the business community to view the schools. It provides the framework to measure the relevance of educational offerings and observe the fit between the changing realities of the world of work and student performance.

The curricular decision support system orders the scope and sequence of knowledge and skills in a developmental fashion. The knowledge and skills are listed as outcome statements that have corresponding criterion-referenced test items attached to the statements. They fall into three broad categories: cognitive, affective, and psychomotor outcome domains.

The local curriculum data bank provides the basis for individual student planning. Appropriate strategies and tactics of instruction are the responsibility of the student's teacher(s) to select and implement. These strategies, tactics, and resource banks make up the interacting instructional support system. The two are linked by the periodic assessment of student progress and planning the next set of appropriate outcomes to guide student planning.

It also is a means to bring different world views and national- and state-validated best practices into the local school district. Advances in communication technology will create the opportunity to validate local curriculum policies and practices within a larger world view. Here again, developing commercial and government-supported data banks will provide local educational agencies with historical and contemporary information by which to plan their own curriculum.

Finally, it provides the access and ownership the community needs to identify with and influence the direction of their public schools. This support system also links the general community with the professional community of educators it charges to instruct their children. With sufficient lead time to change or adjust instructional practices, this window on the schools will help increase public confidence in the schools and the teaching profession.

Policy Decision Support Systems

The policy decision support system (PDSS) is also a dynamic data base that contains past, as well as current, policy that governs the conduct of all participants in the state and local education agency. This decision support system allows the public to view the policies that bound educational practices. It would also suggest the policy options that new curricular or instructional practices might demand as changes are made to update the offerings to students. It would also provide insights into the governance behavior of their elected representatives and offer a means to react to policy options before they take effect. For example, a school board might want to sample public opinion regarding the redistricting of students from two high schools to one or switching from a K-6-3-3 pattern to a K-5-3-4 pattern. The policy decision support system would allow for community values assessments and a gauge of the impact of such values on alternative redistricting plans.

The PDSS for top management and boards of education is primarily geared to helping both groups adjust to environmental and external forces that affect district programs and progress as well as helping determine the key variables that impede progress. With this information they can reallocate resources to get programs and building units back on course, set new courses, or maintain their present one if the analysis yields satisfactory results. The DSS is a tool that can enhance the collective judgment of board and management by providing profiles or snapshots of performance captured during implementation of accepted student-, teacher-, building-, and district-level plans.

Summary

In summary, we have been depicting a scenario that high technology in an information society might bring to public education. Technology, like special education, however, is but one subsystem that interacts interdependently with three other subsystems, namely people, structure, and tasks. All four make up the complex human organization of public education.

In this framework, principals and middle managers are primarily engaged in scanning building-level performance and reports of teacher and student progress toward organizational and individual outcomes. They also can use resource expenditures and estimates of time to monitor progress. Their data analyses are used to create new resource configurations within their current allocations as well as to project still needed resources. They can create new configurations within and between building- and district-wide units. Their planning is essentially tactical rather than strategic or logistical.

Top managers or superintendents can use the bottoming up of data bases to support both policy decisions as well as to project and secure needed resources to facilitate staff and student outcomes. These data bases can serve as a yardstick to measure progress to date. Progress measures allow local boards to modify current or set new directions or maintain their current courses: "Strategic planning is worthless—unless there is first a strategic vision."[17]

It is our belief that district planning should be opportunistic and proceed from a strategic plan of one's technological use. We also believe that what is appropriate for instructional and individual student decision making on a daily basis may have little relevance to higher levels of management.

Figure 10-1 illustrates the articulation between managerial and teacher responsibility to collect information and process it for planning, evaluation, and reporting purposes. While each decision support system is conceptualized as a building block to the next, they are not necessarily cumulative. Planning, design, redesign, choice, and feedback represent the recycling processes personnel in school organizations engage in while creating climates of learning

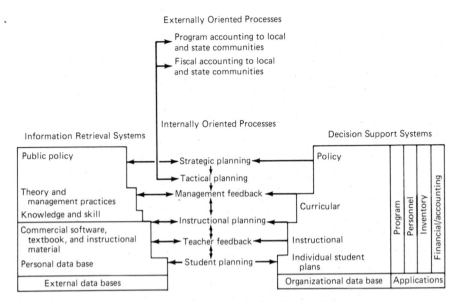

FIGURE 10-1   A Framework for Decision Support Systems in Educational Organizations.

and growth. External to the school organization are information retrieval data banks commercially developed and accessible by subscription or individual use rates. Students, teachers, and managers would have access to these data bases, depending upon planning or implementation needs, through package programs or on-line query capabilities using a telephone modem or individual software packages.

PLANNING FOR THE INTRODUCTION
OF DECISION SUPPORT SYSTEMS
IN EDUCATIONAL MANAGEMENT

The 5 vignettes that follow illustrate a part of the dilemma of planning and introducing the use of electronic technology into the management of public school systems.

> I bought a TRS 80 computer in 1979, I plugged it in 1980, I bought software in 1981, and in 1982, I found out my system was incompatible with the industry standard. Now what am I going to do?
>
> My school system bought 40 Apple's this year, inspite of no money with Proposition Two-and-one half. The computers are locked up because no one knows how to use them, administrators or teachers.
>
> We got an IBM 5650. We have reduced the paperwork of our teachers a hundredfold. We can tell the state anything they want to know about an individual

student, we can produce classlists for teachers, but we can't aggregate the data for planning, supervision, or evaluation of our programs.

My school district has had a mainframe for some time. The district first got a payroll program, then a budgeting and accounting program going, and student scheduling program. But I can't get anything out of it without getting DP to write special routines for me. Now I have a micro and I still can't get DP to help me access the mainframe.

The assistant superintendent launched a comprehensive management information system planning effort in response to a court order. We spent two years identifying data elements needed to complete the court order reports. It was a highly centralized planning effort. Everyone from individual teachers to the superintendent and board members participated. After two years, we still didn't have a management information system that could respond to the the court order.

This part of this chapter outlines the planning approaches that are available to assist district leadership in the introduction of microcomputers into school management. Taylor has prepared an overview of four approaches to planning the introduction of information management systems in social agencies.[18] The four planning approaches he identifies are

1. Automated record systems
2. Incremental
3. Total system development (MIS)
4. Modular

The first two vignettes (at the opening of this section) are really examples of nonplanning; the remaining three correspond to planning approaches 1-3. The modular approach is probably superior as a planning method to bring electronic technology into the management of the public schools. It is essentially an eclectic approach that combines key elements of incremental and MIS approaches.

The modular approach combines the best features of the incremental and MIS approaches. This planning process "uses the incremental, step by step strategy of system design, but each step is guided by a master plan."[19] This approach allows for the development of needed additional modules when necessary, but most important, the development occurs in relation to the existing modules. This enables the end users to access a common format of files—or an interactive data base. It is this feature that makes modular development more like an integrated MIS.

The other major feature of the modular approach is that it remains open for change, enhancement, or termination without jeopardizing the remaining system modules. Repetitious data collection, entry, and storage are eliminated since all modules interact with one another. The major requirement and limitation is that all file structures must be compatible. Many of today's data-based management systems allow the user to build several applications, all of which may be interconnected.

If a district leadership group saw an EDSS as a framework for a comprehensive plan, we would suggest a student referral and placement module first. These two modules can be designed and be up and running within two to three months as opposed to an IEP module, which must be embedded in a larger curriculum DSS. An IEP/CDSS demands much more initial development time and carries an uncertain risk regarding staff acceptance.

Arthur Anderson contrasts system development costs in four phases within two separate approaches (Figure 10-2). The fourth-generation approach is essentially the modular approach described here.[20] It allows developers and end users to examine costs within each phase of development, to change phase development time, and to keep risks within management's control; it is obviously more flexible than traditional approaches.

It is our belief that modular planning combines the best features of other planning approaches without sacrificing relevance and speed of development. It offers the developer a flexible and efficient method of development and introduction into the workplace. This planning approach, however, must occur within a larger framework of the organization. It must attend to the organizational structure, climate, tasks, and personnel. It must also attend to the current methods and communication norms that exist within and between units. With this information, the planner(s) can grasp the scope and nature of the organization and its predisposition to change and accommodate emerging technology.

The Modular Action Planning Model

The action planning model is so named because it should yield results at each step in the process of planning. Figure 10-3 presents the action planning model that fits a modular design strategy. It is designed to provide choice and, therefore, reduce risk for management. It is open and flexible, allowing a range

FIGURE 10-2   System development costs. *Source:* Arthur Anderson & Co., "Factors for Successful Implementation & Payoff," Paper presented at DSS-83 Conference (Boston: The Author, June 27, 1983).

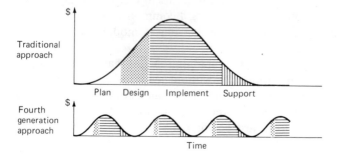

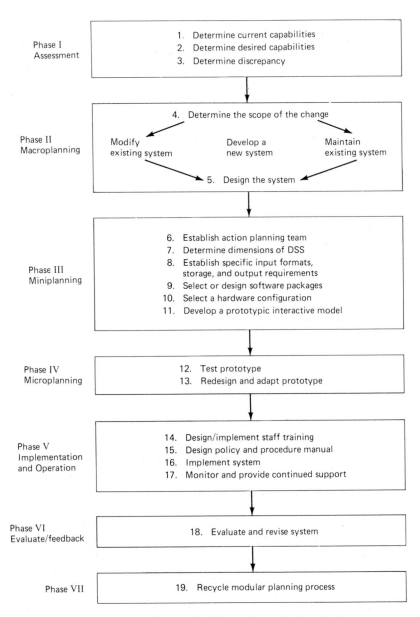

FIGURE 10-3 Steps in the Development of a Decision Support System. *Source: Resource Guide for State and Local Education Agencies* (Washington, D.C.: Management Analysis Center and National Association of State Directors of Special Education, September 1979).

of potential outcomes. It is efficient in its mode of operation because of its guiding principle, which is to identify needed applications within a structure that will allow growth for the future. Finally, the issue of cost is considered throughout to gauge organizational investment. The specific steps in the planning process for an educational decision support system is presented in Appendix A at the end of this chapter. The planning process is divided into managerial and technical dimensions. Within each module development, both sets of questions and decisions arise. The detailed questions allow the planner to access key stakeholders and the eventual end users of the system.

IMPLEMENTATION GOALS AND STRATEGIES

Implementation Goals

Alter suggests two summary measures of quality to determine if the implementation process was successful. His measures are "(1) the degree to which usage is achieved; and (2) the degree of difficulty encountered in attempting to accomplish effective usage."[21] Goal achievement and the quality of the process might be depicted more dynamically as easy to difficult and achieved and not achieved. Alter expresses these two dimensions this way:

	GOAL ACHIEVED	GOAL NOT ACHIEVED
Process, easy	Smooth implementation	Smooth rejection
Process, difficult	Difficulties surmounted	Difficulties not surmounted

The principle that evolved out of Alter's study of business implementation of DSS was that the success of an implementation process was positively related to the degree to which the process could be planned, with certain limits.[22]

What appears critical to an EDSS is the degree of articulation of modules under development and their relationship to one another during the implementation process. If the objective of individually tailored student plans drive the EDSS, users will necessarily need to build a cascading data base that will feed different user needs. An executive-level planning committee must first agree to use a student data base as the foundation of the EDSS. It must be outcome oriented and fall within the boundary of the school district and community values. Teacher and administrator uses evolved out of the relationship between these elements, which represent the key factors in the conceptual framework. The articulation of user levels in development becomes a key implementation factor that is tied to eventual usability of the system in school districts.

The principle we cited earlier from Alter on the relationship of planning to implementation is of great significance. The more an organization can limit its innovation to a single user who understands and plans to use the system with a specific purpose in mind, and have all related programming, maintenance, and support readily available, the more easily will the implementation lead to a successful application.

The factors that inhibit successful implementation identified by Alter include

Nonexistent or unwilling users
Multiple users or implementors
Disappearing or changing users, implementors, and maintenance personnel
Inability to specify purpose or usage pattern in advance
Inability to predict and cushion impact on all parties
Lack or loss of support
Lack of prior experience with similar systems
Technical problems
Cost-effectiveness issues[23]

From our experience, we would add

Failure to complete input or transfer data onto new system, which leads to unreliable data
Requiring input staff to transfer data without making the necessary allowances in their schedule, which builds resistance and slows down implementation and use by others
Failure to prepare modules as prototypes and pilot test extensively before a systems test is conducted
Incomplete systems test before moving on line with the new system
Conflicting expectations within and between internal change agent group and consultants
Past history of neglect and powerlessness between electronic data processing staff and innovating department
Failure of management to communicate and participate at key points in the implementation cycle

How does one overcome these factors? Our most complete response lies in Figure 10-3, where we have delineated our planning model. We would add here that a risk analysis during the planning and development cycle would help the planners to anticipate and, it is hoped, avoid these pitfalls. Brainstorming a similar list, developing an advance warning system, and having at least two alternatives for each eventuality would assist implementors as they come upon the identified problems.

The adage a Chicago planner shared with Harry Truman, " Make big plans, you can always revise them," still holds. Strategic visions spawn strategic plans. The latter must, however, be divisible to be manageable. The essential ingredient must be well understood and accepted. They must be value laden and be pursued with a vengeance. Persistence yet flexibility within the established plan are the key managerial characteristics that lead to a successful set of user outcomes and a smooth implementation process.

Besides divisibility, keeping the solution as simple as possible is advised. The less complex the solution is at first blush, the easier it is to attract converts and interested parties. Sprague and Carlson call this the "quick hit" tactic.[24] Prototypes of an individual module give the developer something to show and demonstrate. The new product, however, simply communicates that it can be done and allows momentum and support to grow.

Developing a sufficient support base is critical at the outset and throughout development of the prototype. It communicates commitment and persistence. It also enhances the probability estimates of those involved in the actual development. They cannot be distracted by questionable support.

Finally, developers really need to tie their information technology innovation to user need. Here we are primarily talking about the discretionary user in contrast to programmers or committed users.[25] Discretionary users participate by choice. They require systems that they believe will enhance their job performance, provide a competitive edge, and increase their own personal sense of effectiveness. For educators, the last value is paramount. It is only after the personal impact has been dealt with and prototypes thoroughly tested with endusers that commitment can be secured and the system can be prepared and institutionalized. Training and support are continuing activities to ensure institutionalization.

Alter has summarized his research on implementation strategies into his four principles which are presented next. He identifies them as strategy statements with corresponding tactics. Using his summary and our examples, we provide a set of implementation strategies within the modular action planning model.[26] Multiple plans require multiple user involvement. What follows is complexity with uncertainty, diversity in terms of users, a new emerging technical environment, and a large number of participants applying the implementation strategies to a specific context. This is the challenge for educators who share our strategic vision.

Implementation Strategy 1

Divide an innovative project into manageable plans to avoid developing a massive plan that has little chance of success.

MATCHING TACTICS

Use prototypes within a modular developmental framework.

Test and retest prototype in both simulated and actual user conditions.

Revise and retest prototype with actual users to increase their ownership, familiarity, and skills.

Use an evolutionary approach.

Throughout recycling during test-retest, demonstrate the relationship between intent and product. Highlight changes and document user participation. Expect frustration with changes and model how to embrace error.

Develop a series of tools.

Develop a series of data bases, small models, and experiments to illustrate system malleability and flexibility.

Implementation Strategy 2

Keep the solution simple by encouraging use and avoid escalating fear and a sense of helplessness. By emphasizing modular development, system complexity can be subsumed.

MATCHING TACTICS

Be simple, at least initially. Demonstrate model complexity over time.

Use the concept of the "black box" to reduce complexity. Allow readiness for complexity to reveal itself through system use and in relation to user's problems.

Automate what is, not what might be to avoid creating a solution to a non-problem.

Implementation Strategy 3

Develop as broad a support base as possible, making frequent attempts to secure interest and commitments through direct person-to-person appeals.

MATCHING TACTICS

Most system efforts fail to obtain enough user participation. Depending on the type of module under development and number of potential users, the sophistication of the application should be limited as a trade off to obtain maximum user involvement.

Getting participation does not necessarily ensure user ownership, especially if the system is imposed from on high. Encourage user ideas and need statements early in defining the change and in module selection. Then demonstrate the relationship between management needs and staff needs. If none exists, propose additional modules that relate closely to staff perceived needs. Encourage staff developer networking.

Sustain management support through their periodic involvement. Choose activities that involve managers and ensure active demonstrations.

Selling the system can only be through tying user needs to it. For managers and other users not involved in all stages of development encourage peer demonstrations.

Implementation Strategy 4

Meet user needs and institutionalize through peer training and timely technical support.

MATCHING TACTICS

Encourage simultaneous mandatory and voluntary use of the system by policy statements, altering work conditions and job responsibilities. With a clear intent to transfer to automated system, communicate to all users that they can get on board as they gain comfort through training and on site technical assistance. A time frame for full-scale implementation should be clearly diffused. As staff prepares to come on board, time should be set aside to allow learning rather than having two full-time jobs.

Start the system with only highly committed and enthusiastic users. Encourage them to share their excitement in training, demonstrations, and on-site technical assistance activities. Acknowledge their contribution as trainers and diffusers.

Keep in mind not all staff will use each of the system's capacities. Therefore, try to match personal capacities to system capacities. Plan for as much of a range as possible and do not confuse personal ability with system requirements. The latter is much more easy to plan for and anticipate. Encourage users to expand the system through training and other incentives.

POLICY AND DECISION SUPPORT SYSTEMS

General to specific policies naturally evolve as the educational organization learns through its planning and implementation cycle. In addition to the general policies that should override any specific set of policies, we have separated policy into three subheadings: development, implementation, and operations. These divisions are consistent with the modular action planning model. We suggested earlier that the priorities for system development grow out of the organizational analysis and assessment phase that results in the general plan and direction of information systems development. The development policies are embedded in the action team model and flow out of the general district policies. Finally, implementation and operations policies eventually bind the actual use of the technology after evaluation and integration into the ongoing organizational operations.

General Policies

The general systems policies cover all forms of technology that are used to manage resources to achieve district or systems goals. McFarlan and McKenney argued that while computers, telecommunications, and word processing have developed separately, policies should be developed centrally to integrate them within the overall organizational objectives.[27] They believe that the tension between innovation and control and between educational data processing professionals and user groups requires a centrally based planning group to oversee development, implementation, and operations.

It has been noted repeatedly that a strategic plan should dictate district investment and utilization of communication and information technologies. Our framework for an educational decision support system broadly defines the role and scope of technology in the policymaking, management, instructional, and learning aspects of educational settings. Each function and constituent group of the educational organization is considered in the EDSS network (see Figure 10-1). The key leadership task is to define the critical objective for each function and each group of participants, keeping in mind how one group's needs can be used by another.

We have adapted and extended Hammer's office information system profile for corporate environments to illustrate the set of choices that should govern general policy development for technology in educational organizations. In Appendix B to this chapter, the choices are illustrated in terms of five questions related to practices, philosophy, user groups, and other technological application choices.[28]

Development Policies

McFarlan and McKenney suggest development policies that should guide the acquisition and development of hardware and software, personnel policies, standards, and support services to endusers.

The first key development policies are to maintain a balance with the three major technologies. This balance is significant as a development policy to ensure a culture that supports technological use through learning and use technology. Second, it encourages all participants in the educational organization to profit from the technological investment. Third, it allows for quick assimilation and installation of applications that may touch people at all levels in the organization.[29]

An additional consideration that flows from the first policy of technological balance is the development of criteria to determine if new applications or modules should be purchased or contracted for with outside vendors and consultants or should be internally developed by a district team. For school districts that have employed technical personnel, this might not be an issue. The issue, rather, is one of flexibility to encourage development and yet attend to the documentation and standards that affect widespread use and applicability to district hardware and software.

The acquisition and maintenance of equipment should be based upon an inventory of current or planned purchases. In addition, standards that relate to (1) telecommunications, (2) languages, (3) documentation procedures by equipment type, (4) district data dictionary, (5) access and user security, and (6) interfaces with other systems should be considered.

This group of policies should also include procedures that ensure the diffusion of applications. Specifically, policies should cover the commitment of resources to assist user target groups that speed or lag behind in development and installation of applications.

Early on, acquisitions take a great deal of time. Determining and writing specifications is a time-consuming task that requires research and study. Development policies should include recommended vendors and suppliers. Exceptions to preferred lists or to bid winners would be made on the basis of these policies.

Finally, policies related to development of new modules should flow out of the planning model described in Figure 10-1. At each transition between phases, policies that determine next steps or criteria for movement between phases should be developed ahead of time. Example policies include the issue of compatibility in the analysis phase, role of endusers in the design and programming phases, and the debriefing at the end of a system's test phase. The set of development policies such as those just described provide the basic framework for the district as a whole.

Implementation Policies

This set of policies governs the transition between development and actual installation and operation of the system or module. These policies represent the district's formal announcement and acceptance of the system or module developed for the district or educational organization. They prescribe what is different and what remains the same. They suggest what will be affected and in what way, including new sets of procedures. These policies set up new relationships and, it is hoped, assist in the adoption of new procedures.

Finally, these policies should include the training program that the staff must complete before the new policy is implemented. Training and orientation by peer developers operating within the norms and problem-solving processes of the operating units are keys to successful implementation and installation. Evidence of competence and the time frame for starting the installation process complete this set of policies.

It is essential that the district maintain an active community relations program during both the development and implementation phases. Policies that direct school management to advertise publicly the school district intent and type of software and hardware, and solicit community reactions to the proposed use of technology that affects instruction and students directly, are critical to fostering cooperation and support of the innovation. Many parents may want to supplement their child's program. Compatibility is an obvious concern. Parent training and computer loan programs are two that Komoski has recommended school boards to consider to maintain parents' support. He also recommends sharing software and hardware evaluations with parents to assist them in selecting the enhancements they choose to provide at home for their children.[30] Extending school library equipment and training to students and parents for supplementary training and practice would reinforce in-school applications and reduce costs to parents unable to provide backup or complementary support systems at home. Considering a homework policy with teacher involvement that would require out-of-school use might be an option some boards of education would find helpful to further student practice and performance. Some districts might also want to develop a district purchasing program with state support, but include parental purchases as part of the agreement. Clearly, software purchasing and rights to diffuse software programs directly or through rental and/or loan agreements with developers would be an excellent way to facilitate home use.

Operations Policies

These policies govern the daily use of the module or system within the schools. First, they should identify who and under what conditions personnel should expect the system to impact upon them. These policies stipulate the access, input form, processing, and sharing of information obtained from the module. They also specify who will receive information from the system, how often, under what conditions, and in what form.

Clearly, issues of confidentiality and security of systems from disruption and sabotage are concerns of the parents, board, and staff. The range of precautions, starting with frequent changes of key code words for selected files might have to be common practice. Backing up key files is an absolute necessity, especially for systems that use floppy disks.

The key point is to develop only those policies you think are critical and add others when needed. Such policies will also evolve out of implementation and actual use of the system. Policy developers then can estimate the need for control without needless interference.

Finally, periodic review and evaluation of the module or system is needed to ensure that the system is operating as planned. The evaluation or review information is passed to end users, executive committees, and ultimately, the central policy group to ensure balance and compatibility of systems. This review also serves as a major input factor in the recommendation for new developments or system enhancements.

Summary

It was noted at the beginning of this section that policy formulation marked the formal acceptance of the organization's technological development efforts. It has been suggested here, though, that policy should be developed at both a general level and at three specific sublevels covering development and introduction of technology, implementation, and operations.

The key focal point of policy development in educational organizations should be end-user involvement and development of personal as well as institutional applications. Kellan writes that it isn't computers that will see us through the future. It's computing. It's not the machines, but the minds behind the machines that will make the difference. He makes the distinction between "personal" and "computing" with the following statement:

> there are computers, and there are computers. As machines they have injected both threat and promise into the age of The Cognitive Revolution in which we live. The crucial distinction between threat and promise lies in understanding of

the meaning of the word "personal." It is not the size of the machine that makes it personal. It is not where the machine is located (classroom, home or office) that distinguishes it and makes it personal. It is not even who owns the system that matters. Rather, it is who has made the decision to use the computer and what it's used for that matters. Personal computing means you have made a decision to use a powerful mental tool to enhance your own personal productivity, to gain your own personal competitive edge.[31]

The policy then is embedded in a value that school board and educational leaders must confront. This confrontation will have profound effects on the structure, tasks, and personnel employed in schools. Once this value is confronted, policy formulation may then proceed. We believe we have asked a series of questions which ultimately each state and a number of local communities must address and answer for themselves.

In closing, we return to McFarlan and McKenney, who believe there are a series of right questions to ask, though the answers will differ among organizations and their individual units. "Analyzing the identifiable but complex forces will help to determine the best answers for each organizational unit—at least for the present."[32]

We believe it would be best to close this chapter with a look at the perspective of Rockart and Flannery who, in contrast to Kellan, have a centralized EDP background. Their suggestions are founded upon Kellan's premise but they go beyond the individual and consider the organizational imperatives that will make or break end-user computing within the organizational framework. From their research, the policies that will support enduser computing most effectively must include (1) an overall strategy, (2) development of enduser priorities, (3) policies governing top management's uses, and (4) control methods to facilitate growth in end-user applications but also not conflict with organizational goals. They recommend the following policies to support end-user practice in computer use. They are:

Emphasis should be placed on "shared environment" where EDP provides support in specific areas, but where the users program, enter some data, operate directly and have some responsibility for systems and applications they develop.

The strategy should be widely promulgated and, obviously, readily supported.

A "distributed" organizational structure should be developed to assist end-user groups through designated liaison personnel, and it must be local and accessible, especially at its initial stages of prototypic development and training in functional areas.

Provide a wide range of products.

Maintain and develop an extensive education program.

Develop effective "data migration" procedures. Once data is stored and located it should be extracted and forwarded to end users.

Flag critical applications to insure documentation and transferability of use, reduce conflicting procedures, and check for confidentiality.

Maintain line control over end users, not EDP personnel, to support valuation and monitoring of usage.

Provide incentives for use and diffusion of model applications for use by others.[33]

Each of these recommendations should be used in conjunction with the four primary concerns noted earlier. It can be used productively or it can create chaos. These recommendations should serve to avoid the pitfalls and ensure success both individually and organizationally.

APPENDIX 10A

MACROPLANNING ORGANIZATIONAL STEPS IN THE DEVELOPMENT OF AN EDUCATIONAL DECISION SUPPORT SYSTEM

PHASE I: ASSESSMENT

TECHNICAL	MANAGERIAL

1. Determining Current Capabilities

(1) (a) What information do you currently gather? (b) From what sources? (c) For what purposes? (2) (a) What process or method do you use to collect the needed information? (b) Who collects the information now? (c) How long does it take to collect the information? (d) How is the information stored? (e) Who has access to the information now?	(1) What job roles are involved in information collection, storage, retrieval, production of organizational reports? (2) (a) What does the staff involved in information processing like and/or dislike about the current system? (b) What is the key data collected? (c) What decisions are made? (d) What information do managers and their constituents want that you cannot obtain now?

TECHNICAL   MANAGERIAL

(f) How is the information trans-
formed and used?

(g) Can you give examples of the
output in reports, files, summaries?

(h) Can you illustrate the current
flow of information and how it
is currently processed?

(3) Are there any problems in the collection of information today?

2. Determining Desired Capabilities

(1) (a) What information would you
like to have that you do not currently collect?

(b) From what sources?

(c) For what purposes?

(d) Can you describe the nature of
the specific data elements you
want?

(e) Has anyone requested this specific information of you?

(1) What will these changes mean in
terms of time for data collection,
processing, and reporting?

(2) Whose job(s) will be affected? In
what ways? At what cost?

(3) Will access to the information be enhanced or limited?

(4) What key data are to be added?

(5) How will the new information be
used? With whom?

3. Determining Discrepancy

(1) Can you build a model of the technical support system you desire?

(2) Assess the changes necessary in the
technical environment to design, develop, and implement the desired
system.

(3) Can the current system be upgraded?
At what cost? If not, can you trade
or redeploy the existing system to
serve some other function?

(1) How much of a discrepancy exists?

(2) Assess the changes necessary in the
managerial environment in the design, development, and implementation.

(3) Is the gap of sufficient magnitude
for you to want to reduce it? At
what cost?

PHASE II: MACROPLANNING FOR SYSTEMS DESIGN

4. Determining the Scope of the Change

(1) What are the technical development
needs suggested by the system development priorities?

(2) Select or designate technical support
personnel to work with managers
and central planning unit.

(1) Identify the primary system development priorities and establish policies
for integrated planning and development.

(2) Designate managerial responsibilities
at each unit and level of the organization.

TECHNICAL	MANAGERIAL
	(3) Establish central planning unit.
	(4) Establish initial planning budget and a system for monitoring costs.
	(5) Orient organizational members, select school and community volunteers to serve in advisory capacities.

5. Designing the System

(1) Specify the information categories, determine data classes, organize data elements into fields, and determine output and frequency by user groups.	(1) Are some areas more important than others?
(2) Develop a time and cost analysis.	(2) What must come first? What can be delayed?
(3) Prepare a technical work plan with support staff, consultants, computer programmers, and hardware specialists.	(3) Do you have the technical or clerical staff, or the managerial resources to assign to continued planning?
(4) Can you illustrate how the additional information might be collected, processed, and organized?	(4) Do you have other fiscal resources needed?
	(5) What other decisions need to be made? With whom? Do other decisionmakers need to be consulted?
	(6) Specify managerial parameters for system planning: information domains/output users time frame job assignments cost limits supervision/liaison performance criteria

PHASE III: MICROPLANNING OF PROGRAMMING/ PROTOTYPING ELEMENTS AND HARDWARE/SOFTWARE INTERFACE

6. Establishing Action Planning Team

(1) Develop record definition and codes for specific data elements and fields.	(1) Establish action planning teams composed of potential implementators and other users.
(2) Review current forms.	(2) Develop a regular pattern of communication to all those involved.

TECHNICAL	MANAGERIAL
(3) Design revised forms and determine most appropriate input formats, method, and retrieval capabilities desired.	(3) Establish direct liaison.
(4) Project the memory/storage capacity needed to handle data needed/desired.	(4) Build a work schedule with consultants.
(5) Can you build a model of the technical support system you desire?	(5) Identify interviews on site with key individuals involved.
(6) Can the current system be upgraded? At what cost? If not, can you trade or redeploy the existing system?	(6) Prepare periodic debriefing sessions with action planning team.

7. Determining Dimensions of Decision Support System

(1) Interview key decisionmakers/users for specific data elements they currently need and desire for the range of decision situations they encounter.	(1) Determine key information domains and set parameters of decision support system.
(2) List specific output requirements for type of decision situation.	(2) Assess staff interest in job changes/reassignments.
(3) Review technical plan with action planning team and consultants to determine its appropriateness to district.	(3) Redesign staff roles and assignments.
	(4) Prepare new job descriptions.

8. Establishing Specific Input, Formats, Storage and Output Requirements

(1) Determine most appropriate software and hardware configuration.	(1) Identify resources and determine the ratio of hardware to software, keeping in mind training/programming or prototyping.
(2) Determine if software already is available in packages, prototyping is in order to speed development, or users should develop their own applications.	(2) Determine storage needs after reviewing state and local policies on file longevity.
(3) Invite software and hardware vendors to react to the technical proposals.	

9. Selecting Software or Contracting for the Design of Appropriate Programs

(1) Technical considerations include structure of data base restrictions on record or field size	(1) Primary consideration in selection is the ease of use.

TECHNICAL

number of records program can contain

flexibility to change data base terms

memory requirements

host language requested or optional

speed of execution (language coded or high-level language or uses interpreter)

cost

MANAGERIAL

(2) Consider adaptability and availability of programming assistance.

(3) Determine staff interest in learning to operate with/without training.

(4) Determine capacity of programmer to communicate with professional and clerical staff.

(5) Assess reliability and commitment of programmers to work to produce to client specifications.

10. Selecting a Hardware Configuration

(1) With technical plan and software select hardware and pilot-test examples on selected hardware.

(1) Determine the appropriate configuration of hardware needed now and the immediate future according to technical plan.

11. Developing a Prototypic Interactive Model

(1) Develop the model from technical plan for the hardware configuration and appropriate software.

(2) Customize programming to local plan if needed.

(3) Provide technical documentation of program if customized.

(4) Prepare input formats consistent with new or revised forms for ease of entry.

(1) Assign liaison to assist programmer if questions should arise.

(2) Prepare action planning team for debugging.

(3) Translate performance criteria.

PHASE IV: MICROPLANNING

12. Testing Prototype

(1) Test prototype off site and on system hardware.

(1) Debug prototype with action planning team and significant users of the DSS.

13. Redesigning and Adapting Prototype

(1) Redesign, modify, and adapt prototype based upon the feedback from action planning team and other users.

(2) Retest revised prototype with system hardware.

(1) Debug revisions with the same group as noted above.

(2) Review changes, decide on modifications.

PHASE V: IMPLEMENTATION AND OPERATION

TECHNICAL   MANAGERIAL

14. Designing/Implementing Staff Training

(1) Initiate training for all personnel who are part of the input, processing, or output procedures.

(1) Assess staff knowledge and skills for DSS.

(2) Observe and evaluate staff performane to determine needed support for implementation.

15. Designing Policy and Procedures Manual

(1) Manual should contain all user roles, functions, and specific directions for their participation in the DSS plan.

(1) Manual should contain policies on longevity, termination, access, updating, revising, and control of related system functions and uses.

16. Implementing System

(1) Establish date and implement new or revised DSS.

(1) Maintain backup system until criteria for success are met.

17. Monitoring and Providing Continued Support

(1) Collect data on system operations and performance.

(1) Assign supervisory responsibility for monitoring, supporting, and evaluating DSS.

(2) Prepare a schedule of evaluation.

PHASE VI: EVALUATION AND FEEDBACK

18. Evaluating and Revising DSS

(1) Mesh technical data on operations with user data.

(2) Request technical changes.

(1) Evaluate DSS with action planning team and a selected group of users.

(2) Revise, where necessary, policies, procedures, information segments, and eventually user manual.

(3) Incorporate changes into data base schemata, include technical documentation for latter analysis.

PHASE VII: RECYCLING THE PLANNING PROCESS

(1) Note implications from evaluation and feedback activities for further refinement, continuation, or termination of module development and diffusion.
(2) Consider technical people, tasks, and structural system and their interrelationships.
(3) Examine resource and further costs implications and level of application along with level of support expected.

APPENDIX 10B

DETERMINING YOUR EDUCATIONAL POLICY PROFILE

PRIORITIES FOR COMPREHENSIVE COMPUTER
INFORMATION SYSTEMS (CCIS)

What will you choose to emphasize when selecting and implementing CCIS? Are you concerned with efficiency or effectiveness? What system purposes and what group of endusers do you want to impact. Seven system uses might be:
data manipulation
problem solving
interpersonal communication
student learning
staff training
experimentation or action research using new technology
overall organizational control and accountability
Other system uses not manifest might include:
appearance of being modern and up-to-date
maintaining control over the release of sensitive data to the public, state legislature, or other influentials
preserving organizational or personnel survival

1. _____ Board-level policy-and decision making
2. _____ Central office management decision making
3. _____ Central office tasks
4. _____ Building unit management decision making
5. _____ Building unit tasks
6. _____ Curricular tasks
7. _____ Instructional tasks
8. _____ Teacher decision making
9. _____ Student decision making
10. _____ Student tasks
11. _____ Clerical tasks

EDUCATIONAL CONSTITUENT/
USER GROUPS

After reviewing the 11 options presented under priorities, ask which constituent groups hold the most influence? What CCIS's are they asking the district to de-

USES BY CONSTITUENT GROUP(S)*

Board members
1 2 3 4 5 6 7 8 9 10 11
Central office personnel Superintendent
1 2 3 4 5 6 7 8 9 10 11

Source: Adapted from Michael Hammer's for "Office Information Systems: What's All the Fuss?" *Management Technology,* 1, no. 2 (June 1983), 33.

* Multiple groups or subdivisions of constituents might all be surveyed to determine their position on selected items in the profile.

EDUCATIONAL CONSTITUENT/ USER GROUPS

velop and purchase? What is their level of understanding and expectations for use? Does a consensus among the constituent groups exist?

USES BY CONSTITUENT GROUP(S)

Assistant superintendents
1 2 3 4 5 6 7 8 9 10 11

Program or Unit Directors
1 2 3 4 5 6 7 8 9 10 11

Data Processing Director
1 2 3 4 5 6 7 8 9 10 11

Clerical Staff
1 2 3 4 5 6 7 8 9 10 11

Building unit level personnel Principal
1 2 3 4 5 6 7 8 9 10 11

Assistant Principals
1 2 3 4 5 6 7 8 9 10 11

Department Heads
1 2 3 4 5 6 7 8 9 10 11

Teachers (K-5, 6-8, 9-12)
1 2 3 4 5 6 7 8 9 10 11

Supportive Service Personnel
1 2 3 4 5 6 7 8 9 10 11

Students (K-5, 6-8, 9-12, 12+)
1 2 3 4 5 6 7 8 9 10 11

Community constituents groups
1 2 3 4 5 6 7 8 9 10 11

EDUCATIONAL ORGANIZATION CCIS PHILOSOPHY

How structured is your thinking regarding CCIS? Can your educational organization tolerate individual building acquisitions or will it have to be centrally controlled by the EDP?

_____Aggressive

_____Cautious

_____Innovative

_____Experimental

_____Tight-Loose controls

_____Centrally focused

_____Building focused

_____User focused

_____Central control

_____Dispersed control

CCIS TECHNOLOGY CHOICES

What uses, products, services, methods, and soft/hardware choices make sense within your organization? What will get each of the tasks done you envision in your master plan? Who will be the end

COMMUNICATION AND INFORMATION TECHNOLOGIES

Types of Communication Applications

_____ Electronic mail

_____ Electronic message and storage center

_____ Teleconferencing

_____ Word processing, electronic fil-

CCIS TECHNOLOGY CHOICES

users? Depending upon the desired outcomes what hardware configuration will meet your present and future needs?

COMMUNICATION AND INFORMATION TECHNOLOGIES

ing, document preparation, editing

_____ Electronic surveys

_____ PBX Networking

_____ Group DSS

_____ Local area network

_____ Scheduling and calendar preparation

Information Technologies

Types of DSS applications

_____ File drawer systems

_____ Data analysis systems

_____ Analysis information systems

_____ Accounting modeling systems

_____ Representation model systems

_____ Optimization model systems

_____ Suggestion model systems

Types of transactional processing applications

_____ Accounts payable

_____ Inventory

_____ Purchasing

_____ Budget projections and expense monitoring

_____ Standard reporting others might include

_____ Expert system or knowledge networks through timesharing agreement

_____ Employment or career counseling systems

CCIS RESPONSIBILITY

Who or what group will make policy recommendations to the board? Who or what group will plan, develop, implement, or track CCIS usage?

_____ Contracted consultants

_____ Superintendent

_____ Central office

_____ EDP group

_____ Business affairs group

_____ Individual program or building units

_____ Team with shared responsibilities

NOTES

[1]Leonard C. Burrello, Michael L. Tracy, and Elsa J. Glassman, "A National Status Report on the Use of Electronic Technology in Special Education Management," *Journal of Special Education,* 17, no. 3 (Fall 1983), 341-353.

[2]Suzanne Ragghianti and Rosemary Miller, "The Micro-computer and Special Education Management," *Exceptional Children,* 49, no. 2 (October 1982), 131-135.

[3]Alan M. Hofmeister, "Microcomputers in Perspective," *Exceptional Children,* 49, no. 2 (October 1982), 115.

[4]Ibid., p. 117.

[5]G. O. Carman and B. Kosberg, "Educational Technology Research: Computer Technology and the Education of Emotionally Handicapped Children," *Educational Technology,* 22, no. 2 (1982), 26-30.

[6]G. P. Cartwright and K. Hall, "A Review of Computer Uses in Special Education," in L. Mann and D. Sabatino (Eds.), *The Second Review of Special Education* (Philadelphia: Journal of Special Education Press, 1974).

[7]Ted Hasselbring, "Remediating Spelling Problems of Learning-Handicapped Students Through the Use of Micro-computers," *Educational Technology,* 22, no. 4 (1982), 31-32.

[8]Hofmeister, "Microcomputers in Perspective," pp. 119-120.

[9]Randy Elliott Bennett, "Applications of Micro-computer Technology in Special Education," *Exceptional Children,* 49, no. 2 (1982), 106-113.

[10]John Thormann, *Public School Use of Computers in Special Education,* Unpublished doctoral dissertation, University of Oregon, 1982.

[11]Leonard C. Burrello, Michael L. Tracy, James E. Siantz and Robert P. Bostrom, *Microcomputers and Educational Management* (Englewood Cliffs, N.J.: Prentice-Hall, in press).

[12]G. A. Gorry and Michael S. Scott-Morton, "A Framework for Management Information Systems," *Sloan Management Review,* 13, no. 1 (Fall 1971), 55-70.

[13]Peter G. W. Keen and Michael S. Scott-Morton, *Decision Support Systems: An Organizational Perspective* (Reading, Mass.: Addison-Wesley, 1978), p. 82.

[14]Steven L. Alter, *Decision Support Systems: Current Practices and Continuing Challenges* (Reading, Mass.: Addison-Wesley, 1980), pp. 73-93.

[15]John Naisbitt, *Megatrends: Ten New Directions Transforming Our Lives* (New York: Warner Books, 1982), p. 151.

[16]Ibid., p. 204.

[17]Ibid., p. 43.

[18]James B. Taylor, *Using Microcomputers in Social Agencies* (Beverly Hills, Calif.: Sage Publications, 1981) pp. 46-49.

[19]Ibid., p. 48.

[20]Arthur Anderson & Co., "Factors for Successful Implementation and Payoff," Paper presented at DSS-83 Conference (Boston: The Author, June 1983).

[21]Alter, *Decision Support Systems,* p. 156.

[22]Ibid., p. 157.

[23]Ibid., p. 157.

[24]Ralph Sprague and Eric Carlson, *Building Effective Decision Support Systems* (Englewood Cliffs, N.J.: Prentice-Hall, 1982), pp. 60-62.

[25]John L. Bennett, "Analysis and Design of the User Interface for Decision Support Systems," in John L. Bennett, ed., *Building Decision Support Systems* (Reading, Mass.: Addison-Wesley, 1983), pp. 41-42.

[26]Alter, *Decision Support Systems,* pp.167-169.

[27]F. Warren McFarlan and James L. McKenney, "The Information Archipelago—Governing the New World," *Harvard Business Review,* 61, no. 4 (July-August 1983), 91.

[28]Michael Hammer, "Strategic Planning for Office Information Systems: What's All the Fuss?" *Management Technology,* 1, no. 2 (June 1983), 33.

[29]McFarlan and McKenney, "The Information Archipelago," p. 99.

[30]Kenneth Komoski, "Computer Policies: Develop Them Wisely," *American School Board Journal,* 170, no. 3 (March 1983), 30-31.

[31]Paul Kellan, "The Future of Computing: Personal with a Capital P," *Personal Computing,* 1, no. 5 (May 1983), 211-214.

[32]McFarlan and McKenney, "The Information Archipelago," p. 99.

[33]John Rockart and Lauren S. Flannery, "Management of End User Computing Communication," *Association for Computing Machinery,* 26, no. 10 (October 1983), 776-784.

CHAPTER 11
FISCAL
MANAGEMENT

The management of fiscal affairs for special education at the level of the local school system can be viewed as falling into two general processes that are related and interactive but that as administrative functions may call for somewhat different skills and knowledge bases. The budget for special education and its related services may well be the major determining force for whatever else occurs. Budget management involves, first, the process of *planning and preparation* and, subsequently, the process of *controlling and monitoring*.

As with many administrative functions taking place in organizational units, particular processes may not be role specific. Persons occupying various administrative and direct service positions within the organization may play a part in each of the processes. Mayer points out that the kinds of information that are likely to be required for the total budgeting process, and the persons who might best provide the information are as follows:

Additional personnel—principals
Instructional materials and equipment—teachers
Space and facilities improvement—director of housing
Projected personnel costs—director of personnel services
Projected enrollments—director of pupil personnel services
Transportation costs—director of transportation

Projected management costs—director of special education
Current year's expenditures—district controller
Projected income—business manager.[1]

While all these individuals may contribute to the total budget process, the program administrator for special education occupies the role bearing the responsibility for adequacy of services and, therefore, must have primary interest in putting it all together. It has been frequently noted where fiscal policy and service operations have been concerned that *program* personnel tend to focus on the nature of the service needed and qualities of that provided, with little understanding or regard for the fiscal details. At the same time, business (financial) managers within the system focus on the flow of funds and tend to steer clear of qualitative program issues. Andersen has described the problems caused by this very natural state of affairs in his analysis of the fiscal problems that occurred early in the implementation of new special education policies in Massachusetts, in which fiscal personnel and program personnel were so separated in their knowledge and perspectives of the total system that massive unintended consequences were the result.[2] He makes the point that differing perspectives of the nature of organizational goals and mechanisms to achieve them are unavoidable, but that remaining aware of the difference between fiscal and programmatic perspectives may be an important tool in both design and implementation.

While a number of different positions have been cited as participants in the budget process, it is reasonable to expect that a single individual or department within a local school system will exercise the major financial functions that must articulate with the programmatic functions that are the responsibility of the special education administrator. It is, therefore, suggested that between those two positions and/or departmental functions, the major communication and interchange of understandings must occur. We are not arguing for gross duplication of effort, but service system benefit can certainly accrue from the sharing of perspectives between these roles. Furthermore, from the standpoint of enlightened self-interest, we suggest that although it may not be possible to control how much interest and knowledge of special education programming can be engendered in the resident financial officer, the program administrator had better assume the obligation of knowing as much as possible about the financial picture. Specifically, this would include understanding revenue sources as well as revenue expenditures.

KNOWING THE FINANCIAL PICTURE

For the special education administrator to deal effectively with the tasks that are concerned with budget planning, allocation, control, and monitoring, a number of specific areas of knowledge are crucial. A primary consideration is the source of revenue. For a particular service organization, the proportion of the budget coming from each source may vary, but some general parameters can be presented here, with some indications as to how much variance can be expected. A second area of knowledge involves the anticipated costs of services, which might be classified according to types of handicaps, levels of service required, age of students, and particular characteristics of the organization and community.

It also should be of considerable importance to employ a systematic procedure for making the connection between program planning and budgeting. Starting with an estimation of service needs and carrying the process through to the establishment of a budget that meets the needs and fits within the available revenue calls for an analytical process. While a number of different systems are capable of adaptation to this process, one approach that seems to hold particular promise in special education will be reviewed here. Together, these items of basic financial knowledge and skills will allow the program administrator at least to converse intelligently with the organization's fiscal officers and thereby place the program in the best possible fiscal advantage.

SOURCES OF FUNDS

With all the attention on special education programming from the federal and state levels of government, it would be easy for the local manager to overlook the importance of the local school district's investment in the services offered. While rather large variances are found among the states, nationwide figures suggest that on the average, the local share of the financial support is about 31 percent of the total special education budget. The average state's share is about 55 percent, whereas the federal level provides about 14 percent.[3] These averages obscure the wide range of proportions. According to some reports, state shares are as high as 98 percent (in Montana) and as low as 17 percent (in Oklahoma).[4] The best picture of a typical situation may be provided by data reported in 1984 by the Department of Education from four geographically diverse states that were selected to illustrate various features about their special education support structure.[5] A number of features about these states will be discussed later, but in terms of the relative contributions from each level of government, the diversity is well illustrated by data reported from a study for the federal Office of Special Education Programs. (See Table 11-1.) The variation in the proportion of federal support must be explained partly by greater or lesser total expenditures per child, since the absolute dollar amount per child from federal programs is based on a flat child-count rate, with discretionary, competitive grants accounting for only a small proportion of total federal funds entering any state's system. However, another source of variation may be the degree to which various federal resources other than education grants are used to purchase related services, which may be calculated

TABLE 11-1   Federal, State, and Local Shares of the Costs of Special Education and Related Services in Four Selected States

Revenue Source	State A (%)	State B (%)	State C (%)	State D (%)
Federal	18.5	9.4	7.1	8.4
State	72.7	41.9	46.4	61.7*
Local	7.5	48.7	46.4	29.9*
Other	1.3**			

* Based on direct state appropriations for handicapped education plus an *estimate* of general fund used for special education.

** Expenditures of the Department of Human Resources for services provided directly to school districts.

Source: Office of Special Education, *Sixth Annual Report to Congress* (Washington, D.C.: U.S. Government Printing Office, 1984), p. 52.

as part of the total expenditures for handicapped school children. These include such sources as Title XIX: Medicaid (for Early and Periodic Screening, Diagnosis and Treatment), Crippled Children's Program, Maternal and Child Health Funds, Mental Health Service Funds, Mental Retardation/Developmental Disabilities Program, Title XX: Social Services, and the Vocational Rehabilitation Program.

The variations between the state and local shares are, of course, a function of the state's general philosophy of educational finance more than the particular formula for distribution of state funding for special education, and the importance of the local program director's mastery of the state distribution procedures versus local budgeting issues will depend on the ratio of state to local sharing in the particular state. Regardless of whether the demand generates from state-imposed cost accounting for state aid or the local district's need for accountability, local managers must be able to identify both revenue sources and costs. Both for estimation in budget planning and for monitoring of expenditures, it is crucial to know what resource commitments are necessary and reasonable.

TRACKING THE COSTS

An important prerequisite to dealing with budget development or monitoring is to have some benchmarks for judging typical costs for special education, totally and categorically by a number of different possible breakdowns. Normative figures based on expenditure history have become available from a variety of cost studies, but most have had rather serious shortcomings. Most studies have focused on limited samples, or from specific states that cannot be extensively generalized. The first comprehensive source of data of this sort was obtained in 1970 from the report of the National Educational Finance

Project (NEFP).[6] Although this study covered 24 school systems across 5 states and included a rather detailed analysis of expenditures by budget categories, the fact that it was broken down strictly by categorical disability programs (with no distinctions drawn for various levels and types of services delivered) made the results of limited value for interpretation.

A major improvement was provided by the federally sponsored study by The Rand Corporation,[7] reporting data collected on the 1977-78 school year from 46 localities in 14 states. The 50 local school systems and 57 intermediate or cooperative service organizations were chosen so as to provide a stratified probabilistic sample, representative of the nation in terms of the conditions known to be influential to the provision of special education services—population density, personal income per capita, type of state special education funding formula, minority enrollment, and so on. Furthermore, the study employed a very detailed and sophisticated data collection and analysis procedure that permitted interpretation from a great variety of perspectives and classifications. The major dimensions of the data collection and analysis utilized will be described here to provide a demonstration of the utility of the information for future budget development and analysis.

Throughout the study, costs of regular education for nonhandicapped students were calculated so as to provide a base for comparison with various special education programs. The *added* costs (and ratio indices) for special education could thereby be considered, so that absolute differences that may exist geographically as a function of general costs of living, and changes that occur as a function of inflation over time, would not unduly limit the interpretive value of the findings. This is extremely important since, as the authors of the report on the study indicate, during the three-year time span between the collection of the data (1977-78) and the publication of the report in 1981, the increase in expenditures was estimated to be 37 percent. While the inflation rate since 1981 has been much less, it is probably appropriate to add about 50 percent to the reported (1977-78) figures to make the translation to 1985.

It should be noted that while the earlier (NEFP) study provided a crude indication of the wide variance in expenditures among handicapping conditions and among school systems, the reporting design of the Rand study included only average figures for the nation as a whole, with no basis for interpreting the variances within any of the multiple categories for which costs were reported. This limitation has significant consequences for both policymakers and managers at all levels.

Identified Cost Categories

The total cost of special education and related services per handicapped child in 1977-78 was estimated to be $3,577, which was 2.17 times the $1,650 estimated for a nonhandicapped student. These costs were broken down into categories relating to instructional costs of special education teachers, regular education teachers, instructional aides (both regular and special); related services personnel, screening, assessment, admission and IEP development, staff inservice training, technical assistance, transportation, instructional supplies and equipment, administration (at the building level, the district level, and for special education personnel), food service, facility operation and maintenance, and facility modification and improvement. While most of the cost categories for nonhandicapped students are also applicable for handicapped, many additional items enter in for the latter. A composite listing of average costs for both handicapped and nonhandicapped is displayed in Table 11-2.

It should be noted that the largest cost category is for *regular teachers'* instructional services, for both the handicapped and nonhandicapped. This is, of course, due to the fact that while the many handicapped children in full-time special classes or special schools would have no costs for regular teachers, the vast majority are served in some fashion wherein assignment to a regular teacher constitutes a major part of their total educational program and must be accounted for accordingly. As is usually the case with averages, these figures fail to communicate the multiple sources of variation in cost figures that were found as a function of type of handicapping condition, type of service delivery model, and age level of the students involved. These three dimensions were used to break down further the collected cost data for analysis.

Cost figures were calculated separately for 13 handicapping conditions, using terminology and categories consistent with federal definitions, which (due to standard reporting requirements) are reasonably similar across all the states in the study. Breakdowns by severity levels within major categories were in accordance with classifications found in use in the various states represented, which appeared to yield reasonably equivalent types of students from one local system to another.

The types of service delivery model, or placements, included 10 different arrangements. Four of these involved regular class as the basic placement but with different additional services (indirect services, related services, itinerant special teacher, part-time special class). Special classes (either full-time or with part-time assignment to a regular class), special day school, homebound instruction, short-term hospital, and full-time work made up the other placements. The latter was a type of program used for a very small number of secondary-aged students who attended no classes but were under partial supervision by public school special education program personnel while employed for occupational training. It should be noted that the study involved only public education agencies and did not include any residential school placements.

Age groups consisting of preschool (age 0 to 4), elementary (age 5 to 11) and secondary (age 12 to 18) provided the remaining dimension for classifying and analyzing the cost data.

TABLE 11-2   Annual Cost of Education per Child in 1977-78*

TYPE OF COST	HANDICAPPED	NON HANDICAPPED
Regular teachers' instruction services	$743	$761
Instructional costs of special education teachers	551	—
Facility operations and maintenance	378	207
Debt service	245	147
School administration	209	96
General district administration	200	105
Related services personnel	191	61
Technical assistance to staff	135	—
Special transportation	111	—
Special education aides	106	—
Admission, placement, IEP development	103	—
Assessment	100	—
Food services	88	84
Special education administrators and secretaries	76	—
Instructional supplies and texts	66	34
Regular transportation	48	73
Facility modification and improvement (general)	44	26
Staff inservice training	40	—
Miscellaneous costs	25	23
Instructional equipment	21	14
Regular education aides	19	8
Related services staff administrators, secretaries, clerks	18	5
Facility modification and improvement (special)	12	—
Special education nonpersonnel administrative costs	11	—
Related services staff, nonclassroom teacher supplies	10	3
Special education program specialists	9	—
Screening for handicapping conditions	8	3
Related services staff, nonclassroom teacher equipment	7	—
Related services staff, nonclassroom teacher transportation	3	—
Total	$3,577	$1,650

*To approximate 1985 costs, add 50 percent.

Source: J.S. Kakalik et al., *The Cost of Special Education,* Rand Note N-1792-ED (Santa Monica, Calif.: The Rand Corporation, 1981), pp. 31–33.

Costs by Handicapping Condition
and Type of Placement

To display the resulting cost figures when broken down by these three dimensions, three tables are necessary, with each one showing one dimension against another. The total annual costs for each handicapping condition, each type of placement, and each age level, as well as all combinations can thus be seen. In addition, since the comparative costs of each to that for nonhandicapped students may provide a better basis for evaluating and predicting the costs in any particular locality and in any condition of general inflationary increase, the tables also indicate cost indices (the ratio of special education costs to regular education costs) based on regular nonhandicapped costs at 1.0. Table 11-3 displays the total annual costs and the cost indices for each handicapping condition against each type of educational placement, combining all age levels together.

Cost Variations by Age Level

These figures mask some rather significant variations that exist between age levels, since there are certain programs that are relatively unavailable at preschool levels and programs that are very different from one age level to another. Combining all handicapping conditions and all types of placements together, elementary age-level programs tend to be slightly less costly and secondary-level programs more costly, with preschool programs falling at about the average. However, within certain handicaps (e.g., the blind and the deaf), the order is reversed. Similarly, within certain types of placements (e.g., itinerant special teacher and special class plus part-time regular class), the elementary-level programs are the more costly. The cost variations as a function of age level within handicapping conditions (combining all types of placements) are displayed in Table 11-4, and those variations as a function of age within types of placements (combining all handicapping conditions) are displayed in Table 11-5.

In interpreting the data presented in these tables, it should be noted that they reflect the expenditure history in those school systems represented, and while the sample was selected to provide maximum generalizability, certain artifacts exist that must be taken into consideration. For example, since speech impaired students constitute such a large proportion of the total, and since virtually all of them (97.86 percent) are served in regular classes with speech therapy provided as a related service, and since the great majority of these (88.48 percent) are at the elementary age level, the impact of speech-impaired students on the cost data at certain points in the total analysis may be distorting. In addition, the preschool age level constituted only about 2 percent of the total sample, whereas elementary age students were about double (65.64 percent) secondary age students (32.25 percent) when all types of handicaps were combined. However, if the speech impaired in the sample are excluded,

TABLE 11-3   Estimated Total Annual Cost per Student and Cost Index by Handicapping Condition and Type of Placement

HANDICAPPED CONDITION	REGULAR CLASSROOM PLUS INDIVIDUALIZED SERVICES	REGULAR CLASSROOM PLUS RELATED SERVICES	REGULAR CLASSROOM PLUS ITINERANT SPECIAL TEACHER	REGULAR CLASSROOM PLUS PART-TIME SPECIAL CLASS	SPECIAL CLASS PLUS PART-TIME REGULAR CLASS	FULL-TIME SPECIAL CLASS	SPECIAL DAY SCHOOL	HOME-BOUND INSTRUCTION	SHORT-TERM HOSPITAL	FULL-TIME WORK	ALL PLACEMENTS COMBINED
Learning disabled	$2,552 1.55	$3,338 2.02	$4,456 2.70	$4,714 2.86	$4,011 2.43	$4,432 2.69	$7,252 4.40	$2,268 1.37	NA	$ 830 0.50	$4,525 2.74
Educable mentally retarded	3,113 1.89	2,488 1.51	3,884 2.35	3,874 2.35	4,058 2.46	3,265 1.98	3,049 1.85	2,629 1.59	2,844 1.72	1,069 0.65	3,795 2.30
Trainable mentally retarded	NA	NA	NA	5,283 3.20	5,660 3.43	5,853 3.55	5,354 3.24	2,400 1.45	NA	807 0.49	5,519 3.34
Severely mentally retarded	NA	NA	NA	NA	6,600 4.00	7,695 4.66	5,997 3.63	2,302 1.40	NA	NA	5,926 3.59
Emotionally disturbed	3,147 1.91	6,501 3.94	7,946 4.82	6,904 4.18	5,417 3.28	5,750 3.48	6,206 3.76	3,167 1.92	2,624 1.59	2,899 1.76	6,269 3.81
Deaf	NA	9,301 5.64	9,276 5.62	5,380 3.26	5,963 3.61	7,691 4.66	7,909 4.79	NA	NA	NA	7,311 4.43

Condition	C1	C2	C3	C4	C5	C6	C7	C8	C9	C10	C11
Hearing impaired	2,181 / 1.32	2,480 / 1.50	4,701 / 2.85	6,979 / 4.23	5,901 / 3.58	6,631 / 4.02	6,896 / 4.18	2,167 / 1.31	3,273 / 1.98	NA	5,091 / 3.09
Blind	NA	NA	11,189 / 6.78	9,874 / 5.98	8,779 / 5.32	5,966 / 3.62	9,126 / 5.53	NA	NA	NA	9,664 / 5.86
Sight impaired	2,936 / 1.78	2,740 / 1.66	4,097 / 2.48	6,369 / 3.86	5,711 / 3.46	5,220 / 3.16	7,913 / 4.80	2,078 / 1.26	NA	NA	4,519 / 2.74
Orthopedic impaired	2,772 / 1.68	4,884 / 2.96	4,986 / 3.02	7,175 / 4.35	5,031 / 3.05	5,495 / 3.33	5,731 / 3.47	2,137 / 1.30	1,911 / 1.16	NA	3,546 / 2.15
Other Health impaired	NA	2,403 / 1.46	2,021 / 1.22	4,973 / 3.01	4,937 / 2.99	4,664 / 2.83	3,676 / 2.23	2,611 / 1.58	1,951 / 1.18	NA	2,502 / 1.52
Speech impaired	2,477 / 1.50	2,244 / 1.36	2,360 / 1.43	4,025 / 2.44	3,500 / 2.12	5,439 / 3.30	2,936 / 1.78	1,509 / 0.91	NA	NA	2,253 / 1.37
Multiple impaired	NA / 1.21	2,004	NA / 6.17	10,187 / 5.32	8,778 / 3.14	5,183 / 5.48	9,048 / 2.05	3,376 / 1.19	1,956	NA	7,642 / 4.63
All conditions	2,550 / 1.55	2,267 / 1.37	5,218 / 3.16	4,709 / 2.85	4,345 / 2.63	4,733 / 2.87	5,352 / 3.24	2,228 / 1.35	1,981 / 1.20	901 / 0.55	3,577 / 2.17

NA–Not available

Source: J. S. Kakalik et al., *The Cost of Special Education* (Santa Monica, Calif.: The Rand Corporation, 1981), pp. 36, 43.

TABLE 11-4   Estimated Total Annual Cost per Student and Cost Index By Handicapping Condition and Age Level

HANDICAPPING CONDITION	AGE LEVEL						ALL AGES COMBINED	
	Preschool		Elementary		Secondary			
	Cost	Index	Cost	Index	Cost	Index	Cost	Index
Learning disabled	$3,392	2.06	$4,488	2.72	$4,856	2.78	$4,525	2.74
Educable mentally retarded	3,465	2.10	3,958	2.40	3,684	2.23	3,795	2.30
Trainable mentally retarded	4,715	2.86	5,078	3.08	6,008	3.64	5,519	3.34
Severely mentally retarded	5,352	3.24	6,013	3.64	5,935	3.60	5,926	3.59
Emotionally disturbed	3,260	1.98	5,871	3.56	6,845	4.15	6,289	3.81
Deaf	7,676	4.65	8,523	5.17	5,200	3.15	7,311	4.43
Hearing impaired	5,853	3.55	4,861	2.95	5,204	3.15	5,091	3.09
Blind	6,603	4.00	11,725	7.11	8,917	5.40	9,664	5.86
Sight impaired	3,254	1.97	4,063	2.46	5,253	3.18	4,519	2.74
Orthopedic impaired	5,097	3.09	3,350	2.03	3,545	2.15	3,546	2.15
Other health impaired	2,319	1.41	2,148	1.30	2,748	1.67	2,502	1.52
Speech impaired	2,490	1.51	2,214	1.34	2,580	1.56	2,253	1.37
Multiple impaired	9,382	5.69	7,165	4.34	7,773	4.71	7,642	4.63
All conditions	3,526	2.14	3,267	1.98	4,099	2.48	3,577	2.17

Source: J. S. Kakalik et al., *The Cost of Special Education* (Santa Monica, Calif.: The Rand Corporation, 1981), pp. 34, 41.

the sample has a virtually equal number of elementary and secondary age students.

Costs of Instructional Personnel

While it is not our purpose to scrutinize the methodology that was necessary to produce the data that the Rand study has provided, some aspects of the analysis can be very instructive in demonstrating the complexity of tracking the total actual costs for special education services. For example, while the cost for teachers is quite straight forward in all full-time placements, the computation in part-time programs requires a proration based on the number of minutes the student is under the instructional care of each teacher.

Costs per pupil for special education teachers were computed in this study by recording actual amounts of time spent in resource rooms or with itinerant teachers. The costs per pupil for regular teachers (for students receiving part-time special education services) was computed by not only counting the handicapped student as one of the total class membership (for the proportion of

TABLE 11-5   Estimated Total Annual Cost per Student and Cost Index By Type of Placement and Age Level

HANDICAPPING CONDITION	AGE LEVEL						ALL AGES COMBINED	
	Preschool		Elementary		Secondary			
	Cost	Index	Cost	Index	Cost	Index	Cost	Index
Regular class plus								
Individualized service	NA	NA	$2,362	1.43	$2,710	1.64	$2,550	1.55
Related service	$1,871	1.13	2,231	1.35	2,601	1.58	2,267	1.37
Itinerant teacher	1,167	0.71	5,588	3.39	4,247	2.57	5,218	3.16
Part-time special class	2,307	1.40	4,481	2.72	4,916	2.98	4,709	2.85
Special class plus Part-time regular class	2,311	1.40	5,038	3.05	3,778	2.29	4,345	2.63
Full-time Special Class	5,352	3.24	5,008	3.04	3,710	2.25	4,733	2.87
Special Day School	5,841	3.54	4,444	2.69	6,669	4.04	5,352	3.24
Homebound	1,629	0.99	2,106	1.28	2,660	1.61	2,228	1.35
Short-Term Hospital	1,921	1.16	1,804	1.09	2,310	1.40	1,981	1.20
Full time work	NA	NA	NA	NA	901	0.55	901	0.55
All placements	3,526	2.14	3,267	1.98	4,099	2.48	3,577	2.17

NA – Not available.

Source: J. S. Kakalik et al., *The Cost of Special Education* (Santa Monica, Calif.: The Rand Corporation, 1981), pp. 35, 42.

the day the child was in the regular classroom) but also adding a factor for the *extra* time the regular teacher spent with the child beyond the time spent on the average nonhandicapped child. This factor was established purely by estimation from interviews with teachers and was the product of a great variety of separate opinions. The grand average for all ages, all handicapping conditions, and all types of placements was 5 extra minutes per day, which calculated to $206 per year. Regular teacher involvement is negligible at the preschool level, and the estimates for this item were slightly higher at secondary than elementary levels. The factor was greatest for placements in regular class with only itinerant service ($746 for all handicaps combined) and in the regular class plus part-time special class ($406). It should be noted that all personnel costs are inclusive of both salary and fringe benefits.

Costs of Aides and Related Services

Costs for special education aides and for related services personnel could be computed directly. While the average cost for aides was $106, this type of service was most used in special day schools (at a cost of $598 per pupil per year) and in full-time special classes (at a cost of $453). Certain types of placements use no aides at all. By handicapping condition, aides were most used with severely mentally retarded (at $1,210), multihandicapped (at $1,143), trainable mentally retarded (at $650), and deaf (at $648). Related services costs were somewhat more evenly distributed around an average cost of $191. Students in special day school placements showed the highest costs ($630 for all ages and handicapping conditions combined) and multihandicapped accounted for the highest cost for related services ($1,179) for all ages and types of placement combined. There are obviously certain conditions, placements, and age levels where the costs for aides and for related services are negligible.

Costs of Other Processes

As with the costs for regular teachers, the time spent by regular education aides, and by the variety of personnel who are involved with screening, assessment, admission, and IEP development must be prorated on the basis of estimated time spent on these activities out of a total work load. To compute an annual cost per child for assessment, it was necessary to determine which personnel were involved, the cost of the time spent by each for each assessment, and the average number of assessments completed on each child per year. The results of such calculation showed an annual cost for the related service and nonclassroom teacher personnel of $72 per child per year and for the involvement of the special education teachers in assessment, a child per year cost of $26. The involvement of regular teachers added another $2, for a total assessment cost of $100 for each handicapped child each year.

The costs of admission, placement, and IEP development processes also are the sum of contributions by a great number of different personnel. The salary and fringe benefits for all the personnel time spent preparing for and attending meetings for this purpose (with the exception of time spent on assessment), as well as writing and revising the IEP, are calculated into this overall function. Of the total cost estimate of $103 per child, the largest single component ($28) was for the special education teacher's time in writing the IEP. Other participants for whom cost accrued included regular teachers, counselors, diagnostic/placement/IEP specialists, nurses, psychologists, social workers, speech therapists, school administrators, special education administrators, and secretaries. As would be expected, the cost of the process varied as a function of handicapping condition, with the highest cost for partially sighted and multihandicapped and the lowest for speech impaired and orthopedic. A similar variation appeared as a function of type of placement, with the highest figures for programs in regular classes with indirect services or with itinerant services and the lowest associated with short-term hospital placements.

The costs of technical assistance to staff and for inservice training was estimated at $135 and $40, respectively. Variation in technical assistance showed the highest costs associated with the blind and the emotionally disturbed and the lowest with speech impaired and orthopedic. Regular class placements with itinerant services and with part-time special class had the highest costs and short-term hospital placements the lowest.

Costs for transportation included both regular and special transportation and are calculated as a total figure for *all* handicapped children. Since many require no transportation, the actual cost for those individuals who do would be much greater than the average figures calculated from this study. However, since the sample was demonstrated to be representative of the national special education population, the figures are predictive of what should be found to be needed. The average cost of $159 per student varied widely as a function of handicapping condition and type of placement, with the highest costs associated with multihandicapped ($980) and severely mentally retarded ($849). Placements in special day schools ($581) and full-time special classes ($410) accrued the highest transportation costs across all handicapping conditions.

Costs of Administration

Administrative costs are usually classified as including a variety of personnel and other necessary resources, most of which cannot be directly associated with specific programs and pupils but must be prorated across the student enrollment. However, with the concept of weighted enrollment, handicapped students can correctly be calculated as requiring a greater share of certain administrative costs than the nonhandicapped counterpart. The most obvious example would be those administrative costs that are associated with the teacher or classroom unit. Facility operations and maintenance costs are to a large degree proportionately attributable to a room in a building. If a special education classroom serves only one-half or one-third as many students as the regular classroom, the per pupil cost of this item would, therefore, be two or three times that of the cost for nonhandicapped. Likewise, the cost of administrative personnel for supervision and similar functions tends to be based on the teacher, regardless of whether that teacher has 8 or 28 students. While some special education classrooms serving a small number of students may actually have less square footage to maintain, and fewer children per teacher may reduce certain administrative chores, the overall costs of administration must be calculated on a weighted pupil basis.

Some of the largest administrative cost items include those that must be totally prorated, as no direct connection to specific programs is possible. The average cost of facility operation and maintenance in the Rand study was computed at $378 and debt service (to pay principal and interest on capital construction) at $245 per pupil per year. For administrative personnel, the largest factor was the school building level, which includes salaries and fringe benefits for principals, assistants, secretaries and other administrative personnel at the school site, administrative supplies and equipment, travel, and so on. This figure was computed at $209, again weighted in accordance with teacher-pupil load. The similar figure for general districtwide administration was $200. The cost for special education administrators and other such program specialists and related staff was much smaller, computed at only $96.

Conclusions Regarding Costs

Interpretation of the extensive data provided by the Rand study can lead one to a number of important conclusions, and perhaps some additional questions about the relationship between program planning and budgeting. The figures point up rather clearly the degree to which special education is integrally involved with the general education program and its budget. Most of the identifiable costs for handicapped students are derived as a prorated share of the general costs for education. It is also clear that very little of the total costs are discretionary. Instructional supplies and equipment, for example, constitute only $87 (about 2.5 percent) of the total annual costs. Costs for assessment, admission, placement, and IEP development are rather well established by regulations reflecting federal requirements. The largest factor in determining what a program for a particular child will cost is the intensity of instructional and related services provided. Instructional service intensity (pupil-teacher ratio) is controlled by state regulation, in most instances, for a particular type of handicap or placement option. The major controllable variation, therefore, lies in the decision as to what type of service option is chosen for each child, and what types of alternatives are promoted as local district policy.

For some children, obvious needs preclude any debate as to type of placement. Homebound instruction and short-term hospital service would usually be unequivocal, but these cases constitute a very small proportion of the total. Special day school placements appear to be the most expensive alternative, but there may well be little choice in the majority of cases assigned to such programs. Itinerant teacher services for students remaining in regular classes appear to be one of the more expensive alternatives, again due to the very low teacher-pupil ratio while that service is being provided.

An interesting conclusion from the Rand data is that the typical resource teacher or resource room model (regular class plus part-time special class) appears to be almost identical in cost to the full-time special class. For certain handicapping conditions (blind, multihandicapped, emotionally disturbed) the resource model yields significantly higher costs than does the full-time special class. If the cost data are an accurate reflection of reasonably appropriate staffing and service provision within each of those service models, there should be little financial incentive for choosing either way between a full-time special class and a resource program. In other words, fiscal neutrality as to actual costs may exist between these choices, leaving only the possible influence of distorted state support formulas to create a bias in placement decisions.

It is important to remember that conclusions drawn from the Rand data can only provide comparative estimates, and complete program planning and budget development must utilize a system that takes into consideration specific factors of the state and local school system. As indicated earlier, the absence of data on the variances among school systems, within the categories of handicapping conditions, service settings, and ages served constitutes a severe limitation. Furthermore, the budgeting procedures that may be peculiar to individual school systems can play a part in dealing with special education costs, for both planning and reporting purposes.

A dramatic example is described by Andersen, in the case of New York City, where special education resources were divided between a special system-wide budget of the Division of Special Education and the regular education budgets of the 32 separate community districts.[8] In that case, the difficulty in establishing the costs of the programming changes necessary for attaining full compliance with mandates was very evident. A report released by the city administration projected staggering cost increases and received wide press coverage, leading to editorial questioning of the appropriateness of such goals.[9] As Andersen points out, closer examination of the published figures revealed that they failed to distinguish between new costs and expenditures merely transferred from one account to another. They also failed to recognize that the increased services would also initiate increased income from state and federal sources. Finally, the figures obscured the fact that the new services were largely for students who would be less costly than those that had been previously provided for if the most appropriate programs for the new students were utilized.

> Therefore, because of the highly politicized nature of the special education cost question, studies such as those reported by the press verge on being artifacts of deception, either by design or error. They fail to define and analyze what is meant by a special education cost.[10]

This situation points up some conceptual problems in dealing with special education costs. Major issues that Andersen mentions include the following:

1. Whether to deal with total program or perpupil costs. While perpupil costs are most useful for comparing various program alternatives, and for highlighting variability, it is sometimes important to emphasize a "bottom line."
2. Whether to focus on full or marginal cost. That is, the cost of adding one more child to the existing system will not be as great as the perpupil cost of those that put the system into place and on which all the necessary overhead is computed.
3. Whether to emphasize new or displaced costs. Almost every child is using some services, somewhere. The total cost of a child's program consists of some portion of new costs and other costs that are merely moved from some other part of the system. Where the system has separate divisional budgets, the displaced costs become an accounting problem, as a savings for one division probably becomes an added cost for another.

4. How best to account for indirect support costs. Since support services often cannot be readily associated with a precise population, it is difficult to determine just what proration to attribute to each subcategory of special program.[11]

Procedures devised for approaching these and other questions systematically will be presented in the next section.

PROGRAM PLANNING AND BUDGETING

It is generally conceded that budgeting in most public service agencies, including schools, usually is a process of looking at what funds were provided and expended in the current and/or immediate past year and making incremental adjustments to the extent that circumstances of resource availability and demand for services dictate. While this process is roundly criticized, it has proven difficult to change. Attempts to implement "zero-based budgeting" have tended to be only partially successful, at best, but to the extent that such efforts have allowed (or forced) program oriented personnel to become better acquainted with the financial facts of life, and thereby be better guided in policy development and program decisions, the attempts have probably had positive effects.

The linkage of program planning to budgeting is an important aspect of the process. At times when change in program structure or magnitude is anticipated, due to such factors as conceptual or attitudinal breakthroughs (e.g., new social policies) or population growth, mobility, or decline, the press for planning may stimulate a need for and interest in more systematic budgeting. One approach to program planning that is closely tied to budget development and that has received favorable attention at both the state and local levels will be described here as an illustration.

The Special Education Planning Model (SEPM), developed under federal contract by Hartman, was originally designed to assist state education agencies to project program needs and necessary financial support.[12] That model was used in over 30 states. An adaptation for local use was then designed to be installed and operated using computer facilities in local school systems.[13] This local model is an interactive computer program, intended for use by personnel without previous computer experience, which calls for data to be introduced from worksheets prepared by special education program personnel who can be expected to have at hand (or be readily able to secure) the necessary raw information.

The steps in using the model include the following:

1. Filling out worksheets calling for district data regarding such items as overall enrollment, anticipated changes, inflation rates, current special education provisions, current resources supplied, prices of resources, program enrollments, desired ratios for students to service providers, and so on.

2. Entering the data into the computer in response to prompts provided by the computer program. This process generates tables that are used for additional worksheet preparation and subsequent alterations.

3. Reviewing the output that consists of 18 reports, to be used as a basis for planning decisions.

4. Making alternative projections to test the effect of adjustments to original "best guesses" about the future special education program. With the initial data entered, it is easy to make additional runs to update or utilize new information.

The data entered into the model include certain factual items, such as actual enrollment and observed rates (e.g., incidence of handicapped students, cost inflation) from which trends can be projected. The model also requires much estimation, based on professional judgment, for which familiarity with the local situation is a crucial requirement. In short, there is no magic in the model or its computerized operation. It simply guides the knowledgeable program specialist systematically through the planning process and budget projection.

The data requirements are based on assumptions regarding standard incidence of various handicapping conditions and normative practices in serving them, attenuated by local circumstances and service delivery history, further adjusted by desired modifications to present practice. To accomplish this process, the following data items are introduced:

1. Total student enrollment
2. Current and projected inflation rate
3. Existing special education program categories (by handicapping condition or by service provided, but with care to avoid overlaps which would produce duplicated counts)
4. Current number served, by category
5. Instructional programs provided
6. Types of resources used for each instructional program (e.g. teachers, aides, materials, travel)
7. Unit price of each instructional resource
8. Amounts of each instructional resource currently used
9. Types of related services provided
10. Resources required for each related service
11. Unit price of each resource
12. Amounts of each related service resource currently used
13. Current student placements in instructional programs, (primary and additional)
14. Current prevalence rate for instructional programs
15. Current student placements in related services programs
16. Current prevalence rate for related services
17. Anticipated student placements (primary and additional) in instructional programs
18. Anticipated student placements in related service programs
19. Current personnel ratios, by program

20. Desired personnel ratios, by program
21. District support services, by type
22. Resources required for each support service
23. Unit price for each resource
24. Service levels (number of units provided)
25. Number of resources (e.g. staff) per unit

After data are entered into the computer program, the output of 18 different reports is as follows:

1. District information
2. Number of students, by category
3. Number of students, by program and service
4. Projected student numbers and placements
5. Program and service description
6. Personnel ratios
7. Number of personnel, by category
8. Number of personnel, by program and service
9. Costs, by category
10. Costs, by programs and services
11. Costs per student, by category—instructional programs
12. Costs per student, by category—related services
13. Total costs per student, by category
14. Costs per student, by program and service
15. Summary by category
16. Summary by program and service
17. District support services description
18. District support services

These reports constitute the initial best guess in the planning process and are of greatest value when subjected to testing by the introduction of alternative choices, estimates, or assumptions regarding what could happen under certain changed circumstances.

The process used in the Special Education Planning Model has been extended more broadly to apply to general state-level fiscal policy development, by employing a more systematic information input process and making necessary refinements to handle all types of regular and special education programs. An overview of that application to budget development within the total system, with its particular use for special education, may also be of value.

THE RESOURCE COST MODEL

The development of the Resource Cost Model (RCM) at the Institute for Research on Educational Finance and Governance has been reported by Chambers and Hartman[14] and by Chambers and Parrish. They describe the RCM as primarily a conceptual framework for sorting out the factors underlying differences in educational costs. It provides a systematic method for allowing program experts and educational policy makers to organize data relevant to the determination of the cost of educational programs. Beyond this, the RCM is a computer program which can organize data on educational resources (i.e., inputs) and resource costs to facilitate estimation of programmatic costs both as they relate to differences in the educational needs of different student populations, to variations in the scale of school and district operations, and to variations in the costs of comparable resources.[15]

A major strength of the approach is that it brings together business and curriculum personnel of a local school system (or an entire state) and leads them through a series of activities that permit a blending of their respective concerns. By allowing all parties to clarify their primary objectives and (through computer simulation) to see the cost implications of various approaches to the pursuit of the total school mission, planning and budgeting can proceed concurrently with immediate feedback as to the probable impact of alternative decision choices.

Whether at a state or district level, the RCM contains three basic elements of data collection and analysis:

1. Program and services specifications (as determined by local district choices within state regulation)
2. Student enrollment patterns
3. Resource price and cost data (from cost of education index, CEI, analysis)

The utilization of these data occurs in a series of steps that can be seen in overview in Figure 11-1. At various points in the model, information from two or more sources are brought together and the computer program produces output that takes the form of an informational report and provides data for a subsequent calculation.

Some details regarding the scope of the various inputs are important to understand. For example, the personnel supplying data need to be conscious of such things as

1. Variations in the types of instructional programs and related services needed
2. Variations in requirements for instructional programs and related services in districts of different sizes
3. Variations in the need for special equipment
4. Variations in the administrative and support requirements in different-sized programs, schools, and districts
5. Variations in the administrative and support requirements in different program areas (e.g., elementary, special education, compensatory education); for different types of schools (e.g., elementary schools, high schools, vocational centers); and for different components of general district operations (e.g., executive administration, personnel, fiscal services, operations and maintenance)[16]

A more detailed breakdown of various inputs points up the need to differentiate clearly among types of items within each variable. For example,

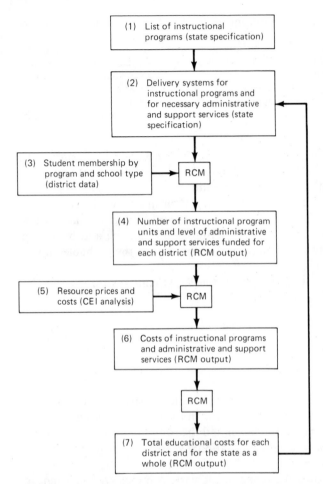

FIGURE 11-1   RCM Data Inputs and Outputs. *Source:* Jay G. Chambers and Thomas B. Parrish, *Adequacy and in state School Financing and Planning: A Resource Cost Model Approach* (Stanford: Institute for Research on Educational Finance and Governance, 1983), p. 30.

delivery systems for instructional programs that must be defined with clarity and avoidance of overlap include self-contained classroom, special class, supplemental instruction or service, supplemental resource, resource center, departmentalized instruction, and external assignment. Similarly, administrative and support services must be differentiated among those that are at the school building level, the program category, and the general district level. The specification of resources must be addressed to each of these identifiable categories.

The derivation of prices and costs of each resource is accomplished by taking known averages and making adjustments to reflect predictable circumstantial variances. Professional salaries, other personnel costs, and energy costs can be expected to be subject to local conditions, but reasonably predictable in relation to average costs. The resulting total cost for a program unit can then be considered, either in terms of its contribution to the bottom line for the system as a whole or as an anticipated obligation per student unit.

When used for statewide planning and projection, or even for multiple program purposes within a single district, the recommended process calls for the appointment of program category committees, consisting of persons who can provide informed judgment as to program needs and resource configurations. Then a single member of each program category committee serves on a central RCM committee, which has a representation extending beyond the interests of education, to reflect the general concerns of the society for both education and other public services. It is through this representation that RCM specifications and recommendations move through the final policy making and fiscal appropriation bodies. An intermediate step (level 2) has the representatives of the various program category committees meeting as a program review panel, for an initial evaluation and standardization of the full set of programs. A schematic representation of the intergroups processes, applied in this case to statewide use, is shown in Figure 11-2.

It is understood that at each level of involvement, evaluation, negotiation, and bargaining must occur. Educational interests will always reside within the context of resource constraints. Recognition of these constraints will occur at each level and will involve both intraprogram and interprogram category pressures and necessary compromises. The recommended process provides for calculations to be made from three different estimates—a desired, or "best guess" figure, a minimum limit figure, and a maximum limit figure. For example, class size for self-contained multiply handicapped might be projected for a target size of 7, but include a calculation for a minimum size of 4 and a maximum of 12. Similar bracketing around optimal "target" estimates may also be used for anticipated needs, prices, and other resource to student ratios. To make these estimates valid, the expertise of the program committee personnel is of course the crucial requisite.

SUMMARY

The major aim of this chapter has been to demonstrate the importance of the interface between program and financial concerns in administering the special education delivery system. Working effectively at the edge of that interface requires knowledge of the facts of the programmatic needs and options, as well as the resource alternatives and limitations. Effective use of that knowledge will be facilitated by a systematic approach to program planning and resource analysis. No one system can be expected to produce correct and unequivocal answers to program and budget questions. The models described here,

Level 1: Program Category Committees

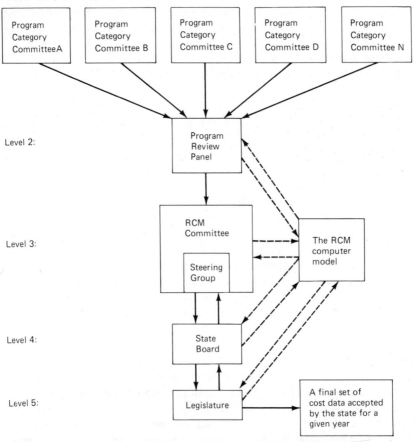

FIGURE 11-2   The Resource Cost Model Process. *Source:* Jay G. Chambers and Thomas B. Parrish, *Adequacy and Equity in State School Finance and Planning: A Resource Cost Model Approach* (Stanford: Institute for Research on Educational Finance and Governance, 1983), p. 14.

however, can lend some order to the process and provide the special education administrator with a basis for active participation, and perhaps leadership in what must always be a complex, multidimensional, professionally shared effort.

NOTES

[1]C. Lamar Mayer, *Educational Administration and Special Education: A Handbook for School Administrators* (Boston: Allyn & Bacon, 1982), pp. 313-314.

[2]David F. Andersen, "Redefining the Implementation of Special Education Programs in Fiscal Terms," *Human Systems Management,* 2 (1981) 294-305.

3"Progress Toward a Free Appropriate Public Education," *A Report to Congress on the Implementation of Public Law 94-142: The Education for All Handicapped Children Act* (Washington, D.C.: U.S. Department of Health, Education and Welfare, 1979), p. 113.

4Mary T. Moore, Lisa J. Walker, and Richard P. Holland, *Finetuning Special Education Finance: A Guide for State Policymakers* (Washington, D.C.: Education Policy Research Institute of Educational Testing Service, 1982), p. 60.

5"To Assure the Free Appropriate Public Education of All Handicapped Children," *Sixth Annual Report to Congress on the Implementation of Public Law 94-142: The Education for All Handicapped Children Act* (Washington, D.C.: U.S. Department of Education, 1984), pp. 48–63.

6Richard A. Rossmiller, James Hale, and Lloyd E. Frohreich, *Educational Programs for Exceptional Children: Resource Configurations and Costs,* National Educational Finance Project Study No. 2 (Madison, Wisc.: Department of Educational Administration, University of Wisconsin, 1970).

7J. S. Kakalik, W. S. Furry, M. A. Thomas, and M. F. Carney, *The Cost of Special Education,* Rand Note N-1792-ED (Santa Monica, Calif.: The Rand Corporation, 1981).

8David F. Andersen, "Problems in Estimating the Costs of Special Education in Urban Areas: The New York City Case," *Journal of Educational Finance,* 7 (1982), 403-424.

9"The Schools and the Handicapped," *The New York Times,* January 8, 1980.

10Andersen, "Problems in Estimating," p. 417.

11Ibid., pp. 417-419.

12William T. Hartman, *Estimating the Costs of Educating Handicapped Children: A Resource-Cost Model Approach,* Final Report, Grant No. G007800013, Office of Education (Stanford, Calif.: School of Education, 1979).

13Peggy L. Hartman and William T. Hartman, *Local Special Education Planning Model: User's Manual,* Project Report No. 82-A20 (Stanford, Calif.: Institute for Research on Educational Finance and Governance, 1982), pp. 1-5.

14Jay G. Chambers and William T. Hartman, *A Cost-Based Approach to the Funding of Educational Programs: An Application to Special Education,* Project Report No. 81-A4 (Stanford, Calif.: Institute for Research on Educational Finance and Governance, 1981).

15Jay G. Chambers and Thomas B. Parrish, *Adequacy and Equity in State School Finance and Planning: A Resource Cost Model Approach* (Stanford, Calif.: Institute for Research on Educational Finance and Governance, 1983), p. 20.

16Ibid., pp. 38-39.

CHAPTER 12
PROGRAM
EVALUATION

The question of the 1980s in education clearly relates to program appropriateness and program quality rather than to one of access. With a legacy of advocacy, litigation, and mandates, disabled students have been guaranteed an education. The issue being raised by constituents is, "Are disabled students now receiving the appropriate specialized educational services?" School boards and superintendents still ask, "What must the school district do to serve the disabled under law? And for what cost?" Yet groups agree that the real issue is more and more "For what benefit? Is the investment worth it?"

Many special educators are asking how they can begin to answer the questions being posed by constituents and superiors. In this chapter, we emphasize defining the context of the evaluation situation as the most critical determining variable in preparing to answer their questions. We then suggest how to proceed to answer them. Identifying the right focus and purpose of the evaluation is the first decision in evaluation planning and contracting for internal or external evaluation services.

With many of the most frequent questions posed, we describe a set of assumptions to guide evaluation activities by the type of purpose the evaluation is to serve. We then present a set of evaluation models, using a variety of evaluative approaches and methods identified in the evaluation literature.

THE PURPOSE OF EVALUATION

Four reasons are often given to conduct program evaluation. They are

1. *Program improvement.* Evaluation serves as a management tool for the program administrator and his or her staff to make specific suggestions in the planning and implementation of a program or service
2. *Program review.* Evaluation serves as a means for top management to review periodically and audit the appropriateness of current program definition, scope, and quality of delivery
3. *Compliance.* Evaluation serves as a means for state agencies to assess if program implementation is being conducted in accordance with state and federal laws and regulations
4. *Community information.* Evaluation serves as a means to secure, maintain, and increase school patronage and taxpayer support for increased school funding and participation in school activities.

Horvath suggests a fifth reason which he labels as policy analysis. In his view, policy analysis as program evaluation is that activity initiated by policymakers regarding programmatic issues that require resolution at a policy level.[1]

Each of these purposes requires different sets of assumptions, planning approaches, and the actual conduct of an evaluation. We make frequent references to these purposes throughout this chapter.

DEFINING THE EVALUATION
DECISION OPTIONS

We would suggest that special educators first assess their organizational context to determine the evaluation opportunities. Using the questions posed below, we believe that the information gathered will save time and embarrassment and, it is hoped, benefit disabled students and their parents. First, it is important to determine what is to be decided by the initiation of a program evaluation. Who or what is to be gained from a positive or a negative evaluation? Put another way, what is to be changed or initiated? What is to be modified that currently exists in some form or another? What or who is to be terminated?

Unfortunately, the program leader cannot always pinpoint the decision(s) to be made and prepare his or her staff until the the evaluation is well underway. Focusing the decision agenda as quickly as possible is desirable for maximizing gains or minimizing losses. Either way, however, knowing what to expect may still not guarantee that a decision will be made on the basis of a formal assessment of the programs and services. The manifest purpose of the evaluation often gives away to more latent values and purposes. Most experienced administrators have learned that both the outcomes and the reasons for making the decisions that affect programs and personnel only become evident, if then, sometime after all is said and done.

A second question is, Who has the need to know in order to make the decision(s) or, at least, influence the outcome? Identifying the key stakeholders in the decision situation and what they value by way of information to control or influence the outcome(s) is the second most important task in defining the decision options. In other words, what's at stake for whom? It is important to probe for stakeholder values/concerns/interests to be served by a program change, modification, or termination. Generally, every current program or service has many more incumbents who seek to keep it intact rather than advocates who may want it changed. Assuming that the incumbent special educator can ascertain stakeholder values/concerns/interest, it is likewise important to sort their positions and weigh their individual or collective power and influence.

Organizing stakeholder positions and estimating their influence serves both political and practical considerations. Politically, it allows the leader to assess support and opposition, and practically, it allows the leader to gather data and information for a range of values/concerns/interests represented by the stakeholding individuals and groups.

Assuming that most of the outcomes can be defined and the stakes identified for the prime movers, the special educator can now turn to consider if the data can be collected. Time, money, and the personnel needed to obtain the information are practical considerations that may preclude the desired evaluation study. As the director contemplates the needed data and information for decision making, he or she should also consider the accuracy, relevance, and the timeliness of the data acquisition task. It is our experience that most evaluation studies are either compromised or aborted because the data demands exceed the capacity or the willingness of decision makers to support its collection. Often recollections and historical perceptions of what is already known substitute for extensive investment in new information. Getting a fix on the necessary data and information to deal with the outcomes desired is more important than determining if it is sufficient. Simon refers to this phenomenon as "satisficing." The program evaluator seldom if ever meets the "optimizing" criteria.[2]

Maher and Bennett[3] describe this set of decision outcomes as the fourth and final phase of a planning and evaluation process. In their terms, as given in Table 12-1, these questions represent outcome evaluation.

Maher and Bennett[4] provide a handy series of evaluation tactics organized around the components of program changes listed under three phases. Their components are presented in Table 12-2.

In summary, diagnosing the decision situation and the options is more what Lindbolm refers to as the "science of muddling through." Major changes

Table 12-1   Decision-Making Concerns Addressed by Outcome Evaluation

DECISION-MAKING CONCERN	EVALUATION FOCUS
To what extent have program goals been achieved?	Goal attainment
Have any positive or negative results not reflected in program goals been produced?	Related program effects
What do consumers think of the program?	Consumer reaction
Did the program cause the observed effects?	Cause-effect relations
What particular program elements were responsible for given effects?	
Was the program worth the resources invested in it?	Cost-effectiveness
How should the program be changed?	All of the above

Source: Charles Maher and Randy Bennett, *Planning and Evaluating Special Education Services*, © 1984, p. 15. Reprinted by permission of Prentice-Hall, Inc., Englewood Cliffs, N.J.

do not generally occur because of a program evaluation. We must expect incremental changes rather than drastic, fundamental change.[5] When we discuss approaches to program evaluation, we detail methods that special education leaders might consider that support long-term effects as well as methods that are employed to cool or defuse a hotbed of controversy.

KEY QUESTIONS

Next we delineate a series of key questions that are driving contemporary evaluation studies in special education. These questions are grouped into program outcomes or summative evaluation questions and process or formative evaluation questions. Some of our assumptions concerning these questions and evaluation in special education follow.

Product Outcomes or Summative Evaluation Questions

Certainly, the first question in this category is related to how disabled students are benefiting from special education programs and services. Are these benefits related to preparing them to return to the regular program? Do these benefits ensure a regular high school diploma? How do these benefits compare to those of their nondisabled peers? How are program graduates faring in community settings? These questions concern student achievement and post-school adjustment. What type of work are the graduates engaged in performing? What contribution are the disabled making in the community for themselves and others? Are they maintaining their own self-esteem? Are program graduates able to live alone in the community? Do they pay taxes?

Table 12-2   Components of a Program Design

I. Purpose
  A. Program rationale
  B. Scope
    1. Activities
    2. Client population
    3. Staff
  C. Major outcomes
II. Implementation
  A. Preconditions for operation
    1. Human resources
      (a) Number, type and qualifications of required staff
    2. Informational resources
      (a) Policies and procedures
        (1) Criteria for selecting program clients
        (2) Evaluation plan
    3. Technological resources
      (a) Materials
      (b) Equipment
    4. Financial resources
      (a) Budgets
        (1) Developmental
        (2) Operational
    5. Physical resources
      (a) Facilities
        (1) Rooms
        (2) Buildings
        (3) Sites
  B. Nature of methods and activities
  C. Roles, responsibilities, and relationships of staff members
  D. Sequence and timing of activities
  E. Amount of permissible variation across sites
III. Outcomes
  A. Program goals
    1. Objectives cross-referenced to activities

Source: Charles Maher and Randy Bennett, *Planning and Evaluating Special Education Services*, © 1984, pp. 13–14. Reprinted by permission of Prentice-Hall, Inc., Englewood Cliffs, N.J.

Process Outcomes or Formative Evaluation Questions

Other questions for school officials relate to how efficiently the special education program operates. They are particularly inclined to ask how long the disabled student will need specialized assistance. Specifically, what specialized programs and services seem to make a difference in student achievement and adjustment? Are all the programs and services equally necessary? Are some more efficient than others? Do some programs and services accomplish the task more efficiently? Which programs and services can be costed out to determine actual cost per pupil?

ASSUMPTIONS REGARDING EVALUATION

Evaluation has never been an apolitical activity, contrary to some professional attempts to rationalize the process. Attempts to make evaluations objective generally fall short of the mark for this reason. We believe responsive or illuminating evaluation in contrast to more goal-based traditional approaches accommodates the pluralistic values that permeate the school community.[6, 7] Values being held by management might not be shared by the school board, the teacher's association or selected community advocacy groups.

Responsive evaluation approaches are grounded in the emergent behavior of organizational members. These behaviors represent the starting point for the evaluation regardless of the purpose for which one seeks to use the data. The evaluation, therefore, is always relative to the organization under study. This approach requires the evaluators to become participant-observers of organizational members within the school setting. In addition, the evaluators serve as recorders of the organizational history, as represented in documents produced by organization members, and by key constituents or other observers of the school community.

Besides trying to make subjective judgments objective, traditional approaches tend to focus on outcomes to the exclusion of more process-oriented approaches. In our view, traditional, goal-based assessments of school programs fail because they proceed from preconceived standard measures that are not grounded in the experience of those to be evaluated. Those measures or values are often inappropriate when applied to the organizational members under study.

Goal-based or outcomes-oriented objective evaluation studies have a place and a use in less complex human social systems. In our view, these studies can be best undertaken when there is a clear consensus on program goals or intent by policymakers, planners, and program operators. In other words, where there is a value consensus and a set of appropriate measures and a set of matching criteria, then goal-based evaluation can be undertaken successfully.

Tracy summaries in outline form a descriptive matrix of six different evaluation models and approaches contrasted across a set of seven factors. Seven considerations and models are displayed in Table 12-3. The factors are defined below.

Focus—the way in which each author places emphasis on his or her approach

Proponents—the major theoretical contributors to each approach

Purpose—the author's goal of the evaluation process

Definition—the way each author has defined the process of evaluation

Design—the content and scope of the study, consistent with both the definition and purpose ascribed to in the evaluation process

Table 12-3 Overview of Evaluation

DIMENSIONS	MODELS			APPROACHES		
	OBJECTIVES	SYSTEM	CONTEXT	PROCESSES	JUDGMENTAL	NATURALISTIC
Focus	Performance measurement	Planning Design	Input, process, and output	Formal/informal Formative/summative	Panels Experts	Responsive effectiveness
Proponents	Tyler Popham	Provus Alkin	Stuffelbeam	Scriven	Eisner Wolf	Guba-Lincoln Stake
Purpose	To determine effectiveness of objectives	To decide whether to change, hold or terminate	To provide data in context for decisions	To identify multiple roles and processes in evaluation	To provide expert judgment	To develop responsive methodologies
Definition	Process to relate objectives to behavior	Process to relate standards to performance	Process to define (etc.) data for decisions	Process to describe and judge performance data with goals	Process to focus on standards and professional judgment	Process to develop responsive and natural methodology
Design	Explicit and include local personnel	Provides feedback loop and information for making decisions	Directed by administrator. Use of systems approach	General structure. Evaluative from within (formative) or from without (summative)	Responsive and based on experience and training	Emergent and responsive
Methodology/procedures	Pre/post comparisons or other appropriate indices of the objectives	Reference in terms of "needs"	Varies, includes needs assessment, case studies and advocate teams	*Modus operandi* analysis	Implicit use of "refined perceptual apparatus"	Naturalistic inquiry
Audiences	Teachers, curriculum developers, students, and parents	All decision makers	All decision makers	Sponsors and consumers	Anyone involved with the entity being evaluated	Anyone involved with the entity being evaluated

Source: Patricanna Tracey, "Supportive Staff and Related Services Evaluation," *CASE Information Packet Series*, ed. Leonard Burrello (Bloomington, Ind.: Council of Administrators of Special Education, 1984), pp. 12–14.

Methodology/procedures—the suggested type of activities recommended for use and how to follow through

Audiences—the groups who should be involved and who can best benefit from this approach[8]

We now move to consider the issue of program evaluation in special education and the assumptions we believe are significant today in conducting program studies for each of the five purposes just described.

ASSUMPTIONS REGARDING PROGRAM EVALUATION IN SPECIAL EDUCATION

These assumptions are grounded in our perception of best practice in program evaluation and the context of special education today and through the 1980s. We have derived these statements from our own practice of evaluation in urban and suburban school systems and rural cooperatives. These assumptions are organized now by one of the five program evaluation purposes noted earlier.

PROGRAM IMPROVEMENT

1. Program evaluation is one of management's tools to introduce or unfreeze organizational members to accept and work toward the introduction of better practices.

2. When special education leaders focus on results, increased evaluation activity follows.

3. Program evaluation should become a regularized activity so that staff and top management come to expect its occurrence and reduce resistance to it.

4. Staff-initiated evaluation for program improvement purposes is defensible and can be more easily budgeted for on a regular basis.

5. Program administrators who initiate program evaluation activities for school improvement purposes will project a positive program image and rarely have to subject themselves or their staff to needless externally driven compliance evaluation.

6. Program evaluation should set the stage for planning and introduction of change or the reinforcement of current practices; if staff changes are needed they should come after a failure to respond to support in the follow-up evaluation.

7. Each program administrator on the special education management team should prepare a program and personal improvement plan on an annual basis and be prepared to share results annually before the annual budget process begins and resources are allocated.

8. Each special education director should establish a non-salary discretionary fund to support innovation or reinforce excellent staff practices documented by annual program and personal improvement projects.

PROGRAM REVIEW

1. Program review evaluation has been instituted in school system and university settings to give top management an external referent by which to judge their special education unit's practice.
2. Regular program review evaluation is instituted to give top management a means to justify expanding or delimiting a program.
3. If top management wants to make a change in leadership or the program under review they will persist until they get the kind of external evaluation that justifies their ends.
4. Program review evaluation gets increasingly more difficult as the number of program and services to be reviewed increases; the corollary to the above is that the more focused the review, the easier it is to obtain the intended outcomes.
5. Program reviews will not necessarily lead to increased top management or community support unless chief stakeholder values are well understood and deeply rooted in organizational evaluation activities.
6. Program reviews are concerned more with the status quo rather than what might be, and for that reason they tend to have limited value and limited futuristic application.

PROGRAM COMPLIANCE EVALUATION

1. Compliance reviews focus on minimum criteria.
2. Compliance reviews are more concerned with what was originally intended than what ought to be.
3. Compliance reviews are static reports.
4. Compliance reviews are concerned with the presence or absence of written statements of assurance and practice.
5. Compliance reviews are valuable as a threat to spur action because they are generally a state agency prerogative that could lead to sanctions and withholding of funds.
6. Compliance reviews are most helpful in immature organizations or with those with new top management who do not trust the local special education leadership.
7. Compliance reviews are also helpful to new special education leadership personnel who need to gain a state as well as local perspective on the status of their new district.

COMMUNITY INFORMATION

1. All forms of program evaluation can be used for this purpose.
2. The degree of utility depends on involvement of key stakeholding groups and their values and concerns.
3. Program evaluation reports can unfreeze staff to future patron participation and volunteer activities as much as the community member.
4. Sharing evaluation data with the media in parts or a series from start to finish may encourage wider and more frequent coverage and follow-up.
5. Program evaluation data should focus on student progress and community contribution in public information releases.

6. Students are untapped consumer evaluators and disseminators of what's right with the schools; program evaluators should share results with students whenever possible so that they can share results with their parents.

7. Program evaluation data should be released in group meetings with community patrons who do not have children in schools as well as identified stakeholder groups with school children.

POLICY ANALYSIS

1. Policy analysis is often initiated at the federal and state levels in response to concerns that transcend the local level.

2. Policy analysis is often initiated because of competition for limited human resources are at stake within education (regular, special, vocational, and higher education) and between education and other human services agencies.

3. Policy analysis are also primarily driven by issues of equity and access to services questions at local as well as state and federal levels.

4. Policy analysis studies demand indepth testimony from key stakeholding audiences.

5. Quantitative evidence is not sufficient to support policy changes, qualitative evidence demonstrating effect on clients and constituents is necessary to portray the effects of current and projected policy changes.

6. The effects of policy changes are rarely immediately known because they demand the test of program implementation.

With these assumptions and observations of each use of program evaluation data, we describe a number of ways local administrators have used evaluation successfully to create a climate for school improvement. These recommendations contain both traditional and emergent responsive evaluation strategies and tactics. Keep in mind that time and costs are constants that vary with the size and scope of the evaluation task. As we suggested earlier, beginning is the toughest part. To assist the reader about to undertake a program evaluation activity, we have presented our outline of a comprehensive evaluation in Appendix 12A.

EXEMPLARS IN SPECIAL EDUCATION EVALUATION

Recent national activity and interest in special education evaluation has been supported by the International Council of Administrators of Special Education (CASE) and the Office of Special Education Programs (OSEP). CASE and OSEP collaborated in 1983-84 in the identification and dissemination of local evaluation models that we have reviewed here.[9] Few models actually used in local school systems have been reported in the literature. We found the same problem in our selection and description of local district organizational structures reported in Chapter 4.

State-Initiated Models
of Local Program Evaluation[10,11]

Massachusetts, North Carolina, and California have supported goal-based evaluation of local education agencies' special education programs. These states have developed very similar models so they will be presented as one, rather than separately. We have also included two other models, the Fort Worth Program Review Model and the Johnson-Gadberry Program Planning and Evaluation Model. Each model is presented within the seven part framework used earlier by Tracy to depict differences in leading evaluation models, approaches and proponents.

Focus.   Performance indicators of student progress and process indicators established by some form of state level consensus. Each state suggests areas for evaluation but encourages local generation of other performance and process indicators of local interest.

Performance Indicators

1. Physical and emotional well-being; values and attitudes
2. Skills and knowledges
3. Citizenship and respect
4. Occupational competence
5. Environment
6. Creative talents and interests

Process Indicators

1. Child identification and evaluation
2. Parent and public involvement
3. Facilities and range of services
4. Staff development
5. Least restrictive environment
6. IEP evaluation

Proponents.   Daniel Stufflebeam, Malcolm Provus, and Ralph Tyler.

Purpose.   To provide data in the local context to determine decision options leading to an action plan.

Definition.   To define evaluation questions initially in 12 areas noted above and establish acceptable performance standards.

Design.   Primarily survey design work, often using state developed prototype, adapted by district task forces of key stakeholding groups organized and directed by the local special education administrator.

Methodology/Procedures.   In addition to above, determine sample sizes, analysis of data in terms of percentages, develop trend analysis and patterns, write action plan, often with regional or state personnel providing technical assistance.

Audiences.   Primarily decision makers and participants in the process.

Other Consideration.   Time frame reported by users is two to three months. State provides technical assistance in providing or actually designing local survey prototypes and training in data collection and reporting writing.

Fort Worth Program Review Model

Focus.   Reviewing current status and direction of school systems' special education program, using an internal panel of stakeholders and expert judges.

Proponents.   Robert Wolf and E. Wisner.

Purpose.   To compare current program and directions with those of an expert panel of judges representing local, state, and national expertise.

Definition.   To assess how the current programs stacks up against the opinion of experts judged to have a national, state, and local perspective in comparable settings and who are wellgrounded in the contemporary practice of special education.

Design.   Review the district's historical and current status and respond to their circumstances in terms of the panel's assessment of what is best practice and possible in the school district context, using the expert panel's experiences and training.

Methodology/Procedures.   The special education leader initiates and gains consensus on a negotiated a set of program review outcomes with top management, an internal audit committee composed of all related program personnel impinging on special education, and a community advisory board; with these outcomes the audit committee generates a set of questions to assess a wider range of regular and special education personnel perceptions of needed changes; these data are provided as evidence along with selected documents the expert panel requested of the director; the final stage of data collection is the interrogation of key staff from the top management groups to teacher aides and site visitations to suspect programs; data analysis is a derivation conference with the panel soliciting needed data when questions arise; draft oral report is shared with top management and the director to tailor the report to district opportunities and constraints; the final steps included sharing the report in written form with internal audit committee and community advisory board before sharing it finally with the superintendent's cabinet; the director is then directed to produce an internal management plan to move the district in new directions prior to a board presentation for discussion of options and eventually sanctioning of resources as policy changes occur.

Audiences.   Any groups concerned with the entity to be evaluated; generally, a comprehensive review will involve at least top and middle building-level management, instructional and related personnel, and finally representatives from school patrons and community agencies.

Other Considerations.   Time—to complete the task can be broken down into director time, internal audit, staff, and expert panel time commitments; 8 days of director's time over a 18-week period, five 2 hour meetings of the internal audit committees, 6 days of three staff members, and 4 days of the expert panel. Cost—approximately $5,000 for external panel fees. Composition of expert panel—local peer director of a well respected local program, a state department consultant, and a national administrative consultant/trainer in special education.

Johnson/Gadberry Program Planning and Evaluation Model[12]

The Johnson/Gadberry Model has been most recently nationally disseminated through the CASE/OSEP evaluation project mentioned earlier. An exemplar of the model was applied by the South Metropolitan Association (SMA), a 55-district cooperative in Illinois and one of its four high-incidence subcooperatives known as SPEED. The SPEED/SMA inquiry is the adaptation that is presented here.

Focus.   Goal-based program development and subsequent evaluation of a locally articulated philosophy, integrated with a set of goals and specific objectives whose achievement can be measured by self-generated criteria.

Proponents.   Ralph Tyler, James Popham, Malcolm Provus in evaluation literature and in special education, Richard Johnson and Eva Gadberry.

Purpose.   To set up a measurable system to determine the effectiveness of program objectives.

Definition.   It is a public process of determining local values and operational objectives that can be measured against a locally determined set of standards.

Design.   The model is explicit in terms of the components Johnson/ Gadberry suggest that the administrator use in planning for and conducting the the evaluation; the 18 components are

1. Statement of philosophy
2. Overall program policies
3. Overall program design
4. Overall planning and coordination
5. Student assessment and program planning
6. Content
7. Method
8. Staff
9. Staff development
10. Instructional resources
11. Physical plan requirements
12. Transportation
13. Parent involvement and training
14. Interagency and advocacy group collaboration
15. Community relations and involvement
16. Fiscal resources
17. Component policies and procedures
18. Total program evaluation

Each component of the model is used in the design of the evaluation from philosophy to goals and objectives. Three criteria are used to measure goal and/or objective achievement. For each program or subprogram component (1) quality, (2) sufficiency of effort and resources, and (3) whether or not the program or component is cost-effective.

Methodology/Procedures.   In the SPEED/SMA Inquiry application of the J-G model, top management decided to focus on four separate topics in their evaluation:

1. Governance structure and the overall relation of the LEAs to the high and low incidence cooperatives (SPEED and SMA)
2. Overall organizational, philosophy, and policy base of the Cooperative
3. Administrative and supervisory support to district regular administrative and instructional staff in special education
4. Program by program and services analysis

With these four foci, the SPEED/SMA cooperative team led an organized series of task forces to generate program descriptions of the current realities in each of the four foci, including criteria statements for each of the 18 components in the J-G model, using the concepts of quality, sufficiency, and cost-effectiveness. Using the criterion statements, the task force groups tackled four interrelated tasks separately and then together to gain a consensus. The four tasks were:

1. Define "what is" happening currently using team-developed criterion statements; this task involved interviewing personnel within the systems and community patrons.
2. Define "what should be" and reach consensus on a "community" set of expectations to guide decision making.
3. Define the discrepancy between the results obtained in tasks 1 and 2.
4. Develop an action plan to reach the desired states defined in task 2.

Audiences.   Top management, cooperative and LEA administrators, SEA representatives, and all staff and community patrons and agencies personnel as appropriate.

Other Considerations.   Adaptation of this model demands a high commitment of top management and the special education administrators; it is not advised to be implemented in a district in a crisis but rather in settings where fundamentally the system participants want a thorough review of the past and seek to establish a new game plan for the future; this type of planning both insures a thoughtful study and builds commitment and acceptance of the future. Time—this type of planning and evaluation project demands 14 to 18 months. Cost—in excess of $10,000 since it demands wide participation and exchange of values and ideas.[13, 14, 15]

Responsive Evaluation Model

Many more examples of responsive evaluation are to be found from studies of federal and state projects than from local school system special education evaluation practices. The next example describes how an evaluation of a major SEA/LEA training project was conducted using the responsive evaluation model. The authors have used some of the naturalistic methods described next in assessing the effectiveness of evaluation efforts, in a large urban school district, and a large special education cooperative. Baker has designed a state model for Vermont. It is currently being pilot tested there.[16]

Focus.   To assess key stakeholders' perception of the effectiveness of LEA planning and implementation of training projects within a statewide network supported by SEA discretionary money and a university based technical assistance group.

Proponents.   Egon Guba, Yvonna Lincoln, and Robert Stake.

Purpose. To determine if task force planning and implementation of quality practices in personnel development could be replicated in local school districts and cooperatives with regular and special educators effectively; in short, the evaluation assesses the values of the project participants in terms of the merit of the planning versus the worth of the plan produced and the training actually provided.

Definition. To determine the values held by SEA, technical assistance group, and local planning team members and whether or not the intent of the SEA project was in fact apparent and operational in the behavior of the planning team and others affected by the planning and training activities in their backhome situations.

Design. The design of a naturalistic inquiry is emergent rather than preordinated; the evaluator seeks to discover the values held by multiple audiences and attempts to richly describe the patterns (if any exist) in their divergent values regarding the merit of the process or the worth of the plan or training actually delivered.

Methodology/Procedures. Evaluator(s) is (are) the chief instrument in a naturalistic inquiry; the evaluator seeks to determine the general intent of the project by garnering a collection of data sources (both oral and written) including a thorough review of the grant proposal documents, letters of introduction, and letters of agreement between the parties in the interagency arrangement; from these documents an unstructured interview schedule is developed and a sample of school districts progressing well and not so well are selected from the opinions of the SEA staff and technical assistance group; a set of 10 to 15 interviews are conducted with the sample of teachers and administrators from both regular and special educators' planning team and non-team members; the sample grows as the evaluator solicits names of others during the conduct of the interviews to seek out unique perceptions or distinct values that emerged from the interviews with the initial sample; plans are reviewed, as well as evaluation reports, training sessions observed, and participants queried during and after training sessions with the evaluator in attendance; finally, (where possible) the evaluator attends staff and planning meetings on the backhome site.

Data analysis occurs during and after reviewing initial interviews; the evaluator is searching for the patterns of themes that emerge from the interviews; these patterns result through the dissection and rebuilding of the participants' values and observations; they are shared with the participants to clarify and ensure their meaning and with others to confirm their validity.

Reports are written with much of the participants' actual words; the report is more of a portrayal, giving the readers a sense of actually being there and framing recommendations that fit their own context.

Audiences.   Anyone involved or representative of the project or program under study.

Other Considerations.   Time—depending upon the size of the entity being evaluated. The time frame for program in a district of 2,000 disabled youngsters might be four months with an internal or outside person working 16-24 days. Costs—$5,000 and $6,000.

OTHER RECOMMENDATIONS

It may be apparent that combining qualitative and quantitative evaluation methods, especially in large evaluation efforts, is highly recommended. In large organizations or in programs having multiple audiences, one is likely to confound the original intent and diffuse implementation as the program implementors get farther away from the policymakers. We recommend this combined approach, however, more because it should increase scope and the focus of the evaluation and consequently be more effective. Quantitative approaches may appear more efficient and generally are, but they can miss the target by a wide margin. Qualitative approaches, while labor intensive, lead to rich descriptions of reality that build rapport and acceptance of change if participants have been involved from the beginning.

A second recommendation we wish to make involves the use of the work of the Evaluation Training Consortium (ETC) at Western Michigan University. The ETC has a long history in evaluation training and has produced a set of volumes that contain descriptions of the evaluation focusing and design process. We have included one of its displays of the evaluation functions, key issues and questions, and the key evaluation tasks that correspond to both the functions and issues. See Appendix 12B for the format.[17]

One final comment—begin before it's too late!

APPENDIX 12A

A COMPREHENSIVE OUTLINE FOR EVALUATION IN SPECIAL EDUCATION

I. *Guiding Principles*

Operative assumptions

A. When a system can operate under a continuous set of objectives, its effectiveness and efficiency are probably increased.

B. Major objectives should be appropriately operationalized at all levels of the system.

C. No part of the system should view itself as divorced from the operational framework defined by the program objectives.

D. A person at any position in the system should know

1. What the systems' objectives are

2. How his or her "division" fits into meeting those objectives

3. How those objectives prescribe, operationally, what he or she does in the system

4. How he or she gives operational clarity to those subordinate to him

5. How he or she shares personal and professional expectations and resources amongst peers and subordinates

II. *Organization for Service Delivery*

Assumptions regarding a "good" system

A. Personnel must be of adequate quantity and quality to provide

1. Major policy leadership

2. General administrative management

3. Technical supervision/consultation

4. Ancillary support

5. Direct instructional service

B. Procedures must be established, clearly understood, and consistently implemented concerning

1. Screening within the system

2. Case finding outside the system

3. Referral for evaluation

4. Diagnostic-prescriptive services

5. Placement in programs providing continuing instructional services

    6. Evaluation of progress in programs

    7. Changes in placement within and between programs and the mainstream

  C. Program alternatives must be available to meet varied pupil needs considering

    1. Type of major exceptionality

    2. Degree of deviance

    3. Approach to instructional intervention

    4. Intensity of service required

  D. Consumer involvement must be evident in terms of parents'

    1. Input to decisions regarding placement

    2. Understanding of objectives of program

    3. Knowledge of pupil progress

    4. Awareness of alternatives for pupils

  E. Related community agencies must be involved cooperatively with the school system in the provision of services for pupils in such areas as

    1. Health

    2. Social Services

    3. Psychological assessment

    4. Parent counseling

  F. System monitoring must be possible, in order to assure assessment of

    1. Achievement of overall program objectives

    2. Instances of unmet needs (excluded pupils, inappropriate placements, etc.)

III. *Curriculum*

Assumptions concerning an appropriate curriculum

  A. Curriculum will evidence

    1. Congruence with major program objectives

    2. Sequence between maturational levels

    3. Articulation between special and mainstream

    4. Relationship between school, home, and adult role in society

    5. Community-based training activities

IV. *Physical Facilities*

Assumptions concerning appropriate facilities

  A. Facilities will reflect program philosophy in terms of

    1. Recognition of special needs

    2. Maximum feasible normalization

  B. Facilities will make provisions consistent with

    1. Variety of types of pupils served

    2. Variety of instructional methodologies utilized

V. *Instructional Approaches*

Assumptions concerning "good" instruction

  A. Teachers' activities will reflect

    1. Awareness of major program objectives

    2. Consistency with objectives

    3. Maximum flexibility to match pupil differences

    4. Provision of input from home

    5. Maximum relationship between present and long range needs

    6. Demonstrating effective teaching practices grounded in instructional effectiveness research

B. Teachers' characteristics will include

    1. Basic certification

    2. Demonstrated competence

    3. Individual development plan

    4. Engaging in growth and development activities

C. Instructional materials will be adequate in terms of

    1. Quantity to serve all pupils

    2. Variety to serve all types of needs

    3. Consistency with major objectives

D. Evaluation of results of instruction will be

    1. Systematically implemented

    2. Usable for continued prescriptive guidance

    3. Transmittable to relevant targets outside the school

VI. *Outcomes*

Assumptions regarding desired outcomes

A. Output of programs will be manifested in students who have

    1. Good human relationships

    2. Maximum participation in normal living

    3. Minimal stigma associated with their handicap

    4. Positive self concept

    5. Demonstrated progress in meeting individual achievement objective

    6. Productive occupation

B. Global effects of programs will be to facilitate growth in larger society in terms of positive attitudes toward human deviance

APPENDIX 12B

KEY ISSUES AND TASKS, BY FUNCTION, IN AN EVALUATION PROCESS

FUNCTION	KEY ISSUES	TASKS
Focusing the evaluation	1. What will be evaluated?	1. Investigate what is to be evaluated
	2. What is the purpose for evaluating?	2. Identify and justify purpose(s)
	3. Who will be affected by or involved in the evaluation?	3. Identify audiences
	4. What elements in the setting are likely to influence the evaluation?	4. Study setting
	5. What are the crucial evaluation questions?	5. Identify major questions
	6. Does the evaluation have the potential for successful implementation?	6. Decide whether to go on with evaluation
Designing evaluation	1. What are some alternative ways to design an evaluation?	1. Determine the amount of planning, general purpose, and degree of control
	2. What does a design include?	2. Overview evaluation decisions, tasks, and products
	3. How do you go about constructing a design?	3. Determine general procedures for the evaluation
	4. How do you recognize a good design?	4. Assess the quality of the design
Collecting information	1. What kinds of information should you collect?	1. Determine the information sources you will use

Source: Robert O. Brinkerhoff, Dale M. Brethower, Terry Hluchyj, and Jeri Ridings Nowakowski, *Program Evaluation: A Practitioner's Guide for Trainers and Educators* (Boston: Kluwer-Nijhoff, 1983).

FUNCTION	KEY ISSUES	TASKS
	2. What procedures should you use to collect needed iinformation?	2. Decide how you will collect information
	3. How much information should you collect?	3. Decide whether you need to sample and if so, how
	4. Will you select or develop instruments?	4. Determine how precise your information must be and design a means to collect it
	5. How do you establish reliable and valid instrumentation?	5. Establish procedures to maximize validity & reliability
	6. How do you plan the information collection effort to get the most information at the lowest cost?	6. Plan the logistics for an economical information collection procedure
Analyzing and interpreting (evaluation)	1. How will you handle returned data?	1. Aggregate and code data if necessary
	2. Are data worth analyzing?	2. Verify completeness and quality of raw data
	3. How will you analyze the information?	3. Select and run defensible analyses
	4. How will you interpret the results?	4. Interpet the data using prespecified and alternative sets of criteria
Reporting	1. Who should get an evaluation report?	1. Identify who you will report to
	2. What content should be included in a report?	2. Outline the content to be included
	3. How will reports be delivered?	3. Decide whether reports will be written, oral, etc.
	4. What is the appropriate style and structure for the report?	4. Select a format for the report
	5. How can you help audiences interpret and use reports?	5. Plan postreport discussions, consultation, followup activities
	6. When should reports be scheduled?	6. Map out the report schedule
Managing	1. Who should run the evaluation?	1. Select, hire, and/or train the evaluator
	2. How should evaluation responsibilities be formalized?	2. Draw up a contract or letter of agreement
	3. How much should the evaluation cost?	3. Draft the budget

FUNCTION	KEY ISSUES	TASKS
	4. How should evaluation tasks be organized and scheduled?	4. Draft a time/task strategy
	5. What kinds of problems can be expected?	5. Monitor the evaluation and anticipate problems
Evaluating evaluation (meta-evaluation)	1. What are some good uses of meta-evaluation?	1. Determine whether you need to meta-evaluate; if so, when
	2. Who should do the meta-evaluation?	2. Select a meta-evaluator
	3. What criteria or standard should you use to evaluate the evaluation?	3. Select or negotiate standards
	4. How do you apply a set of meta-evaluation criteria?	4. Rank order standards, determine compliance

NOTES

[1]Les Horvath, "Quantitative Program Evaluation," *Program Evaluation: Matching Quantitative and Qualitative Assessments to the Organizational Context,* eds. Theodore Riggen and Leonard Burrello (Bloomington, Ind.: Council of Administrators of Special Education, Fall l984).

[2]Herbert Simon, "A Behavioral Model of Rational Choice," *Models of Man* (New York: John Wiley, l957), pp. 241-260.

[3]Charles A. Maher and Randy Bennett. *Planning and Evaluating Special Education Services* (Englewood Cliffs, N.J.: Prentice-Hall, 1984), p. 15.

[4]Ibid., pp. 13-14.

[5]Charles Lindbolm, "The Science of Muddling Through," *Public Administration Review* (Spring l959), pp. 151-169.

[6]Egon G. Guba and Yvonna S. Lincoln. *Effective Evaluation: Improving the Usefulness of Evaluation Results through Responsive and Naturalistic Approaches* (San Francisco: Jossey-Bass, 1982).

[7]M. Parlett and D. Hamilton. Evaluation as illumination: A new approach to the study of innovative programs. *Evaluation Studies Review Annual* (1976), 1, 140-57.

[8]Patricanna Tracy, "Supportive Staff and Related Services Evaluation," *CASE Information Packet Series,* ed. Leonard C. Burrello (Bloomington, Ind.: Council of Administrators of Special Education, 1984), pp. 12-14.

[9]Conference Report Institute on Special Education Programs:"Molds for Evaluation and Related Services at the Local Level," Contract no. 300840016 (Washington, D.C.: U.S. Department of Education, Office of Special Education Programs, December 30, 1983).

[10]Ibid., pp. 11-39.

[11]Theodore R. Drain and Linda G. Rowe, eds. *Program Quality Evaluator Manual* (Raleigh, N.C.: Department of Public Instruction, Division for Exceptional Children, 1983).

[12]Conference Report Institute, "Molds for Evaluation," pp. 40-53.

[13]Linda Beitz, "Participants' Views of Interorganizational Arrangements in Education, A Case Study," Unpublished doctoral dissertation (Bloomington, Ind.; August 1983).

[14]Robert Owens, "Indiana Comprehensive System of Personnel Development Project: An Evaluation Report" (Indianapolis: Department of Education, July 1981).

[15]Edith E. Beatty, "Qualitative Responsive Approaches," *Program Evaluation: Matching Quantitative and Qualitative Assessments to the Organizational Context,* eds. Theodore Riggen and Leonard Burrello (Bloomington, Ind.: Council of Administrators of Special Education, Fall 1984).

[16]Lynn Baker, "The Guide to the Vermont Special Education Program Evaluation Model" (Montpelier, Vt.: State Department of Education, 1983).

[17]Robert Brinkeroff, Dale M. Brethower, Terry Hluchyj, and Jeri Ridings Nowakowski, *Program Evaluation: A Practitioner's Guide for Trainers and Educators* (Boston: Kluwer-Nijhoff, 1983).

INDEX